The Infallible Word

The Infallible Word

A Symposium by the Members of the Faculty of Westminster Theological Seminary

Edited by N. B. Stonehouse
and Paul Woolley

Second edition

Foreword by D. M. Lloyd-Jones

P&R PUBLISHING
P.O. BOX 817 • PHILLIPSBURG • NEW JERSEY 08865-0817

Second edition ("third revised printing") published by P&R
Publishing Company 1967 and reissued 2002.

Published under the provisions of the Harry A. Worcester
Lectureship and Publication Fund of Westminster
Theological Seminary, Philadelphia.

Printed in the United States of America

ISBN: 0-87552-543-1

PREFACE

THE title of this volume, *The Infallible Word,* is derived from the language of the first chapter of the Westminster Confession of Faith and serves to epitomize its classic formulation of the doctrine of Holy Scripture. All sixty-six books of the Old and New Testaments are declared to be "given by inspiration of God, to be the rule of faith and life." The authority of Holy Scripture, "for which it ought to be believed and obeyed," is said to depend "wholly upon God . . . the author thereof and therefore it is to be received, because it is the Word of God." And the "full persuasion and assurance of the infallible truth and divine authority thereof" is held to be derived "from the inward testimony of the Holy Spirit, bearing witness by and with the Word in our hearts."

When this symposium was undertaken Presbyterians were celebrating the tercentenary of the convening, on July 1, 1643, of the assembly of divines which produced the historic Westminster standards of faith. This event raised a series of urgent questions. Did this celebration of their labors also evoke a cordial reaffirmation of their faith? Can we in particular, after three hundred years of discovery and research, still accept their doctrine of Scripture? Can we now in good conscience subscribe, as Presbyterian officials are generally still called upon to do, to belief in the Scriptures as "the Word of God, the only infallible rule of faith and practice"? It has been the vogue in many circles to represent this view of the Bible as a hopelessly outmoded point of view, which long ago should have been totally abandoned or radically transformed. Yet this historic view of Scripture will not down. Writers on the general theme of Christianity are occupied with the subject of revelation as they have not been for decades, and in these discussions the traditional view cannot be ignored. The writings produced by the movement which has found its most conspicuous figure in Karl Barth are proof of this fact. Although Barth polemicizes against the ancient Protestant doctrine of Scripture, he is compelled to deal with it and, in stating his own position, largely to employ the old terminology.

The point of view of this volume is that of a cordial acceptance of the high Protestant doctrine of the Bible. It is the position of Westminster Theological Seminary, which was established in 1929 to carry on the tradition of loyalty to the Bible and the Reformed Faith which was the distinguishing mark of Princeton Theological Seminary until its reorganization in that year. We welcome the illumination of the Scriptures which discovery and research provide. We are as much concerned with the light which may yet break forth from the Scriptures and with the knowledge to be gained from a study of the world in which the Scriptures originated as any student of the Bible. In that sense we have no desire to remain where the Westminster divines of the seventeenth century stood. However, their formulation of the doctrine of Scripture in our judgment remains valid today. It does not need to retreat in the face of modern scholarship.

It is not obscurantism that accounts for our intransigence on this matter. The fundamental issue is not that of the knowledge or even of the interpretation of details. It is rather the issue whether the total view of the world and of life which the Bible presents is true. To approach the Bible in terms of an antibiblical philosophy of reality is to transform the Bible into something quite at variance with what it purports to be. To approach it, however, in the perspective provided by its own Christian theistic philosophy is to acknowledge it at its face value. Unless this fundamental matter is recognized at all times in the modern debate, confusion and distortion must result. The discussions in this volume at least possess the merit of taking account of the presuppositions of the writers.

We hope that this symposium may serve to clarify the position of orthodox Christianity with respect to the Bible. The issues of the day require us to take stock of this doctrine in a far more comprehensive way than is done in some of the brief formulations of faith which have gained favor in certain circles. And the fact that all too frequently modern writers have been occupied with a caricature of the orthodox doctrine rather than with the formulations of those who have defended it most ably adds urgency to this effort.

Although the subjects treated in this symposium have been suggested by the formulation of the doctrine of Scripture in the Westminster Confession and the principal aspects of the doctrine come under review in these discussions, we should perhaps make clear that we make no pretense of offering an exposition of the Confession. The contributors have been left free to discuss the several themes as they have seen fit. Although this has brought about considerable diversity of approach and treatment, we believe that the readers of the volume will agree that the common effort to expound this doctrine, and to evaluate it in relation to modern thought and life, secures sufficient unity to justify its publication as a single work.

We take pleasure in expressing here our grateful acknowledgment of the generous assistance received from several persons. To Miss Margaret S. Robinson for help in the preparation of the typescript, to Arthur W. Kuschke, Jr., for the makeup of the indexes, and to Thomas R. Birch for many services in connection with the publication of the volume, we hereby convey our heartfelt thanks.

N. B. STONEHOUSE,
PAUL WOOLLEY,
Editors.

FOREWORD

The proposal to republish "The Infallible Word" comes to me as most welcome news and I regard it as a real privilege to be asked to write this brief foreword.

When it first appeared this book rendered great service in helping and strengthening the faith of true evangelical people throughout the world. It was needed then, but now, alas, the need is even greater.

The problem of authority has always been crucial in the life of the individual and the Church; and to Protestants that authority has always been found in the Lord Jesus Christ Himself mediated to us through "the infallible Word." The Bible and our attitude to it has always therefore been at the very heart and center of the conflict between true evangelicals and Roman Catholicism on the one hand, and liberal and modernistic Protestantism on the other hand. The fight has gone on for two and a half centuries, reaching its climax perhaps in the 20's of the present century. The very existence of the Westminster Theological Seminary is a living reminder of this.

But, it is not yet over, and alas, it is assuming a new form which to those of us who belong to the Reformed and evangelical tradition is most grievous. For it has now become a civil war within that very camp. Where all were agreed until some fifteen years or so ago there is now an obvious and increasing divergence of opinion. Once more the Reformation cry of *"Sola Scriptura"* is being questioned and that in a most subtle manner. A new authority is being set alongside the Scripture as being co-equal with it, and in some respects superior to it — the authority of modern scientific knowledge. The Scriptures are still regarded as being authoritative in all matters of religious experience. But not only is their authority in such matters as the creation of the universe and man, and even historical facts which play a vital part in the history of salvation, and which were accepted by our Lord Himself, being questioned and queried; it is even being asserted that it is foolish of us to look to the Scriptures for authoritative guidance in such matters. It has recently been remarked that some well-known evangelical writers are arguing that there is a distinction between the Bible's teaching and what is found in that book which is incidental. They believe that the scientific assumptions are usually in the category of incidentals and do not belong to the infallible teaching. In like manner certain historical data are not a part of the infallible message of Scripture.

All this of course is not new; it is but the old Ritschlian dichotomy with regard to facts and judgments. What is new is that men who are the successors of those who fought the old battle so nobly and successfully, and who themselves once saw so clearly the subtle danger of this type of thinking, should be succumbing and even defecting to the ranks of liberalism and what one of the

writers of this book has described as "The New Modernism." There is nothing to justify this. There are no
new facts or discoveries which have in any way changed
the position and which could therefore justify this
change. It is part of the indifferentist attitude and spirit
fostered and encouraged by ecumenical thinking of a
wrong sort, which, in some, places fellowship before
truth, and bonhomie and intellectual respectability before integrity — and in others allows the "problem of
communication" so to occupy their attention that they
forget that that is the prerogative of the Holy Spirit,
and that our task is to be faithful to "the truth once and
for ever delivered to the saints."

I say all this to show that the arguments presented in
this volume are not only as cogent as ever, but are as
urgently relevant today as they were when it was first
published.

I can but thank God for its re-appearance at this time
of unprecedented confusion, and urge all who are
anxious to stand steadfastly against the alarming drift
even among evangelicals to read it and study it with
diligence. It will inform their minds, warm their hearts,
and strengthen their resolution.

D. M. Lloyd-Jones

Westminster Chapel
London, England

Preface
to the
Third Revised Printing

It is a pleasure to note that the people of God have called for a third printing of this symposium. The chapters written by the Rev. Professors John Murray, Edward J. Young and John H. Skilton have undergone pervasive revision. The chapters by the late Professors N. B. Stonehouse and R. B. Kuiper are printed unchanged, as are those by the Rev. Professor Cornelius Van Til and the undersigned.

The changes in some of the chapters do not reflect any lowering of the high view of Scripture set forth in previous editions. Rather they are designed to strengthen and confirm the affirmation of that view. It continues to be our conviction that this is the basic position of the divines who made up the Westminster Assembly which convened in 1643, and whose labors have been such a continuous blessing to the church of God since that time. Although their views are denigrated in many circles which still bear the names "Presbyterian" and "Reformed," we are happy to draw out for the people of the last half of the twentieth century what seem to us to be the implications of these views for the present day.

Paul Woolley
Editor

November, 1967

CONTENTS

THE ATTESTATION OF SCRIPTURE

By JOHN MURRAY

I. THE OBJECTIVE WITNESS

CHRISTIANS of varied and diverse theological standpoints aver that the Bible is the Word of God, that it is inspired by the Holy Spirit and that it occupies a unique place as the norm of Christian faith and life. But such general confessions do not of themselves settle for us the view entertained with respect to the origin, authority, and character of Holy Scripture. A passing acquaintance with the literature on this subject will show that such propositions are made to do service for wholly diverse views of the nature of Scripture. It becomes incumbent upon us, therefore, to define and examine the statement that the Bible is the Word of God.

Diversity of viewpoint with respect to this proposition has generally, if not always, taken its starting-point from the recognition that the Bible has come to us through human instrumentality. Every book of the Bible has had its human author. The Bible did not come to us directly from heaven; in its totality and in all its parts it has come to us through human agency. Since this is the case, every serious student of the Bible has to take cognizance of the human factor in the preparation, composition, and completion of what we know as the canon of Holy Writ.

1

If, then, human instruments have performed a function in producing the Bible, does it not necessarily follow that the marks of human fallibility and error must be imprinted on the Bible? Since the fall of our first parents, no perfect human being has walked upon this earth. It is true there was one, indeed human, who was holy, harmless, undefiled, and separate from sinners. But he was more than human; he was the eternal Son of God manifest in the flesh. If he had written the Bible, then the question with which we are now faced would not need to be asked. In any case, there would be at hand a very ready answer to the question. The infallibility of Christ's human nature would provide us with a simple answer to the urgent and difficult question: How can the Bible be the Word of God and at the same time the work of man? The resolution of the apparent antinomy would be provided by the fact that the person who wrote it was himself perfect God and perfect man.

The Lord Jesus Christ, however, did not write the Bible nor any part of it. When he left this world and went to the Father, he left no books that were the product of his pen. So in every case the Bible and all the Bible was written by those who were mere men and therefore by men who, without exception, were themselves imperfect and fallible.

This plain and undisputed fact has led many students of the Bible to the conclusion that the Bible cannot be in itself the infallible and inerrant Word of God. Putting the matter very bluntly, they have said that God had to use the material he had at his disposal and, since the material he had was fallible men, he was under the necessity of giving us his Word in a form that is marred by the defects arising from human fallibility. In the words of Dr. J. Monro Gibson:

"It is important at the outset to remember that the most consummate artist is limited by the nature of his material. He may have thoughts and inspirations far above and beyond what he can express in black-and-white or in colours, in marble or in bronze, in speech or in song; but however perfect his idea may be, it must, in finding expression, share the imperfections of the forms in which he works. If this very obvious fact had only been kept in mind, most of the difficulties which beset the subject of inspiration need never have arisen."[1]

And then Dr. Gibson proceeds to enumerate some of the limitations with which God had to deal, the limitations of human agency, human language and literary forms.

It is by plausible argument of this sort that students of the Bible have too rashly come to the conclusion that the human factor or, as we should prefer to call it, human instrumentality settles this question and that the Bible, though God's Word, must at the same time be errant and fallible, at least in scientific and historical detail, simply because it came to us through the ministry of men. Dr. Gibson is very jealous that we should follow the facts and let the Bible speak for itself rather than approach the Bible with a preconceived notion of divine infallibility. It is, however, just because we are jealous that the Bible should speak for itself that we must not take it for granted that human authorship necessitates errancy and fallibility.

[1] John Monro Gibson: *The Inspiration and Authority of Holy Scripture* (New York, n.d.), p. 146; *cf.* Emil Brunner: *Revelation and Reason,* E. T. (Philadelphia, 1946), pp. 128 f.

The fact of human authorship does indeed seem to provide a very easy argument for the errancy and fallibility of Scripture. Or, to state the matter less invidiously, human authorship seems to provide a very easy and necessary explanation of what are alleged to be the facts of errancy and fallibility. We must accept the facts, it is said, rather than hide behind the theory of inerrancy.[2]

Those who thus contend should, however, be aware of the implications of their position. If human fallibility precludes an infallible Scripture, then by resistless logic it must be maintained that we cannot have any Scripture that is infallible and inerrant. All of Scripture comes to us through human instrumentality. If such instrumentality involves fallibility, then such fallibility must attach to the whole of Scripture. For by what warrant can an immunity from error be maintained in the matter of "spiritual content" and not in

[2] It must be emphasized that the proponents of Biblical inerrancy do not ignore "facts" nor do they fail to take these into account in their construction of inspiration. "It must be emphatically stated that the doctrine of biblical inerrancy . . . is not based on the assumption that the criterion of meticulous precision in every detail of record or history is the indispensable canon of biblical infallibility. To erect such a canon is utterly artificial and arbitrary and is not one by which the inerrancy of Scripture is to be judged. It is easy for the opponents of inerrancy to set up such artificial criteria and then expose the Bible as full of errors. . . . Every one should recognize that in accord with accepted forms of speech and custom a statement can be perfectly authentic and yet not pedantically precise. Scripture does not make itself absurd by furnishing us with pedantry" (Calvin on Scripture and Divine Sovereignty, by the present writer, Grand Rapids, 1960, p. 30; cf. Ned B. Stonehouse: Origins of the Synoptic Gospels, Grand Rapids, 1963, pp. 109 f.) .

the matter of historical or scientific fact? Is human fallibility suspended when "spiritual truth" is asserted but
not suspended in other less important matters?[3]

Furthermore, if infallibility can attach to the "spiritual truth" enunciated by the Biblical writers, then it
is obvious that some extraordinary divine influence
must have intervened and become operative so as to
prevent human fallibility from leaving its mark upon
the truth expressed. If divine influence could thus in-
trude itself at certain points, why should not this same
preserving power exercise itself at every point in the
writing of Scripture? Again, surely human fallibility is
just as liable to be at work in connection with the
enunciation of transcendent truth as it is when it deals
with the details of historical occurrence.

It is surely obvious that the appeal to human fallibility in the interest of supporting, or at least de-

[3] The phrase "spiritual truth" is used here by way of accommo-
dation to the views of those who in the discussion of this question
stress the distinction between the outward form of the Bible and
the religious content of which the Bible is the vehicle. *Cf., e.g.,*
W. Sanday: *The Oracles of God* (London, 1892), pp. 29 f.; R. H.
Malden: *The Inspiration of the Bible* (London, 1935), pp. 5 f.
Karl Barth is consistent in this respect. Fallibility, he claims,
applies to the religious and theological as well as to the historical
and scientific. Referring to the witnesses to revelation "as fallible, erring men like ourselves" he says: "We can read and try
to assess their word as a purely human word. It can be subjected to all kinds of immanent criticism, not only in respect of
its philosophical, historical and ethical content, but even of its
religious and theological" *(Church Dogmatics,* E. T., Vol. I, 2
Edinburgh, 1956, p. 507; *cf.* also, p. 509). Barth can do this,
compatibly with his position, because he does not equate Scripture with the revelatory Word; Scripture only witnesses to
revelation.

fending, Biblical fallibility is glaringly inconsequent, if it is maintained that God has at any point given us through human agency an infallible and inerrant Word. Either *a priori* argument from human fallibility has to be abandoned or the position must be taken that human fallibility has left its mark upon all of Scripture and no part of it can be called the infallible Word of God, not even John 3:16. We cannot too strenuously press the opponents of Biblical inerrancy to the implications of their position. Human fallibility cannot with any consistency be pleaded as an argument for the fallibility of Scripture unless the position is taken that we do not have in the Scriptures content of any kind that is not marred by the frailty of human nature.

This plea for consistency does not mean however, that Biblical infallibility is thereby proven. While it is necessary to remove any *a priori* argument, drawn from human fallibility, that would do prejudice to the evidence, the doctrine of Biblical inerrancy must rest upon the proper evidence. In this case, as in all other doctrine, the evidence is the witness of Scripture itself. Does the Scripture claim inerrancy for itself and, if so, must this claim be accepted?

It must be freely admitted that there are difficulties connected with the doctrine of Biblical infallibility. There appear to be discrepancies and contradictions in the Bible. Naturally we cannot be expected to believe what we perceive to involve a contradiction. Furthermore, disingenuous and artificial attempts at harmony are to be avoided, for they do not advance the cause of truth and of faith. The conscientious student has, therefore, great difficulty sometimes in resolving problems raised by apparent contradictions. It is true that many such resolve themselves when careful study is applied to them, and oftentimes the resolution of the difficulty in the light of the various factors involved becomes the occasion for the discovery of a harmony and fullness of meaning that otherwise would not have been recognized by us. But some difficulties, perhaps many, remain unresolved. The earnest student has no adequate answer and he may frankly confess that he is not able to explain an apparent discrepancy in the teaching of Scripture.

It might seem that this confession of his own inability to resolve seeming discrepancy is not compatible with faith in Scripture as infallible. This is, however, at the best, very superficial judgment. There is no doctrine of our Christian faith that does not confront us with unresolved difficulties here in this world, and the difficulties become all the greater just as we get nearer to the center. It is in connection with the most transcendent mysteries of our faith that the difficulties multiply. The person who thinks he has resolved all the difficulties surrounding our established faith in the Trinity has probably no true faith in the Triune God. The person who encounters no unresolved mystery in the incarnation of the Son of God and in his death on Calvary's tree has not yet learned the meaning of I Timothy 3:16. Yet these unanswered questions are not incompatible with unshaken faith in the Triune God and in Jesus Christ, the incarnate Son. The questions are often perplexing. But they are more often the questions of adoring wonder rather than the questions of painful perplexity.

So there should be no surprise if faith in God's inerrant Word should be quite consonant with unresolved questions and difficulties with regard to the content of this faith.

The defense of the foregoing position that faith is not inconsistent with unresolved questions is far more crucial in this debate than might at first appear. It lies very close to the vital question of what is the proper ground of faith in the Bible as the Word of God. The ground of faith emphatically is not our ability to demonstrate all the teaching of the Bible to be self-consistent and true. This is just saying that rational demonstration is not the ground of faith. The demand that apparent contradictions in the Bible should have to be removed before we accord it our credit as God's infallible Word rests, therefore, upon a wholly mistaken notion of the only proper ground of faith in the Bible. It is indeed true that we should not close our minds and researches to the ever-progressing resolution of difficulties under the illumination of the Spirit of truth, but those whose approach to faith is that of resolution of all difficulty have deserted the very nature of faith and of its ground.

The nature of faith is acceptance on the basis of testimony, and the ground of faith is therefore testimony or evidence. In this matter it is the evidence God has provided, and God provides the evidence in his Word, the Bible. This means simply that the basis of faith in the Bible is the witness the Bible itself bears to the fact that it is God's Word, and our faith that it is infallible must rest upon no other basis than the witness the Bible bears to this fact. If the Bible does not witness to its own infallibility, then we have no right to believe that it is infallible. If it does bear witness to its infallibility then our faith in it must rest upon that witness, however much difficulty may be entertained with this belief. If this position with respect to the ground of faith in Scripture is abandoned, then appeal to the Bible for the ground of faith in any other doctrine must also be abandoned. The doctrine of Scripture must be elicited from the Scripture just as any other doctrine should be.[4] If the doctrine of Scripture is denied its right to appeal to Scripture for its support, then what right does any other doctrine have to make this appeal? Faith in the Trinity does not have to wait for the resolution of all difficulties that the teaching of Scripture presents to us on this question; it does not have to wait for the resolution of all apparent contradictions in the teaching of Scripture on the Trinity. So neither does faith in Scripture as the inerrant Word of God have to wait for the resolution of all difficulties in the matter of inerrancy.

The real question then becomes: What is the witness of Scripture with reference to its own character? It is important to appreciate the precise scope of this question; it is to elicit from the Scripture the evidence it contains bearing upon its origin, character, and authority. This approach is very different from the approach that too many claim to be the only scientific and inductive approach. It is often said that we must not go to the Bible with an *a priori* theory of its infallibility but we must go to the Bible with an open mind and find out what the facts are and frame our theory from the facts rather than impose our theory upon the facts.

---

4 W. Sanday states this principle well enough when he says that "we may lay it down as a fundamental principle that a true conception of what the Bible is must be obtained from the Bible itself" (*op. cit.*, p. 47). But he does not apply this principle consistently.

There is an element of truth in this contention. It is fully granted that we should never approach Scripture with an *a priori* theory of its character and impose that theory upon the evidence. We just as vigorously repudiate any such method as do others, and we have to impute to many liberal and radical students the very fault which they are too ready to impute to the orthodox believer. But while the *a priori* method of approach must on all accounts be condemned, it does not follow that the proper approach is that of the alleged inductive and scientific method. We do not elicit the doctrine of Scripture from an inductive study of what we suppose determines its character. We derive our doctrine of Scripture from what the Scripture *teaches* with respect to its own character—in a word, from the testimony it bears to itself.

This procedure does not by any means imply that the believer in Biblical infallibility can afford to be indifferent to the difficulties that may arise in connection with apparent discrepancies nor to the attacks made upon infallibility from various sides on the basis of what are alleged to be disharmonies and contradictions. The believer cannot at any time afford to be obscurantist; and orthodox scholarship must set right criticism over against wrong criticism. The motto of faith must be: "prove all things, hold fast that which is good." The believer must always be ready to give a reason for the faith that is in him. But he must also remember that the character and content of his faith in Scripture as the Word of God must be dictated by the divine witness bearing directly upon that precise question. What then is the testimony of the Scripture regarding itself? For to this question we must now address ourselves.

First of all, there is the negative evidence. The Scripture does not adversely criticize itself. One part of Scripture does not expose another part as erroneous. It goes without saying that, if Scripture itself witnessed to the errancy and fallibility of another part, then such witness would be a finality, and belief in the inerrancy of Scripture would have to be abandoned. But it is a signal fact that one Scripture does not predicate error of another. It is true that the Scripture contains the record of much sin and error in the history of men, of Satan and of demons.[5] The Bible, of course, is to a large extent historical in character and, since history is strewn with sin, the Bible could not fail to record the dark and dismal story. Indeed, the frankness and candor of the Bible in this regard is one of its most striking features. The openness with which it exposes even the sins of the saints is one of the most signal marks of its authenticity. But the condemnation of the sin and error the Bible records is not witness to its own fallibility. It is rather an integral part of the witness to its own credibility and, so far from constituting any evidence against itself as inerrant Scripture, it thereby contributes evidence that is most germane to the establishment of its infallibility.

[5] The statement in Gen. 3:4: "Ye shall not surely die" is not the word of God but of the tempter. But the *information* given us respecting the lie of the tempter is the Word of God and is brim full of revelatory significance. It is that of which our Lord's word is the commentary, "He was a liar from the beginning" (John 8:44). It is this obvious distinction that is applicable to all falsehoods of which Scripture informs us and exemplifies how Scripture is not merely a record but is itself revelatory, not even simply a record of revelation but is itself revelation.

It is also true that the Bible fully recognizes the temporary and provisional character of many of the regulations and ordinances which it represents as imposed by divine authority. The most relevant case in point here is the temporary character of many of the regulations of the Mosaic law. That the observance of these preparatory and temporary precepts, rites and ceremonies has been discontinued with the advent and establishment of the Christian economy is the express teaching of the New Testament. But in such teaching there is no reflection whatsoever on the divinely authoritative character of such provisions under that economy in which they were operative and, far more, no reflection upon the infallibility of that Old Testament Scripture which embodies the revelation to us of that divine institution. For example, when Paul in the epistle to the Galatians writes, "Behold, I Paul say unto you, that if ye be circumcised, Christ shall profit you nothing" (Gal. 5:2), he in no way casts any aspersion on the truth of those Old Testament books which inform us of the institution of circumcision and of its divinely authorized practice among the people of God from Abraham onwards. In fact, the same Paul lends the strongest corroboration to the truth of the Old Testament in this regard when he says elsewhere with reference to Abraham, "And he received the sign of circumcision, a seal of the righteousness of the faith which he had yet being uncircumcised" (Rom. 4:11).

Our thesis at this point will, of course, be challenged. It will be said that abundant evidence can be produced to show that Scripture does expose as erroneous the distinct representations of other parts of Scripture. To put the opposing argument otherwise, it is said that one part of Scripture says one thing and another part of Scripture dealing with the same situation says something else. For example, the Pentateuch represents the Levitical laws with respect to sacrifice as ordained by divine revelation and authority after the children of Israel came out of Egypt and while they were sojourning in the wilderness. It cannot be questioned that this is the story of the Pentateuch. But the prophet Jeremiah writes as the word of the Lord, "For I spake not unto your fathers, nor commanded them in the day that I brought them out of the land of Egypt, concerning burnt offerings or sacrifices: but this thing commanded I them, saying, Obey my voice, and I will be your God, and ye shall be my people: and walk ye in all the ways that I have commanded you, that it may be well unto you" (Jer. 7:22, 23).

It must be replied that the argument based on this antithesis in the prophecy of Jeremiah fails to appreciate one of the basic principles of Biblical interpretation, namely, that a relative contrast is often expressed in absolute terms. What is being protested in Jeremiah 7:22, 23 is the externalism and formalism of Israel. Mere ritual, even when the ritual is of divine institution, is religiously worthless, indeed is hypocrisy, if the real religious import of that ritual is not understood and particularly when the moral requirements of God's law are trampled under foot. Ceremonial ritual without ethical integrity and particularly without regard to spiritual attachment and obedience to the Lord God is mockery. And it is just of this formalism and hypocrisy that Isaiah writes, "Your new moons and your appointed feasts my soul hateth: they are a trouble unto me; I am weary to bear them" (Isa. 1:14).

The objection arising from such passages, however, confuses the precise question of our present thesis. Such passages as these, however great may appear to be the discrepancy in the witness of Scripture, do not fall into the category with which we are now dealing. For they are not, even on the most radical interpretation of the discrepancy, exposures of error on the part of one writer of Scripture of statements made by another writer. Jeremiah in other words does not quote the Pentateuch and then say that the statement concerned is an error and must therefore be corrected. While Jeremiah 7:22, 23 constitutes an apparent discrepancy in the testimony of Scripture, Jeremiah does not quote another writer and overtly or impliedly say that this writer was in error. It is in that particular question we are now interested.

The passages in what is generally called the Sermon on the Mount, where Jesus appears to set up an antithesis between his own teaching and the regulatory statutes of the Pentateuch, might plausibly be appealed to in this connection as instituting criticism of some of the Mosaic ordinances. Even though Jesus did not write Scripture, yet the finality of his teaching would make an appeal to his authority quite relevant to the present phase of our discussion. If it could be demonstrated that these passages in Matthew do involve criticism of the Mosaic regulations which Jesus quotes, then the divine character of the Pentateuch would in these particulars be impugned.

It must be recognized at the outset that, even if Jesus could be shown to appeal to his own authority as setting aside the Mosaic provisions concerned, this does not establish the errancy of these provisions nor overthrow the fact of their divine authority and sanction under the Mosaic dispensation. We have already shown that the abrogation of the temporary legislation of the Pentateuch does not in the least impugn its authenticity, infallibility, or divine character and authority. So Jesus might well have abrogated the observance of certain Mosaic ordinances and yet not in the least reflected upon their divine origin and character nor upon their divine authority during the period of their application and operation.[6] Surely nothing more than this could with any reason be elicited from these passages in Matthew and it is obvious that such does not provide us with any evidence that Jesus taught the errancy or fallibility of the five books of Moses.

We must, however, insist that it is not at all apparent that the notion of abrogation is the key to the interpretation of these antitheses. It should be remembered that the preface to this whole section in Jesus' teaching is in these words:

"Think not that I am come to destroy the law, or the prophets: I am not come to destroy, but to fulfill. For verily I say unto you, Till heaven and earth pass, one jot or one tittle shall in no wise pass from the law, till all be fulfilled. Whosoever therefore shall break one of these least commandments, and shall teach men so, he shall be called the least in the kingdom of heaven: but whosoever shall do and teach them, the same shall be called great in the kingdom of heaven" (Matt. 5:17-20).

A careful reading of this passage will show that any reflection upon the character of the law and the proph-

---

[6] The word "abrogated" is used in this sentence with reference merely to the discontinuance of *observance* and should not be understood to conflict with what will be later maintained respecting the permanent validity and meaning of the law.

ets or any insinuation of their errancy is entirely out of the question. As we shall see later, the import of such references to the law and the prophets is to the opposite effect. But, with more precise reference to our present discussion of the idea of abrogation, it would seem very strange indeed that Jesus would have made such an unequivocal appeal to the inviolability of every jot and tittle of the law and to the sanctions attending the breach of one of these least commandments as well as to the divine blessing accruing to the observance of them, and then have proceeded forthwith to teach the abrogation of these very commandments. There would be contradiction in any such view of the sequence and in such an interpretation of the import of the antitheses. We must therefore turn in some other direction for the meaning of Jesus' teaching in these verses. Dr. Stonehouse has admirably shown that

"Understood as illustrations of Jesus' fulfillment of the law, the antitheses then provide no support of the thesis that they involve an abrogation of the objective authority of the law. In the single instance where an enactment through Moses is set aside as provisional, namely, in the instance of the provision for a bill of divorcement, Jesus appeals decisively to the teaching of the law which is not circumscribed by reference to a temporary state of affairs. In the five other cases the design of Jesus is to show that current interpretations are inadequate as abiding by the externals or are in error as to the actual requirements of the law."[7]

These antitheses then constitute no evidence that Jesus taught or even insinuated that any part of the

---

[7] Ned B. Stonehouse: *The Witness of Matthew and Mark to Christ* (Philadelphia, 1944), p. 209; *cf.* by the present writer: *Principles of Conduct* (London and Grand Rapids, 1957), pp. 149-180.

Pentateuch or of the Old Testament was in error and therefore calculated to misinform us as to fact or doctrine.

We must now turn, in the second place, to the positive evidence the Scripture contains with respect to the character of Scripture. However significant and important the absence of evidence calculated to deny the inerrancy of Scripture may be, it is upon positive evidence that the doctrine of Biblical infallibility must rest.

In the Old Testament we find a great deal of evidence that bears directly upon the divine character and authority of what is written. Much that is written by the prophets, for example, is, by introductory statements such as "Thus saith the Lord," asserted to be divine in origin, content and authority. In the most express way the divine seal is attached to what is written. Obviously, if error could be discovered in or predicated of any of the passages bearing this seal, then there are only two alternatives. The claim to be the Word of the Lord must be rejected or fallibility must be predicated of the divine utterance. From the latter every Christian must recoil. The former must reject the testimony of Scripture with respect to the character of its own content. If that is done then our argument is at an end. The premise of our whole thesis, indeed our thesis itself, is that the doctrine of Scripture must be based upon the witness of Scripture just as any other doctrine in the whole realm of Christian confession. So the adoption of this alternative means the abandonment of the witness of Scripture as the basis of Christian doctrine. If the witness of Scripture is not accepted as the ground of the doctrine of Scripture, if it is not reliable in this department of doctrine, then by what right can its witness be pleaded as the authority in any department of truth?

Again, in the Old Testament the way in which the later books of the Old Testament appeal to the laws enunciated in the Pentateuch presupposes the divine authority and sanction of these laws. For example, there is the indictment which the last of the Old Testament prophets, Malachi, brings against his people.

"Ye said also, Behold what a weariness is it! and ye have snuffed at it, saith the Lord of hosts; and ye brought that which was torn, and the lame, and the sick; thus ye brought an offering: should I accept this of your hand? saith the Lord. But cursed be the deceiver, which hath in his flock a male, and voweth, and sacrificeth unto the Lord a corrupt thing: for I am a great King, saith the Lord of hosts, and my name is dreadful among the heathen" (Mal. 1:13, 14).

"Even from the days of your fathers ye are gone away from my ordinances, and have not kept them. Return unto me, and I will return unto you, saith the Lord of hosts. But ye said, Wherein shall we return? Will a man rob God? Yet ye have robbed me. But ye say, wherein have we robbed thee? In tithes and offerings" (Mal. 2:7, 8).

Such accusations are meaningless on any other assumption than that of the divine authority and obligation of the Levitical law (cf. Mal. 2:4-8). And the endorsement of Moses is put beyond all question when at the end of his prophecy Malachi writes, "Remember ye the law of Moses my servant, which I commanded unto him in Horeb for all Israel, with the statutes and judgments" (Mal. 4:4). It is surely of the greatest weight that the long line of Old Testament prophetic witness should come to its close with so insistent an appeal for devotion to the law of Moses, the Lord's servant, and that the intertestamentary period should be bridged, as it were, by the retrospective and the prospective, the appeal to Moses, on the one hand, and the promise of the resumption of the prophetic voice in him than whom there should not have arisen a greater, namely, John the Baptist, on the other (*cf.* chap. 4:5).

It is not, however, in the Old Testament that the most cogent evidence of a positive character, relative to this question, appears. For we do not have in the Old Testament any reference on the part of its writers to that collection of canonical writings in its entirety. In the nature of the case this could not reasonably be expected. Consequently we should not expect in the Old Testament any express predication or witness with respect to the whole collection of Old Testament books looked at in their unity as a fixed canon of sacred writings. In the New Testament the perspective is quite different. When the New Testament era opens to our view, the Old Testament books comprise a fixed collection of sacred writings. They exist before the speakers and writers of the New Testament period as a distinct corpus of authoritative writings viewed not only in their diversity but also and very distinctly in their unity as the canon of faith. Consequently, we find in the New Testament the most express and distinct estimate of the character of this body of writings viewed in their sum and unity as an entity capable of such characterization. It is such witness that is most directly pertinent to the present subject. What is the witness of the New Testament to the character of the Old Testament?

When we say the witness of the New Testament we mean, of course, the authoritative speakers and writers of the New Testament. First and foremost among such

authoritative witnesses is our Lord himself. His word is
a finality; on any other supposition the whole super-
structure of Christian faith must totter and crumble.
What then is our Lord's testimony with respect to the
Old Testament?

We have had occasion to quote and discuss the passage in Matthew 5:17-19 in another context. It is relevant to our present purpose in that it provides us with
one of the most striking testimonies to the estimate of
the Old Testament entertained by Jesus. It is highly
probable that, when Jesus says "the law or the prophets," he denotes by these two designations the whole of
the Old Testament, the law denoting what we know
as the Pentateuch and the prophets the rest of the Old
Testament. It is possible that by the prophets he means
the specifically prophetic books of the Old Testament,
and by the law he may have had in mind the law of
Moses in the more specific sense of the legislative economy embodied in the Pentateuch. If he is using these
terms in the more specific sense it would be wholly
arbitrary, indeed casuistic and contrary to all of the
evidence, to suppose that there is the least hint in such
a specific use of the terms "law" and "prophets" that
other parts of the Old Testament are in a different category in respect of authority. In this passage, then, Jesus
gives us his estimate of at least a very large part of the
Old Testament and his conception of the relation that
it sustained to his messianic work. He came not to destroy the law or the prophets; he came to fulfill.

The word "destroy" ($\kappa\alpha\tau\alpha\lambda\acute{v}\omega$) is peculiarly significant. It means to abrogate, to demolish, to disintegrate,
to annul or, as J. A. Alexander points out, "the destruction of a whole by the complete separation of its parts,

as when a house is taken down by being taken to pieces."[8] His emphatic denial of any such purpose in reference to either the law or the prophets means that the discharge of his messianic mission leaves the law and the prophets intact. He utters, however, not only this emphatic denial but also adds the positive purpose of his coming—he came to fulfill, to complete. And so his work with reference to both law and prophets is completory, not destructive. He who can speak in the immediately succeeding context with such solemn asseveration and imperious authority brings all that is involved in such asseveration and authority to bear upon the confirmation of the abiding validity, stability, and authority of both law and prophets. And not only so, but he also grounds his own mission and task upon such permanent validity, and defines his work in terms of fulfillment of all that the law and the prophets provided.

In verse 18 Jesus proceeds to apply the general statement of verse 17 to the minutiae of the law. It is this application of the general assertion to the minutest details that is particularly pertinent to our present topic. General statements may sometimes not cover, or provide for, certain exceptions in detail. But here Jesus precludes any possibility of discrepancy between the general and the particular. He is saying in effect, "This proposition that I came not to destroy but to fulfill applies not simply in general terms but also to the minutest particulars." And not simply is this the case; the connection expressed by the conjunction is also that the

[8] *The Gospel according to Matthew Explained* (London, 1884), p. 126.

general statement of verse 17 is grounded in the fact
that not one jot or tittle, not the minutest detail, will
pass from the law till all be fulfilled. To enforce and
seal the veracity of this, Jesus uses the formula that
combines asseveration and authority, "Verily I say unto
you."

The "jot" is the smallest letter of the Hebrew alphabet and the "tittle" is the minute horn or projection
that distinguishes consonants of similar form from one
another. It would be impossible to think of any expression that would bespeak the thought of the meticulous
more adequately than precisely this one used here by
our Lord. In respect of the meticulous, our English expression "one letter or syllable" is scarcely equivalent.
Could anything establish more conclusively the meticulous accuracy, validity, and truth of the law than the
language to which Jesus here attaches his own unique
formula of asseveration? Many professing Christians
recoil from the doctrine of verbal inspiration, the doctrine which means simply that the inspiration of Scripture extends to the very words as well as to the thoughts.
It is difficult to understand why those who assent to
inspiration should stumble at *verbal* inspiration. For
words are the media of thought and, so far as Scripture
is concerned, the written words are the only media of
communication. If the thoughts are inspired, the words
must be also. But whatever the case may be in the
sphere of logic, the antipathy to verbal inspiration has
little in common with the very obvious import of Jesus'
representation in this passage. The indissolubility of
the law extends to its every jot and tittle. Such indissolubility could not be predicated of it if it were in any
detail fallible, for if fallible it would some day come to

nought. And this is just saying that in every detail the law was in his esteem infallible and therefore indissoluble. It is indeed strange prejudice that professes adherence to the infallibility of Christ and yet rejects the clear implications of his teaching. Nothing could be plainer than this, that in the smallest details he regards the law as incapable of being made void and that in the smallest details it is taken up by him and finds, in his fulfillment of it, its permanent embodiment and validity. By the most stringent necessity there is but one conclusion, namely, that the law is infallible and inerrant.[9]

[9] Dewey M. Beegle evades the force of Matt. 5:17, 18 by appeal to what he alleges to be the contrast in Paul's teaching between the letter of the law and its spirit (*The Inspiration of Scripture*, Philadelphia 1963, pp. 75 f.). If anything should point to the fallacy of this interpretation of both Paul and Jesus, it is Matt. 5:17, 18. In II Cor. 3:6, to which Beegle appeals, the contrast between the letter and the Spirit is the contrast between the law in its condemning and death-inflicting power and the life-giving efficacy of the Holy Spirit. To find in this passage or others the outworn popular notion of a contrast between the letter and the spirit of the law is to abandon exegesis; it is alien to Paul's thought and misses completely the contrasts of the passage. *Cf.* J. Gresham Machen: *What is Faith?* (Grand Rapids, 1946), pp. 187 ff.

It should also be remembered that when speaking of verbal or jot and tittle inspiration, we are never thinking of words, or letters, or tittles in themselves or in abstraction. This would not be verbal inspiration, for the simple reason that no such words (or letters or tittles) occur in Scripture. They are always words in relationship, in clauses, sentences, paragraphs, books, and, in fact, relationship to the whole of Scripture. Their significance resides in this relationship and only in that relationship are they inspired. It is easy to show how far-reaching the change of a letter or tittle could be. It is to this Matt. 5:17, 18 bears witness.

In our discussion of Matthew 5:17-19, we left open the possibility that Jesus was using the terms "law" and "prophets" in a more restricted and specific sense. It is far from being certain that this interpretation of the scope of his words is justifiable. It is far more reasonable to believe that he had the whole Old Testament in mind. But we must not prejudice the argument by insisting upon this, for the argument we are now pursuing does not rest upon it. The witness of our Lord to the character of the Old Testament is so copious that what is not supplied by one passage is supplied by another. If the books other than those of Moses and the prophets are not expressly alluded to in Matthew 5:17-19 they certainly are in other places. One of the most striking of these is John 10:33-36, and to this part of his witness we may now turn.[10]

The occasion for his speaking these words was that created by the reaction of the Jews to his claim, "I and the Father are one." The Jews rightly interpreted this claim as meaning that Jesus placed himself on an equality with God. This they regarded as blasphemy and they took up stones to stone him. Jesus' claim was, of course, a stupendous one and there are only two alternatives. Either his claim was true or he did utter blasphemy. Here Jesus did not simply claim to be the Messiah; he claimed to be equal with the Father. The charge brought by the Jews was not a whit too severe if their conception of Jesus were correct. Quite logically on their own presuppositions their charge struck at the

10 It is not within the scope of this study to discuss the critical questions raised with respect to John's Gospel and other New Testament writings.

center of Jesus' claim and therefore at the basis of his mission and work. The charge denied his deity and his veracity. If validated, it would have exposed Jesus' claim as the most iniquitous imposture.

It was a charge with such implications that Jesus had to answer. If ever the resources of effective rebuttal needed to be drawn upon, it was at such a juncture. How did he meet the charge? "Jesus answered them, Is it not written in your law, I said ye are gods? If he called them gods unto whom the word of God came, and the scripture cannot be broken, say ye of him whom the Father sanctified and sent into the world, Thou blasphemest, because I said I am the Son of God." As we read this reply, we are amazed at what appears to be the facility and composure with which it is given as well as at what appears to be its restraint. Indeed, on superficial reading it might appear to be weak and ineffective. But the facility, composure, and restraint, which we believe are real, as well as the apparent weakness, which is not real, all converge to demonstrate the significance for our present purpose of his appeal to Scripture. He staked his argument for the rebuttal of the most serious allegation that could be brought against him upon a brief statement drawn from Psalm 82:6. It is this appeal to Scripture that is the pivot of his whole defense. This cannot be explained on any other basis than that he considered the Scriptures as the unassailable instrument of defense. For "the scripture cannot be broken."

Just as eloquent of Jesus' use of Scripture is, what appears to us, the obscurity of the passage to which he appeals. It would seem to have no direct bearing upon the question at issue. Yet Jesus uses this apparently obscure and less important passage as his argument to answer an attack that was aimed at the center of his person and teaching and work. And furthermore, this passage is drawn from that part of the Old Testament that possibly, so far as our argument is concerned, did not come within his purview in Matthew 5:17. Does this not show that his attitude to every jot and tittle of the Psalms was identical with that to every jot and tittle of the law? Upon any other supposition his appeal to a brief and relatively obscure statement of the book of Psalms would be quite forceless and inconclusive.

Finally, the force of the brief parenthetical clause, "the scripture cannot be broken," has to be noted. It might be plausibly argued that Jesus in his reply to the Jews was simply taking advantage of an *ad hominem* argument. In the question, "Is it not written in your law?", Jesus is meeting his adversaries on their own assumptions. And so, it might be said, no argument bearing upon Jesus' own view of Scripture could be based on this passage. But Jesus' remark, "the scripture cannot be broken," silences any such contention. In this remark Jesus expresses not simply the attitude of the Jews to Scripture but his own view of the inviolability of Scripture. He appeals to Scripture because it is really and intrinsically a finality. And when he says the Scripture cannot be broken, he is surely using the word "Scripture" in its most comprehensive denotation as including all that the Jews of the day recognized as Scripture, to wit, all the canonical books of the Old Testament. It is of the Old Testament without any reservation or exception that he says, it "cannot be broken." Here then there can be no question as to how much of the Old Testament came within the purview or scope of his assertion. He affirms the unbreakableness of the Scripture in its entirety and leaves no room for any such supposition as that of degrees of inspiration and fallibility. Scripture is inviolable. Nothing less than this is the testimony of our Lord. And the crucial nature of such witness is driven home by the fact that it is in answer to the most serious of charges and in the defense of his most stupendous claim that he bears this testimony.

In passages such as those with which we have just dealt, our Lord's view of Scripture comes to explicit expression and exposition. It is not, however, in a few passages that his viewpoint is attested. There is a mass of evidence that corroborates the express teaching of the more explicit passages. Indeed, corroboration is too weak a word to do justice to the import of the mass of evidence bearing upon the question. Rather should we say that the teaching of our Lord is so steeped in the appeal to Scripture, so steeped in the use of the formula, "it is written," so pervaded by the recognition that what Scripture says God says, so characterized by the acceptance of the finality of the word of Scripture, that the doctrine of Scripture clearly enunciated in some passages is the necessary presupposition of the correlative evidence. The inescapable fact is that the mass of direct and indirect statement leads to one conclusion that, for our Lord, the Scripture, just because it was *Scripture,* just because it fell within the denotation of the formula, "it is written," was a finality. His attitude is one of meticulous acceptance and reverence. The only explanation of such an attitude is that what Scripture said, God said, that the Scripture was God's Word, that it was God's Word because it was Scripture and that it was or became Scripture because it was God's Word. That he

distinguished between the Word of God borne to us by
Scripture and the written Word itself would be an im-
position upon Jesus' own teaching wholly alien to the
identifications Jesus makes and to the reverence for the
letter of Scripture so pervasive in all of his witness.

To institute a contrast between the teaching of our Lord
and of his apostles on the question of Scripture would, of
course, disrupt the harmony of the New Testament witness.
The establishment of such disharmony would admittedly be
a serious matter and it would have far-reaching consequences for the whole construction of Christian truth.
Regarding the respective views of Scripture, discrepancy
between Jesus and the writers of the New Testament could
be sought in either of two directions. It could be sought in
the direction of trying to find a more liberal view of Scripture reflected in the writers, or at least in some of the
writers, of the New Testament, or it might be sought in
the direction of showing that in the writings of the New
Testament there is a petrifying and mechanizing process at
work so that the more organic and elastic view of Jesus is
transformed and brought into accord with the allegedly
more scholastic and legalistic bias of later developments.
We already found what our Lord's teaching was. We found
it to be nothing less than that of the infallible character
and authority of the Old Testament. A higher view of
plenary or verbal inspiration we could not expect to find.
If discrepancy between Jesus and the writers of the New
Testament is to be sought it would not be reasonable, in
view of the evidence, to seek it in the greater liberalism of
Jesus. When we turn in the other direction, do we find any
relaxation of the rigidity of Jesus' teaching in those who
were his appointed witnesses?

Any adequate examination of this question would lead
us far beyond our space in this volume. But is it not of the
greatest pertinence that the books of the New Testament

show that same characteristic which is so patent in the teaching of Christ, namely, appeal to what had been written? It is singular that the New Testament, not only in the reporting of Jesus' teaching but also as a whole, should as it were rest its case so frequently upon the adduction of Scripture proof and should authenticate the history of the Old Testament by such copious reference to it. Its witness in general is to the same effect as is summed up in the words of Paul, "For whatsoever things were written aforetime were written for our learning, that we through patience and comfort of the scriptures might have hope" (Rom. 15:4), an appraisal of the whole of the Old Testament that is preceded by a thoroughly typical appeal to the Old Testament as testifying beforehand to the example of Christ that he pleased not himself and as therefore not only witnessing to the fact that Christ pleased not himself but as also supporting the exhortation, "Let every one of us please his neighbour for his good to edification" (Rom. 15:2). It is precisely in such estimation of the Scriptures and in such allusion to them, as not only prophetic of what took place in the fullness of time but also as having direct bearing upon the most practical and abiding of Christian duties, that the New Testament abounds. And this is just saying that the Old Testament is not simply true as history, prophecy, and law but that it is also of abiding validity, application, and authority.

But, just as we found in the case of our Lord that the high view of the inspiration of Scripture not only underlies the formulae and allusions in which his teaching abounds but also comes to explicit expression in specific passages, so is it in the case of the other authoritative New Testament witnesses. The doctrine of Scripture becomes in some passages the subject of express teaching. Perhaps most notable among these is II Timothy 3:16, "All scripture is given by inspiration of God."[11]

In the preceding context of this passage, Paul refers to the "holy writings" which Timothy knew from a child. These "holy writings" can be none other than the sacred Scriptures of the Old Testament. It is with these Scriptures in mind that Paul says, "All scripture is God-breathed." The word that Paul uses predicates of all Scripture or of every Scripture a certain quality. More particularly, the predicate reflects upon its origin; it is the product of God's creative breath. The terseness of Paul's affirmation here must not be allowed to obscure its significance. It is that Scripture, the denotation of which is placed beyond all doubt by the context, is God's mouth, God's breath, and therefore God's oracle. Paul makes no qualifications and no reservations. Every Scripture is God-breathed and therefore, so far as divine origin and resultant character are concerned, there is no discrimination. And in respect of the benefit accruing to men, all of Scripture is, for the reason that it is God-inspired, also profitable for doctrine, for reproof, for correction, for instruction in righteousness, that the man of God may be perfect, thoroughly furnished unto every good work.

Paul was, of course, well aware that God used human instruments in giving us these Scriptures. In his epistles he makes repeated allusion to the human authors of the sacred books. But the recognition of human instru-

[11] See, for an examination of the meaning of θεόπνευστος, B. B. Warfield: *Revelation and Inspiration* (New York, 1927), pp. 229-280, *The Inspiration and Authority of the Bible* (Philadelphia, 1948), pp. 245-296 and, for an exegesis of II Tim. 3:16, these same, respectively, pp. 79 ff. and pp. 133 ff.

mentality did not in the least inhibit Paul from making the stupendous affirmation that all Scripture is God-breathed, which means that Scripture is of divine origin and authorship and therefore of divine character and authority.

The predication which Paul here makes is nothing less than the high doctrine of plenary inspiration. For Paul is not here speaking of an inbreathing on the part of God into the writers of holy Scripture nor even into holy Scripture itself. The term Paul uses represents the concept of "breathing out" rather than that of "breathing in" and is far removed from the notion that a human product or witness is so interpenetrated with divine truth or influence that it becomes the Word of God. The whole emphasis is upon the fact that all Scripture proceeds from God and is therefore invested with a divinity that makes it as authoritative and efficient as a word oracularly spoken by God directly to us.

In II Timothy 3:16 Paul says nothing with respect to the human authors of Scripture nor with respect to the way in which God wrought upon the human authors so as to provide us with God-breathed Scripture. The apostle Peter, however, though not by any means furnishing us with a full definition of the mode of inspiration, does go farther than does Paul in II Timothy 3:16 in stating the relation that obtained between the Holy Spirit and the inspired human witnesses. "No prophecy of scripture," he writes, "is of private interpretation. For not by the will of man was prophecy brought aforetime, but as borne by the Holy Spirit men spake from God" (II Pet. 1:20, 21). That Peter's statement here bears upon the agency of the Holy Spirit in the giving of Scripture is obvious from the phrase, "prophecy of scripture."

Peter's teaching in this passage is both negative and positive. Negatively, he denies that the prophecy of Scripture owes its origin to human initiative, volition, or determination. It is not the product of individual reflection or imagination. Positively, human instrumentality is asserted. "Men spake from God." False inferences that might be drawn from the absolute terms of the preceding negations are obviated by the recognition of human agency. But while men spake, they spake from God, and it is this datum that harmonizes the fact of human agency with the negations of private interpretation and the will of man. They spake from God because they were borne along or borne up by the Holy Spirit.[12] Here there is plainly the conjunction of human and divine agency. But the divine character of the prophecy is insured by the peculiar character of the Spirit's agency. He took up the human agents in such a way that they spoke God's Word, not their own.

In this context it is the stability of the prophetic Word that is being emphasized. The ground upon which this stability rests is that it came from God, that the Holy Spirit was not only operative in the writers of Scripture but carried them to his destination and that this prophetic Word is not a momentary utterance or passing oracular deliverance but the Word of God that has received through Scripture permanent embodiment and authentication.

Summing up the witness of the New Testament, we

12 Cf. B. B. Warfield: op. cit., respectively, pp. 82f. and pp. 135f.

find that human authorship or instrumentality is fully recognized and yet human agency is not conceived of as in any way impairing the divine origin, character, truth, and authority of Scripture. It is divine in its origin because it is the product of God's creative breath and because it was as borne by the Holy Spirit that men spoke from God. For these reasons it bears an oracular character that accords it an authority as real and divine as if we heard the voice of God speaking from heaven. This oracular character is a permanent feature and so Scripture has an abiding stability and application—it is unbreakable and indissoluble.

The witness with which we have so far dealt confines itself to the express testimony of the New Testament with reference to the Old. What then of the evidence on which may be founded a similar judgment with respect to the character of the New Testament? It must be acknowledged that the great mass of the evidence we possess bearing upon the inspiration of Scripture is the witness of the New Testament with reference to the Old. We do not have from the New Testament writers or authoritative witnesses the same abundance of testimony to the inspiration of the New Testament. That this should be the state of the case should not surprise us. When the New Testament witnesses spoke or wrote there was no finished New Testament canon to which they could refer as a unified and completed corpus of writings. Particularly is this true of our Lord himself. None of the books of the New Testament was written when he spoke upon earth. Witness to the character of the New Testament as a whole such as we find in the New Testament with reference to the Old would have been impossible for any writer of the New Testament except the last and only then as an appendix to his own last canonical writing. This type of witness it would be unreasonable for us to demand as the necessary seal upon the divine character and authority of the entire New Testament.

While we do not have the same mass of testimony to the inspiration of the New Testament as to the Old, and while the circumstances were such that we could not expect the same kind of inclusive characterization, it does not follow that we have no evidence upon which to maintain the divine origin and character of the New Testament. We have sufficient evidence, and to such we now turn our attention.

The organic unity of both Testaments is the presupposition of the appeal to the authority of the Old Testament and of allusion to it in which the New Testament abounds. This fact of organic unity bears very directly upon the question of the inspiration of the New Testament. For if, as we have found, the authoritative witness of the New Testament bears out the unbreakable and inerrant character of the Old, how could that which forms an organic unit with the Old be of an entirely different character as regards the nature of its inspiration? When the implications of organic unity are fully appreciated, it becomes impossible to believe that the divinity of the New Testament can be on a lower plane than that of the Old. Surely then, if the Old Testament, according to the testimony that in this matter has the greatest relevance or authority, is inerrant, the New Testament must also be.

This argument from organic unity has peculiar force when we properly understand the implications of progressive revelation. The New Testament stands to the

Old in the relation of consummation to preparation; it embodies a fuller and more glorious disclosure of God's character and will. This is signalized by the fact that in these last days God hath spoken unto us by his Son who is the brightness of his glory and the express image of his being (Heb. 1:1-3). In Paul's language the glory of the New Testament is the glory that excels (II Cor. 3:10, 11). The New Testament Scripture enshrines and conveys to us the content of that new and better covenant, established upon better promises. Is it at all consonant with the completory nature of the New Testament, with the more excellent glory inherent in the New Testament and with the finality attaching to the revelation of God's own Son to suppose that the Scripture of such an economy should be lacking in that inerrancy which the authoritative witnesses—our Lord and his apostles—predicate of the Old Testament? It would be contrary to all sound analogy and reason to entertain such a supposition.[13]

The cogency of this argument is made all the more apparent when we bear in mind the meaning of Pentecost. The Old Testament was God-breathed, possessing unshakable stability and permanent validity, because it was as borne by the Holy Spirit men spoke from God. Yet so much more abundant were the operations of the Spirit introduced by Pentecost that it can be described in terms of "giving" and "sending forth" the Holy Spirit. Are we to believe that this greater fulness and abundance of the Spirit's operation gave us a Scripture less reliable and less inerrant than the Scripture that the Spirit gave before the abundant effusion

[13] Cf. L. Gaussen: *Theopneustia* (Cincinnati, 1859), pp. 74f.

of Pentecost took place? Are we to believe that the
Scripture that is the only abiding witness to and embodiment of the full and abundant administration of
the Spirit is a Scripture less characterized by the activity of the Spirit that imparted divinity and authority
to the Old Testament? To ask these questions is to show
that once the witness of the New Testament to the inspiration and inerrancy of the Old is accepted, once the
relations which the two Testaments sustain to one another are understood and appreciated, the infallible
character of the Old Testament furnishes us with the
most cogent considerations in support of a similar judgment with respect to the character of the New Testament.

We must not think, however, that these considerations
constitute the whole basis of faith in the New Testament as inerrant Scripture. For the New Testament is
not without direct witness to its own character. It is
true that we do not have the mass of testimony that
we have in connection with the Old Testament. But,
in a manner analogous to the witness the Old Testament bears to its own divinity, the New Testament
not only bears the unmistakable marks of its divine
origin but also bears direct witness to its own divine
character and authority.

If the New Testament is the Word of God with all the
fulness of meaning that the authoritative witnesses of
the New Testament ascribe to the Old, it must be by
reason of that same plenary inspiration of the Holy
Spirit operative in the writing of the Old Testament.
The promises that Christ gave to his disciples with respect to the Holy Spirit have, therefore, the closest bearing upon this question. When Jesus sent out his disciples

to preach the kingdom of God he said to them, "But when they deliver you up, take no thought how or what ye shall speak, for it shall be given you in that hour what ye shall speak. For it is not ye that speak but the Spirit of your Father that speaketh in you" (Matt. 10:19, 20; cf. Mark 13:11; Luke 12:12; Luke 21:14, 15). Such a promise assures to the disciples that in the "passing exigencies" and "to subserve interests of the narrowest range"[14] there would be afforded to them an inspiration of the Holy Spirit that would make their spoken words not simply their words but the words of the Holy Spirit. This same promise of the Spirit is given greatly increased scope and application when on the eve of his crucifixion Jesus said, "It is expedient for you that I go away. For if I go not away, the Comforter will not come unto you, but if I depart I will send him unto you.... He will guide you into all the truth" (John 16:7, 13). After his resurrection Jesus performed what must be construed as the act of official impartation of the Holy Spirit when he breathed on his disciples and said, "Receive ye the Holy Ghost" (John 20:22). And before his ascension he assured them, "Ye shall receive power after that the Holy Spirit is come upon you, and ye shall be my witnesses both in Jerusalem and in all Judea and in Samaria and unto the uttermost part of the earth" (Acts 1:8). The work and functions of the disciples are therefore to be discharged, in accordance with the promise and commission of Christ, by the direction and inspiration of the Holy Spirit. It is no wonder then that we find in the writings of the New Testament a note of authority, of certainty and of final-

14 L. Gaussen: *op. cit.*, p. 77.

ity that it would be presumptuous for men to arrogate to themselves, a note of authority that is consistent with truth and sobriety only if the writers were the agents of divine authority and the subjects of inspiration by the Holy Spirit. Relevant to the question of inspiration, this note of authority is one of the most significant features of the New Testament.

The passage in I Corinthians 7:10-12 is sometimes understood as if Paul were instituting a contrast between the authoritative teaching of Christ and his own unauthoritative judgment on questions bearing upon marriage and separation—"But to the married I give charge, not I but the Lord.... But to the rest I say, not the Lord." A careful reading of the whole passage will, however, show that the contrast is not between the inspired teaching of Christ and the uninspired teaching of the apostle but rather between the teaching of the apostle that could appeal to the express utterances of Christ in the days of his flesh, on the one hand, and the teaching of the apostle that went beyond the cases dealt with by Christ, on the other. There is no distinction as regards the binding character of the teaching in these respective cases. The language and terms the apostle uses in the second case are just as emphatic and mandatory as in the first case. And this passage, so far from diminishing the character of apostolic authority, only enhances our estimate of that authority. If Paul can be as mandatory in his terms when he is dealing with questions on which, by his own admission, he cannot appeal for support to the express teaching of Christ, does not this fact serve to impress upon us how profound was Paul's consciousness that he was writing by divine authority, when his own teaching was as mandatory in its terms as was his reiteration of the teaching of the Lord himself? Nothing else than the consciousness of enunciating divinely authoritative law would warrant the terseness and decisiveness of the statement by which he prevents all gainsaying, "And so ordain I in all the churches" (I Cor. 7:17).

That Paul regards his written word as invested with divine sanction and authority is placed beyond all question in this same epistle (I Cor. 14:37, 38). In the context he is dealing specifically with the question of the place of women in the public assemblies of worship. He enjoins silence upon women in the church by appeal to the universal custom of the churches of Christ and by appeal to the law of the Old Testament. It is then that he makes appeal to the divine content of his prescriptions. "If any man thinketh himself to be a prophet or spiritual, let him acknowledge that the things I write unto you are the commandment of the Lord. And if any man be ignorant, let him be ignorant." Paul here makes the most direct claim to be writing the divine Word and coordinates this appeal to divine authority with appeal to the already existing Scripture of the Old Testament.

In the earlier part of this epistle Paul informs us, in fashion thoroughly consonant with the uniform teaching of Scripture as to what constitutes the word of man the Word of God, that the Holy Spirit is the source of all the wisdom taught by the apostles. "God hath revealed them unto us through the Spirit. For the Spirit searcheth all things, yea, the deep things of God" (I Cor. 2:10). And not only does Paul appeal here to the Holy Spirit as the source of the wisdom conveyed through his message but also to the Spirit as the source of the very media of expression. For Paul continues, "which things also we speak, not in the words which man's wisdom teacheth, but which the Spirit teacheth, combining spiritual things with spiritual" (I Cor. 2: 13).[15] Spirit-taught things and Spirit-taught words! Nothing else provides us with an explanation of apostolic authority.

Much else that supports and corroborates the foregoing position could be elicited from the witness of the New Testament. But in the brief limits of the space available enough has been given to indicate that the same plenary inspiration which the New Testament uniformly predicates of the Old is the kind of inspiration that renders the New Testament itself the Word of God.

Frequently the doctrine of verbal inspiration is dismissed with supercilious scorn as but a remnant of that mediaeval or post-Reformation scholasticism that has

---

[15] It is possible that συγκρίνοντες could be rendered "interpreting." But, in that event, the immediately preceding context would indicate that the rendering of the clause would be: "interpreting spiritual things by spiritual words." This would have the same effect for the question being discussed as the rendering given above. The rendering that has been proposed: "interpreting spiritual things to spiritual men" is quite unnatural and cannot compete with the other renderings. The clause in question surely stands in apposition to what precedes: "which things also we speak, not in words taught of human wisdom, but in words taught of the Spirit." The thought is the combination of *the things* of the Spirit and *words* taught of the Spirit. The well-established meaning of συγκρίνω, namely, "combine," together with the thought of the preceding context and the syntax of the whole sentence point clearly to the translation: "combining spiritual things with spiritual words."

tended to petrify Christianity.[16] Such contempt usually
accompanies the claim that open-minded scientific research has made adherence to Biblical inerrancy inconsistent with well-informed honesty and therefore untenable. This boast of scientific honesty is plausible, so
much so that it is often the password to respect in the
arena of theological debate. The plea of the present
contribution has been, however, that the summary dismissal of Biblical infallibility is lamentably unscientific
in its treatment of the very data that bear directly on
the question at issue and that such dismissal has failed
to reckon with the issues at stake in the rejection of
what is established by straightforward scientific exegesis
of the witness of Scripture to its own character. If the
testimony of Scripture on the doctrine of Scripture is
not authentic and trustworthy, then the finality of
Scripture is irretrievably undermined. The question at
stake is the place of Scripture as the canon of faith. And
we must not think that the finality of Christ remains
unimpaired even if the finality of Scripture is sacrificed.
The rejection of the inerrancy of Scripture means the
rejection of Christ's own witness to Scripture. Finally

16 Verbal inspiration is not to be equated with a theory of
mechanical dictation. The classic exponents of the doctrine of
verbal inspiration have not attempted to define the mode of
inspiration. It is true that the term "dictation" sometimes occurs, but its use was not intended to specify the mode of
inspiration as that of dictation. Full allowance is made for the
manifold activities and processes by which the books of Scripture
were brought into being and full recognition given to the
diversity characterizing those who were the instruments in the
production of Scripture. *Cf.* B. B. Warfield: *op. cit.,* respectively,
pp. 99-106 and pp. 153-160; *Calvin and Calvinism* (New York,
1931), pp. 62 ff.

and most pointedly, then, the integrity of our Lord's witness is the crucial issue in this battle of the faith.

II. The Internal Testimony

The thesis maintained above in our examination of the objective witness is that Scripture is authoritative by reason of the character it possesses as the infallible Word of God and that this divine quality belongs to Scripture because it is the product of God's creative breath through the mode of plenary inspiration by the Holy Spirit. The rejection of such a position has appeared to many to involve no impairment of the divine authority of the Bible because, even though the infallibility of Scripture has to be abandoned, there still remains the ever abiding and active witness of the Holy Spirit, and so infallible authority is fully conserved in the internal testimony of the Holy Spirit. Scripture is authoritative, it is said, because it is borne home to the man of faith by the internal testimony of the Spirit.

That there is such an activity of the Holy Spirit as the internal testimony is beyond dispute, and that there is no true faith in Scripture as the Word of God apart from such inward testimony is likewise fully granted. It might seem, therefore, that it belongs to the situation in which we are placed, relative to the Holy Spirit, to say that the divine authority that confronts us is not that emanating from a past and finished activity of the Spirit but rather the influence of the Spirit which is now operative with reference to and in us. Does not the positing of divine authority in an activity of the Spirit that to us is impersonal and external, as well as far distant and now inactive, do prejudice to the real meaning of that directly personal and presently operative address of the Holy Spirit to us and in us?

This question is that which defines what is the most important cleavage within Protestantism today. It is the cleavage between what is called Barthianism and the historic Protestant position. The Barthian view is that Scripture is authoritative because it witnesses to the Word of God; it is the vessel or vehicle of the Word of God to us. In that respect Scripture is said to be unique and in that sense it is called the Word of God. But what makes Scripture really authoritative, on this view, is the ever-recurring act of God, the divine decision, whereby, through the mediacy of Scripture, the witness of Scripture to the Word of God is borne home to us with ruling and compelling power. The Scripture is not authoritative antecedently and objectively. It is only authoritative as here and now, to this man and to no other, in a concrete crisis and confrontation, God reveals himself through the medium of Scripture. Only as there is the ever-recurring human crisis and divine decision does the Bible become the Word of God.

It is apparent, therefore, that for the Barthian the authority-imparting factor is not Scripture as an existing corpus of truth given by God to man by a process of revelation and inspiration in past history, not the divine quality and character which Scripture inherently possesses, but something else that must be distinguished from any past action and from any resident quality. The issue must not be obscured. Barth does not hold and cannot hold that Scripture possesses binding and ruling authority by reason of what it is objectively, inherently and qualitatively.

An objection to this way of stating the matter is easily

anticipated. It is that this sharp antithesis is indefensible. For, after all, it will be said, Scripture is unique. It is the Word of God because it bears witness to God's Word. It occupies a unique category because there was something unique and distinctive about that past activity by which it came to be. It differs radically from other books written at the time of its production and also from all other books. It can, therefore, have no authority in abstraction from that quality that belongs to it as the human witness to the revelation given by God in the past. So, it may be argued, the factor arising from past events and activities enters into the whole complex of factors that combine and converge to invest Scripture with that unique character which makes it the fit medium for the ever-recurring act of divine revelation. It is not then an *either or* but a *both and*.

The objection is appreciated and welcomed. But it does not eliminate the issue. After making allowance for all that is argued in support of the objection, there still remains the fact that, on Barthian presuppositions, it is not the divine quality inherent in Scripture nor the divine activity by which that quality has been imparted to it that makes Scripture authoritative. That past activity and the resultant quality may constitute the prerequisites for the authority by which it becomes ever and anon invested, but they do not constitute that authority. It is rather the ever-recurring act of God that is the authority-constituting fact. This ever-recurring activity of God may be conceived of as the internal testimony of the Spirit and so it is this testimony that constitutes Scripture authoritative.[17]

---

[17] *Cf.* Karl Barth: *Church Dogmatics*, Vol. I, 1, E. T. (Edinburgh, 1936), pp. 207 ff.

It is sometimes supposed that this construction of the authority of Scripture represents the classic Protestant or indeed Reformed position. Even the Westminster Confession has been appealed to as enunciating this position when it says that "our full persuasion and assurance of the infallible truth and divine authority thereof, is from the inward work of the Holy Spirit bearing witness by and with the Word in our hearts" (I:V). A little examination of Chapter I of the Confession will expose the fallacy of this appeal. Indeed, the Westminster Confession was framed with a logic and comprehension exactly adapted not only to obviate but also to meet this construction. Section V, from which the above quotation was given, does not deal with the nature or ground of the authority of Scripture. The preceding section deals with that logically prior question. It states clearly that the authority of Scripture resides in the fact that it is the Word of God. "The authority of the Holy Scripture, for which it ought to be believed and obeyed, dependeth not upon the testimony of any man, or Church; but wholly upon God (who is truth itself) the author thereof: and therefore it is to be received because it is the Word of God." In one word, Scripture is authoritative because God is its author and he is its author because, as is stated in Section II, it was given by inspiration of God. Nothing could be plainer than this: that the Confession represents the authority of Scripture as resting not upon the internal testimony of the Holy Spirit but upon the inspiration of the Spirit, a finished activity by which, it is clearly stated, the sixty-six books enumerated were produced and in virtue of which they are the Word of God written.

It is, however, by "the inward work of the Holy Spirit

bearing witness by and with the Word in our hearts"
that we become convinced of that authority. The authority of Scripture is an objective and permanent fact
residing in the quality of inspiration; the conviction on
our part has to wait for that inward testimony by which
the antecedent facts of divinity and authority are borne
in upon our minds and consciences. It is to confuse the
most important and eloquent of distinctions to represent the former as consisting in the latter. The Confession has left no room for doubt as to what its position
is, and in formulating the matter with such clarity it
has expressed the classic Reformed conception.

What then is the nature of this internal testimony
and what is the Scriptural basis upon which the doctrine rests?

If, as has been shown in the earlier part of this discussion, Scripture is divine in its origin, character, and
authority, it must bear the marks or evidences of that
divinity. If the heavens declare the glory of God and
therefore bear witness to their divine Creator, the Scripture as God's handiwork must also bear the imprints
of his authorship. This is just saying that Scripture
evidences itself to be the Word of God; its divinity is
self-evidencing and self-authenticating. The ground of
faith in Scripture as the Word of God is therefore the
evidence it inherently contains of its divine authorship
and quality. External evidence, witness to its divinity
derived from other sources extraneous to itself, may
corroborate and confirm the witness it inherently contains, but such external evidence cannot be in the category of evidence sufficient to ground and constrain faith.
If the faith is faith in the Bible as God's Word, obviously the evidence upon which such faith rests must

itself have the quality of divinity. For only evidence with the quality of divinity would be sufficient to ground a faith in divinity. Faith in Scripture as God's Word, then, rests upon the perfections inherent in Scripture and is elicited by the perception of these perfections. These perfections constitute its incomparable excellence and such excellence when apprehended constrains the overwhelming conviction that is the only appropriate kind of response.

If Scripture thus manifests itself to be divine, why is not faith the result in the case of every one confronted with it? The answer is that not all men have the requisite perceptive faculty. Evidence is one thing, the ability to perceive and understand is another. "The natural man receiveth not the things of the Spirit of God: for they are foolishness unto him: neither can he know them, because they are spiritually discerned" (I Cor. 2:14). It is here that the necessity for the internal testimony of the Spirit enters. The darkness and depravity of man's mind by reason of sin make man blind to the divine excellence of Scripture. And the effect of sin is not only that it blinds the mind of man and makes it impervious to the evidence but also that it renders the heart of man utterly hostile to the evidence. The carnal mind is enmity against God and therefore resists every claim of the divine perfection. If the appropriate response of faith is to be yielded to the divine excellence inherent in Scripture, nothing less than radical regeneration by the Holy Spirit can produce the requisite susceptibility. "Except a man be born again, he cannot see the kingdom of God" (John 3:3). "The natural man receiveth not the things of the Spirit of God" (I Cor. 2:14). It is here that the internal testimony of the

Spirit enters and it is in the inward work of the Holy
Spirit upon the heart and mind of man that the internal testimony consists. The witness of Scripture to
the depravity of man's mind and to the reality, nature, and effect of the inward work of the Holy Spirit
is the basis upon which the doctrine of the internal
testimony rests.

When Paul institutes the contrast between the natural man and the spiritual and says with respect to the
latter, "But he that is spiritual judgeth all things, yet
he himself is judged of no one" (I Cor. 2:15), he means
that the "spiritual" person is the person endowed with
and indwelt by the Holy Spirit. It is only such an one
who has the faculty to discern the things revealed by the
Spirit. By way of contrast with the natural man he
receives, knows, and discerns the truth.

Earlier in this same chapter Paul tells us in terms that
even more pointedly deal with our present subject that
the faith of the Corinthians in the gospel was induced
by the demonstration of the Spirit and of power. "And
my speech and my preaching was not in persuasive
words of wisdom, but in demonstration of the Spirit
and of power, in order that your faith might not be in
the wisdom of men but in the power of God" (I Cor.
2:4, 5). No doubt Paul here is reflecting upon the manner of his preaching. It was not with the embellish-
ments of human oratory that he preached the gospel
but with that demonstration or manifestation that is
produced by the Spirit and power of God. He is saying,
in effect, that the Spirit of God so wrought in him and
in his preaching that the response on the part of the
Corinthians was the solid faith which rests upon. the
power of God and not that evanescent faith which de-

pends upon the appeal of rhetorical art and worldly wisdom. It is in the demonstration of which the Holy Spirit is the author that the faith of the Corinthians finds its source. It is, indeed, faith terminating upon the Word of God preached by Paul. But it is faith produced by the accompanying demonstration of the Spirit and manifestation of divine power.

In the first epistle to the Thessalonians Paul again refers to the power and confidence with which he and his colleagues preached the gospel at Thessalonica. "For our gospel came not unto you in word only, but also in power and in the Holy Spirit and much assurance" (I Thess. 1:5). In this text the reference to power and assurance appears to apply to the power and confidence with which Paul and Silvanus and Timothy proclaimed the Word rather than to the conviction with which it was received by the Thessalonians. The gospel came in the Holy Spirit and therefore with power and assurance. But we must not dissociate the reception of the Word on the part of the Thessalonians from this power and confidence wrought by the Spirit. For Paul proceeds, "And ye became imitators of us and of the Lord, having received the word in much affliction with joy of the Holy Spirit" (vs. 6). The resulting faith on the part of the Thessalonians must be regarded as proceeding from this activity of the Holy Spirit in virtue of which the gospel was proclaimed "in power and in the Holy Spirit and much assurance." That the Thessalonians became imitators of the Lord and received the Word with joy is due to the fact that the gospel came not in word only, and it came not in word only because it came in the power of the Holy Spirit. Their faith therefore finds its source in this demonstration of the

Spirit, just as the joy with which they received the Word is the joy wrought by the Spirit.

When the Apostle John writes, "And ye have an anointing from the Holy One and ye know all things. I have not written to you because ye do not know the truth, but because ye know it, and that no lie is of the truth" (I John 2:20, 21; *cf.* vs. 27) , he is surely alluding to that same indwelling of the Spirit with which Paul deals in I Corinthians 2:15. This anointing is an abiding possession and invests believers with discernment of the truth and stedfastness in it.

Summing up the conclusions drawn from these few relevant passages, we may say that the reception of the truth of God in intelligent, discriminating, joyful, and abiding faith is the effect of divine demonstration and power through the efficiency of the Holy Spirit, and that this faith consists in the confident assurance that, though the Word of God is brought through the instrumentality of men, it is not the word of man but in very truth the Word of God. We again see how even in connection with the internal testimony of the Spirit the ministry of men in no way militates against the reception of their message as the Word of God.

This witness of the Holy Spirit has been called the internal testimony of the Spirit. The question arises, why is the inward work of the Spirit called *testimony?* There does not appear, indeed, to be any compelling reason why it should be thus called. There is, however, an appropriateness in the word. The faith induced by this work of the Spirit rests upon the testimony the Scripture inherently contains of its divine origin and character. It is the function of the Holy Spirit to open the minds of men to perceive that testimony and cause the Word of God to be borne home to the mind of man with ruling power and conviction. Thereby the Holy Spirit may be said to bear perpetual witness to the divine character of that which is his own handiwork.

The internal testimony of the Spirit has frequently been construed as consisting in illumination or in regeneration on its noetic side. It is illumination because it consists in the opening of our minds to behold the excellence that inheres in Scripture as the Word of God. It is regeneration in its noetic expression because it is regeneration manifesting itself in our understanding in the response of the renewed mind to the evidence Scripture contains of its divine character. Anything less than illumination, in the sense defined above, the internal testimony cannot be.

The question may properly be raised, however, whether or not the notion of illumination is fully adequate as an interpretation of the nature of this testimony. On the view that it consists merely in illumination, the testimony, most strictly considered, resides entirely in the Scripture itself and not at all in the ever-present activity of the Spirit. And the question is, may we not properly regard the present work of the Spirit as not only imparting to us an understanding to perceive the evidence inhering in the Scripture but also as imparting what is of the nature of positive testimony? If we answer in the affirmative, then we should have to say that the power and demonstration with which the Holy Spirit accompanies the Word and by which it is carried home to our hearts and minds with irresistible conviction is the ever-continuing positive testimony of the Spirit. In other words, the seal of the Spirit belongs to the category of testimony strictly considered. If this construction should be placed upon the power and seal of the Spirit, there is a very obvious reason why this doctrine should be called, not only appropriately but necessarily, the internal testimony of the Spirit.

The most relevant passages (I Cor. 2:4, 5; I Thess. 1:5, 6) speak of this witness of the Spirit as demonstration (ἀπόδειξις) and power (δύναμις) and as such is supplementary to the word of the gospel itself. These terms, especially the term "demonstration," convey the notion of proof, of attestation, of confirmation. Since this activity of the Spirit is not inherent in the Word (cf. I Thess. 1:5) and produces the full assurance of faith (cf. also I Thess. 2:13), it must be construed as additional attestation, as a sealing witness of the Holy Spirit by which there is induced in us the irresistible conviction of the truth conveyed. This means that the work of the Spirit concerned is itself positive testimony collateral and correlative with the evidence which the Scripture contains of its divine origin and authority. This collateral witness coalesces with and confirms the witness resident in Scripture. It must never be identified or confused with the witness borne by our consciousness. It is witness *to* our consciousness and is wholly the work of the Spirit.

Whether we view the internal testimony as merely illumination or as illumination plus a positive supplementation construed as testimony in the stricter sense of the word, there is one principle which it is necessary to stress, namely, that the internal testimony does not convey to us new truth content. The whole truth content that comes within the scope of the internal testimony is contained in the Scripture. This testimony terminates upon the end of constraining belief in the divine character and authority of the Word of God and upon that end alone. It gives no ground whatsoever for new revelations of the Spirit.

When Paul writes to the Thessalonians, "Our gospel came not unto you in word only, but also in power and in the Holy Spirit and much assurance," he is surely making a distinction between the actual content of the gospel and the attendant power with which it was conveyed to them and in virtue of which it was carried home with conviction to the hearts of the Thessalonians. In like manner in I Corinthians 2:4, 5 the content of Paul's word and preaching will surely have to be distinguished from the demonstration of the Spirit and of power by which Paul's message was effectual in the begetting of faith in the Corinthian believers. And we are likewise justified in recognizing a distinction between the truth which John says his readers already knew and the abiding anointing of the Spirit which provided them with the proper knowledge and discernment to the end of bringing to clearer consciousness and consistent application the truth which they had already received (I John 2:20-27). In each case the illumining and sealing function of the Spirit has respect to truth which has been received from another source than that of his confirming and sealing operations.

The internal testimony of the Spirit is the necessary complement to the witness Scripture inherently bears to its plenary inspiration. The two pillars of true faith in Scripture as God's Word are the objective witness and the internal testimony. The objective witness furnishes us with a conception of Scripture that provides the proper basis for the ever-active sealing operation of the Spirit of truth. The internal testimony insures that this objective witness elicits the proper response in the human consciousness. The sealing function of the Spirit finds its complete explanation and validation in the pervasive witness that Scripture bears to its own divine origin and authority. And the witness to plenary inspiration receives its constant confirmation in the inward work of the Holy Spirit bearing witness by and with the Word in the hearts of believers.

THE AUTHORITY OF THE OLD TESTAMENT

By Edward J. Young

In the versions of the Old Testament commonly in use in Christendom there are thirty-nine books. These same thirty-nine books are also found in the Hebrew Scriptures. By the Jews they have been looked upon as sacred, and by the Christian church they are considered to be the very Word of God.

It is interesting to note that throughout the entire present era, the Christian church has accepted the Scriptures of the Old Testament as the infallible revelation of God. Nor is such an attitude toward them representative merely of a portion of the church; it is, rather, the expression of a conviction which appears to have characterized the church universal.

This conviction was also shared by our Lord himself. Christ regarded the Hebrew Scriptures as divinely revealed and as absolutely authoritative. He appealed to them constantly to support his claims. "Till heaven and earth pass," he said, "one jot or one tittle shall in no wise pass from the law, till all be fulfilled" (Matt. 5:18). Our Lord's earthly life was lived in the very atmosphere of the Old Testament Scriptures, and because he believed them to be God's Word, his church has followed him in this respect.

Was Christ, however, justified in so regarding the Old Testament, and are Christians today justified in sharing

55

his opinion? This question is pertinent, indeed; for now, as probably never before, this traditional attitude is being questioned and doubted and attacked. What grounds has the Christian for his belief that the Old Testament Scriptures are the very Word of God? How may he be sure that these writings are indeed authoritative and reliable? What assurance does he possess that, in the law and the prophets and the writings, God has spoken, and that he, the Christian, may rest upon these promises, convinced that he is heeding, not the word of man, but the word of the living God? These are the questions which will occupy our attention in the present chapter.

A. CHRIST AND THE OLD TESTAMENT

At first sight it might appear that for the devout Christian the answer to the questions which have just been raised is not at all difficult. "Jesus Christ was indeed justified in considering the Old Testament to be the Word of God and therefore I also may so regard it," is no doubt the response which many a true believer in Christ would offer. And his response, we think, would be perfectly correct for, as a matter of fact, Jesus Christ did look upon the Old Testament as inspired Scripture.

So simple a solution to the problem, however, will by no means meet with universal approval. It is necessary to examine more fully, therefore, what is involved in the assertion that Christ considered the Old Testament to be the Word of God. In making such an examination, we shall proceed upon the assumption that the words of Christ as they are presented in the New Testament are fully worthy of trust. This is not the place to discuss certain questions raised by form and source criticism which would appear to impair the New Testament picture of Jesus. The subjective nature of these types of criticism will, as time passes, more and more force itself into the open, and the day will come, we believe, when they will be largely discarded as legitimate methods of studying the Bible. At any rate, we shall regard the witness to our Lord which the New Testament offers as completely authoritative.

It must be apparent to anyone who reads the Gospels carefully that Jesus Christ, in the days of his flesh, looked upon that body of writings which is known as the Old Testament as constituting an organic whole. To him the Scriptures were a harmonious unit which bore a unique message and witness. Nothing could be farther from the truth than to say that he thought of the Scriptures as merely a group of writings which were in conflict among themselves and which bore no particular relationship to one another. This may easily be seen by the consideration of one or two relevant passages.

When, for example, the Jews took up stones to cast at our Lord, believing him to have been guilty of blasphemy, he opposed them by an appeal to the Old Testament (cf. John 10:31-36). In this appeal he quoted Psalm 82:6, and assumed the truth of what was stated in the Psalm by asserting that "the scripture cannot be broken." The force of his argument is very clear, and may be paraphrased as follows: "What is stated in this verse from the Psalms is true because this verse belongs to that body of writings known as Scripture, and the Scripture possesses an authority so absolute in character that *it cannot be broken*." When Christ here employs the word Scripture, he has in mind, therefore, not a particular verse in the Psalms, but rather the entire group of writings of which this one verse is a part.

That Christ regarded the Scriptures as constituting a unit is also seen when, at the time of his betrayal, he acknowledged the need for his arrest and sufferings if the Scriptures were to be fulfilled (*cf.* Matt. 26:54). Indeed, he was concerned that the Scriptures must be fulfilled. To him it was more important that this should take place than that he should escape from arrest. By his use of the plural, he made it abundantly clear that there existed a plurality of writings, each of which had this in common with the others: that it belonged to the category of Scripture and that, taken as a whole, it had direct reference to the sufferings which he was about to undergo. Thus, by his manner of speech, did he bear witness to the fact that the Old Testament is an organic whole and so, by implication, to the consent and harmony of all its parts.

This testimony of our Lord to the nature of the Old Testament is by no means an isolated phenomenon. Rather, not only is it made expressly clear by certain individual passages,[1] but also it underlies his entire treatment of the Scriptures. In adopting such an attitude Christ placed himself squarely in opposition to those views, so prevalent in our day, which look upon the Old Testament as merely a collection of more or less loosely related, heterogeneous material, a library rather than a Book.

Not only did Jesus Christ look upon the Old Testament as forming an organic whole but also he believed

[1] *Cf.* Matthew 21:42, 22:29; Mark 14:49; John 6:45, 15:25.

that both as a unit and in its several parts it was finally and absolutely authoritative. To it appeal might be made as to the ultimate authority. Its voice was final. When the Scriptures spoke, man must obey. From them there was no appeal. When, for example, the Tempter would have the Son of God command the stones to be made bread, he was silenced by the assertion, "It is written." This appeal to the Old Testament ended the matter. That which was written was for Christ the deciding voice.

Not only, however, was such authority attributed to the Scriptures as a unit and to particular verses or utterances, but it was also extended to include individual words and even letters. This is shown by a statement such as the following, "It is easier for heaven and earth to pass, than for one tittle of the law to fail" (Luke 16:17). In some instances Christ based his argument merely upon a word, as for example when, seeking to refute the Jews, he singled out the word "gods" in Psalm 82:6. A careful reading of the Gospels will reveal the fact that the Scriptures of the Old Testament, in all their parts, were believed by Christ to be authoritative.

Is there, however, any dependable method by which one may determine precisely what books Christ regarded as belonging to the category of Scripture? Is it not possible that some books upon which he placed the stamp of his approval have been irretrievably lost, whereas others which would not have been recognized by him are now looked upon as part of the Old Testament?

It may with confidence be said that Christ recognized as canonical the same books as those which comprise the

Old Testament as we have it today. Of course, he did not leave a list of these books nor did he expressly quote from each of them. Hence, we must look elsewhere for evidence to support our statement.

From our Lord's references to the Old Testament it is possible to determine the extent of the canon which he recognized. He quoted abundantly, and the nature of his quotation often lends its sanction not only to the book in which the quotation is found, but even to the entire collection itself. The force of this impresses itself upon us more and more as we notice how Christ chose from this and that book statements which would enforce and support his arguments. It appears that his earthly life was steeped in the teaching of the Old Testament. Not only were whole verses frequently upon his lips, but also his own speech was clothed with expressions from the Scriptures.

There is, however, one passage in particular in which he gives a clue as to the extent of the Old Testament of his day. On the walk to Emmaus, after his resurrection, he said to his companions, "These are the words which I spake unto you, while I was yet with you, that all things must be fulfilled, which were written in the law of Moses, and in the prophets, and in the psalms, concerning me" (Luke 24:44). Here he clearly recognizes that there are three divisions to the Old Testament, and that the things which were written in each of these divisions must be fulfilled. The designation "law of Moses" refers, of course, to the first five books of the Bible; the "prophets" includes the historical books and the works of the great writing prophets. As to the identity of these two divisions there would seem to be little doubt.

What, however, is meant by Christ's use of the word "psalms"? Did he thereby intend to refer to all the books in the third division of the canon, or did he merely have in mind the book of Psalms itself? The latter alternative, we think, is probably correct. Christ singled out the book of Psalms, it would appear, not so much because it was the best known and most influential book of the third division, but rather because in the Psalms there were many predictions about himself. This was the Christological book, *par excellence,* of the third division of the Old Testament canon.

Most of the books of this third division do not contain direct messianic prophecies.[2] Hence, if Christ had used a technical designation to indicate this third division, he would probably have weakened his argument to a certain extent. But by the reference to the Psalms he directs the minds of his hearers immediately to that particular book in which occur the greater number of references to himself.

This does not necessarily mean that he did not make reference to the messianic prophecies which appear, for example, in the book of Daniel. Nor does it mean that the third division of the canon was not yet complete. It would appear, rather, that by his language Christ

[2] The following books are reckoned as belonging to the Writings or *Hagiographa:* the three poetical books, Psalms, Proverbs, Job; the five *Megilloth:* Song of Solomon, Ruth, Lamentations, Ecclesiastes, Esther; and Daniel, Ezra, Nehemiah, I-II Chronicles. Apparently, however, this classification has not always been held. See R. D. Wilson, "The Rule of Faith and Life," in *The Princeton Theological Review,* Vol. xxvi, No. 3, July, 1928; Solomon Zeitlin, *An Historical Study of the Canonization of the Hebrew Scriptures* (Philadelphia, 1933).

set the seal of his approval upon the books of the Old
Testament which were in use among the Jews of his
day, and that this Old Testament consisted of three
definite divisions, the Law, the Prophets and a third
division which as yet had probably not received any
technical designation.[3]

B. THE CANONIZATION OF THE SCRIPTURES

When Christ thus set the seal of his approval upon
the Jewish Scriptures of his day, it meant that he considered those Scriptures to be divinely inspired. When,
however, did the Jewish people who lived before him so
come to regard them? To this question many answers
are given, and it is to this question that we must now
direct our attention.

By the term canonical writings is meant those writings which constitute the inspired rule of faith and life.
Canonical books, in other words, are those books which
are regarded as divinely inspired. The criterion of a
book's canonicity, therefore, is its inspiration. If a book
has been inspired of God, it is canonical, whether accepted by men as such or not. It is God and not man
who determines whether a book is to belong to the
canon. Therefore, if a certain writing has indeed been

[3] There is every reason for believing that the canon of Christ
and the canon of the Jews of his day were identical. There is no
evidence whatever of any dispute between him and the Jews as
to the canonicity of any Old Testament book. What Christ opposed was not the canon which the Pharisees accepted but the
oral tradition which would make this canon void. From statements in Josephus and the Talmud, it is possible to learn the
extent of the Jewish canon of Christ's day.

the product of divine inspiration, it belongs in the canon from the moment of its composition.

That this is so, appears from the very nature of the case. If man alone were capable in his own strength of identifying accurately the Word of God, then man would be equal in knowledge with God. If God is truly God, the creator of all things and utterly independent of all that he has created, it follows that he alone can identify what he has spoken. He alone can say, "This is my Word, but that has not proceeded from my mouth."

Hence, it will be seen that the word "canon" means far more than merely a list of books. If this low view of the meaning of the word be adopted, we by no means even begin to do justice to the various factors which are involved. The reason why many discussions of the problem of the canon are unsatisfactory is that they proceed upon the assumption that the canon is merely a list of books which the Jewish people itself came to regard as divine, and they neglect the theological aspect of the question almost entirely.[4] To the Christian, however, the word "canon" has a far higher connotation; to him it constitutes the inspired rule of faith and practice. The writings of the Bible claim to be the Word of God, and their contents are in entire harmony with this claim. The Christian recognizes the Scriptures as inspired, because they are such, and bear in themselves the evidences of their divinity. Basic, therefore, to any consideration of how man comes to recognize the Bible as God's Word is the fact that it is indeed divine.

[4] This question will be discussed more fully at a later point.

It is one of the strengths of the Westminster Confession that it so clearly and forcefully states this fact. All the canonical books of the Old and New Testaments are expressly said to be the Word of God written (I.2), and to be given by inspiration of God to be the rule of faith and life. Furthermore, the Confession presents several of the reasons why the Bible evidences itself to be the Word of God. It mentions "the heavenliness of the matter, the efficacy of the doctrine, the majesty of the style, the consent of all the parts, the scope of the whole (which is to give all glory to God), the full discovery it makes of the only way of man's salvation, the many other incomparable excellencies, and the entire perfection thereof" (I.5).

In themselves, however, these arguments do not bring us to full persuasion that the Bible is God's Word, and the reason for this is that the human understanding is darkened by sin. What is needed is an opening of the eyes that man may see what is so clear. This opening of the eyes of the understanding is the work of God's Spirit, as the Confession says, "our full persuasion and assurance of the infallible truth and divine authority thereof, is from the inward work of the Holy Spirit bearing witness by and with the Word in our hearts" (I.5). What the Confession teaches is the teaching of the Scriptures. For example, Paul writes: "But as it is written, What no eye has seen, nor ear heard, nor the heart of man conceived, what God has prepared for those who love him, God has revealed to us through the Spirit. For the Spirit searches everything, even the depths of God" (I Cor. 2:9, 10; cf., also, Heb. 4:12; I Cor. 2:3-5; I Thess. 1:5a; I John 2:20, 27).

Without attempting to give a full definition of this

doctrine of the internal testimony of the Holy Spirit we may say that bearing witness by and with the Word in our hearts the Holy Spirit convinces and persuades us that the Scriptures are the Word of God.

These points will perhaps be more clearly understood if we examine the history of the collection of the Old Testament Scriptures. No complete history of this process has been preserved, but certain important statements are made in the Bible itself, and these statements must be taken into consideration in any discussion of the subject.

The Law of Moses

In the first place, therefore, we turn to the first five books of the Old Testament, which are commonly known as the Pentateuch or the Law of Moses. Traditionally, by both Jews and Christians, Moses has been regarded as the author of these books. We believe that tradition is in this point correct, and that the essential Mosaic authorship of the Pentateuch may be maintained. There may indeed be certain few minor additions, such as the account of Moses' death, which were inserted into the Pentateuch under divine inspiration by a later edition, but this by no means runs counter to the common tradition that Moses is the author of these books.

To maintain that Moses was the author of the Pentateuch does not imply that he received by direct divine revelation everything that he wrote. Quite probably large portions of the Law had existed in written form before the time of Moses. If this were so it would account for some of the variations in style and emphasis which are often erroneously attributed to different documents. Moses may very well have pieced together different fragments which had been written long before his time. In a certain sense he may have engaged in the work of compiling. He, however, was responsible for the finished work, and in composing this finished work, the writings which we call the Pentateuch, he labored under the superintendence of the Spirit of God.

When these writings had been completed they were accepted by the devout in Israel as divinely authoritative. Express provision was made for their protection and custody. "And it came to pass, when Moses had made an end of writing the words of this law in a book, until they were finished, that Moses commanded the Levites, who bare the ark of the covenant of Jehovah, saying, Take this book of the law, and put it by the side of the ark of the covenant of Jehovah your God, that it may be there for a witness against thee" (Deut. 31:24-26). The priests were commanded to read the Law to the people, ". . . thou shalt read this law before all Israel in their hearing" (Deut. 31:11). When Israel would have a king, that king was to possess a copy of the Law (Deut. 17:18, 19). Joshua was commanded to guide the people in the light of the Law. "This book of the law shall not depart out of thy mouth, but thou shalt meditate thereon day and night, that thou mayest observe to do according to all that is written therein" (Josh. 1:8).

Throughout the history of Israel, the Law was regarded as divinely authoritative. David charged Solomon to give his obedience thereto. Jeroboam was denounced because of disobedience to God's commands. Some of the kings of Judah are particularly commended because of their adherence to the Law, whereas others are condemned for their lack of such adherence. The very exile itself is considered by the sacred writers to be due to infractions of the statutes and the covenant which God made with Israel's ancestors. And on the return from exile, the Israelites governed themselves in accord with the Law of Moses.

It will be seen then that upon the testimony of the only contemporary writings of ancient Israel, the Law of Moses was regarded from the earliest times as divinely inspired and authoritative. It was final. What it commanded was to be obeyed, and what it prohibited was not to be done. Such is the picture which the Old Testament itself presents, if it be accepted as it stands.

The Prophetical Books

Not only was the Law of Moses regarded as God's Word, but the words and writings of the prophets were also so considered. In Deuteronomy it had been said of the prophets that God would put his "words in his [*i.e.*, the prophet's] mouth, and he shall speak unto them all that I shall command him" (Deut. 18:18). The prophets themselves believed that they spoke in the Name of the Lord and that they declared his very word to men. How frequently do they exclaim, "The word of the Lord came unto me, saying...," "Thus saith the Lord...," "Hear the word of the Lord!" The message which they proclaimed, therefore, was, according to their own testimony, not a message of their own devising, but the actual Word of God.

The prophets demanded that same obedience to their words which was due unto the Law of God. They had no hesitation in candidly telling Israel that her calamities and misfortunes had befallen her, not only because of her disobedience to the Law, but also because she had transgressed their words. And they frankly assert that, unless she gives heed to their message, dire distress and suffering will come upon her. The evidence to support these statements is not isolated. Rather, if one will read the prophetical writings to see what is the testimony of the prophets to their authority, he will note how frequently and consistently they assert that they are declaring the final, absolute Word of Jehovah. (*Cf., e.g.,* Isa. 8:5, 31:4; Jer. 3:6, 13:1; Ezek. 21:1, 25:1; Amos 3:1; 7:1ff., etc.)

If, therefore, we are to accept the testimony of the Bible itself, we see that the words of the prophets were regarded in Israel as authoritative, decisive, and inspired. Consequently, it may easily be understood how these words in their written form would be preserved in the church and regarded as the Word of Jehovah.

It is true that the Old Testament does not relate how the books which are commonly called the Former Prophets (*i.e.,* Joshua, Judges, I-II Samuel, I-II Kings) came to be included with the other canonical books. However, the answer to this question, it would appear, is readily at hand. The authors of these books, whoever they may have been, were men who occupied the office of prophet. In ancient Israel this was a special and unique office. The prophet was an Israelite who acted as a mediator between God and man. Just as the priest represented the people before God, so the prophet represented God before the people. In a very special sense, therefore, he was the recipient of revelation. God so implanted his words in the prophet's mouth, that the resultant delivered message was the actual Word of God.

Not all prophets wrote down their messages. As we have seen, Israel did gather and preserve the words of those prophets who committed their messages to writing. But no doubt many messages were delivered which were not recorded. However, when men of the status of prophets wrote an interpretative history of Israel, it may readily be understood why such a history would be accepted by the Israelitish church as the Word of God. For in their interpretation of history, these authors often profess to speak as in the Name of God. These writings, therefore, are historical in character, and profess to trace the hand of God in Israel's history.

Furthermore, despite the assertions of some critics, these writings are in harmony with the written prophecies. Not only are they a perfect complement to those written prophecies, but they are a necessary completion to the history contained in the Law of Moses. Upon the basis of the Law of Moses we should expect such a history of the subsequent developments in Israel. Without this interpretative history, much in the prophets would be obscure. So far as is known, none of these books has ever been disputed as to its canonicity. The former prophets, then, were accepted as part of the Word of God, and therefore as canonical, because they were written by men who held the high office of prophet, and who, as inspired prophets, interpreted Israel's history.

The Writings

How did the third division of the Old Testament, the so-called *Hagiographa,* or Writings, come to be collected and regarded as canonical? There is no direct answer given to this question in the Scriptures. The Bible does not tell us who collected these books nor at what time they were gathered. The books which belong to this third division of the canon were written by men inspired of God who nevertheless did not occupy the office of prophet. Some of the authors, however, such as David and Daniel, did possess the prophetic gift although not occupying the official status of prophet. This accounts for the fact that a book such as Daniel is found not among the Prophets but among the Writings. The official status of Daniel, as a careful study of the Old Testament will reveal, was not that of prophet, but of statesman. Daniel, however, did possess the gift of prophecy.

An objection is often made to this argument. If it is true that the status of the authors of the *Hagiographa* was that of inspired men who did not occupy the prophetic office, then the book of Amos, it is claimed, should be included among the *Hagiographa* and not among the Prophets. Amos, it is asserted, distinctly maintained that he was neither a prophet nor the son of a prophet (Amos 7:14). However, this argument is based upon a fallacious interpretation of the passage to which appeal is made. In this passage Amos is relating his prophetic call. He disclaims that he is earning his livelihood by being a prophet, since he is a shepherd and a plucker of sycamore fruit. However, God called him to be a prophet. "Go, prophesy unto my people Israel," the Lord had said to him. These are the words by which he was inducted into the prophetic office. This objection to our argument, therefore, is without merit.

In the prologue to *Ecclesiasticus* (written about 130 B.C.) mention is made of "the law itself, and the prophecies, and the rest of the books." Here is witness to a third division, namely, "the rest of the books." The language does not tell how many or which books were considered by the author as coming under this category. However, it does imply a fixed group of books, and also implies, we think, that these books had been in existence for some time. The designation here given of the third group is as definite and explicit as are those given to the first two divisions of the canon.

The writer of the prologue also speaks of the "law and the prophets and the others that followed after them" and states that his grandfather, the author of *Ecclesiasticus* (c. 190 B.C.), gave himself largely to the reading of "the law and the prophets and the other books of the fathers." In the mind of the writer of the prologue, then, there existed three definite divisions to the Old Testament Scriptures.

We need not be alarmed because the author does not use a technical term to designate the third division. As a matter of fact, he is not consistent even in his reference to the second division. He speaks of it now as "the prophecies" (αἱ προφητεῖαι) and now as "the prophets" (τῶν προφητῶν). The technical designation *Writings* was only applied to these books long afterward. The miscellaneous character of their contents would make it difficult to employ an adequately descriptive designation, such as was enjoyed by the Law and the Prophets. Upon the basis of what is stated in the prologue to *Ecclesiasticus,* there does not appear to be warrant for assuming that the third division of the canon was still in process of collection.

In all probability these books were gathered by Ezra and those who immediately followed him. Concerning this period very little is known, but it seems to have been a time when attention was given to the Scriptures, and it may well have been that these sacred books were then collected. Nor does this necessarily mean that some inspired additions were not made to certain books at a later time. Such may very well have been the case.

It need not be maintained that from the beginning there was a recognition of a threefold division of the canon. For this reason, some lists may contain books which from the standpoint herein presented would seem to be in the wrong division of the canon. Nevertheless, this threefold division flows naturally from the position of the writer in the Old Testament economy. When the threefold division as such was first recognized we may not be able to tell. That it is a Scriptural division would seem to admit of no doubt.

To sum up, we may say that the books of the Old Testament, being immediately inspired of God, were recognized as such by his people from the time when they first appeared. That there may have been questions and minor differences of opinion about certain books does not at all detract from this fact.

It is well-known that in the later Jewish schools there were certain disputes as to the canonicity of particular books, notably, Esther and Ecclesiastes. However, it is questionable whether these disputes were really more than academic. It is questionable whether they really represented the attitude of the people to any great extent.

How the books were gathered we are not told. Apparently, no religious council in ancient Israel ever drew up a list of divine books. Rather, in the singular providence of God, his people recognized his Word and honored it from the time of its first appearance. Thus was formed the collection of inspired writings which are known as the canonical books of the Old Testament.

It has sometimes been held that a Jewish Synod was held at Jamnia in Palestine and that this synod made pronouncements concerning the extent of the canon. After Titus and his armies had destroyed Jerusalem in 70 A.D. Rabbi Johanan ben Zakkai settled in Jamnia and carried on his literary activity there. Jamnia did become a center of Biblical study and the canonicity of certain books was discussed, and in particular, it would seem, whether these books should be excluded from the canon. But that there was a Synod which discussed whether certain books were to be included in the Canon is very questionable. Professor H. H. Rowley has written very wisely concerning Jamnia: "It is indeed, doubtful, how far it is correct to speak of the Council of Jamnia. We know of discussions that took place there amongst the Rabbis, but we know of no formal or binding decisions that were made, and it is probable that the discussions were informal, though none the less helping to crystallize and to fix more firmly the Jewish tradition" (*The Growth of the Old Testament*, London, 1950, p. 170).

C. CRITICAL VIEWS OF THE CANONIZATION OF THE SCRIPTURES[5]

[5] Strictly speaking, every careful student of the Old Testament and of the problem of its canonization may be called a critic. However, in common parlance the word "critical" has come to connote an attitude towards the problems of Old Testament study which is generally destructive of and hostile to traditional views. It is in this latter sense that the words "critic" and "critical" are employed in this paper, and this merely to avoid confusion in the mind of the reader who may not be well acquainted with the present state of Old Testament studies.

The view of the collection of the canon of the Old Testament which has just been outlined by no means finds universal acceptance today. However, it would appear to be the view which is most congruous with what is related in the Old Testament as it stands. It would seem too that essentially this position has been traditionally embraced by the Christian church.

At the present time, however, it is not only being set aside but is even strongly attacked in many quarters. In its place, diverse theories are being offered.

The theory of canonization which has been outlined above, it will be remembered, finds tnat that which determines the canonicity of any book is the book's inspiration. A book which is inspired of God, therefore, is *ipso facto* canonical. Furthermore, the book is canonical whether it is bound up with other canonical books or not. It is God who sets the limits to the canon and not man. Due, however, to God's providential leading and due to the inward testimony of the Holy Spirit in the hearts of his people, the people of God have been enabled to recognize his Word. And remarkable, indeed, has been the unanimity of their witness to the identity of the canon.

The theories which are now about to be considered, however, although differing among themselves in many respects, nevertheless have this in common, that they reject inspiration as the determining principle in the formation of the canon. Such rejection, indeed, is not always conscious. Furthermore, there may truly be, among those who advance critical theories of the formation of the canon, some who are firm believers in the supernatural. Nevertheless, it must be confessed that among the advocates of recent critical theories the greater number do reject the working of God in any adequate sense in Israel's history.

The question involved in the formation of the Old Testament canon is basically the question of the supernatural. If one firmly believes in the triune God, he will, if he is consistent, adopt essentially the theory of the canon which has been presented because this theory alone adequately takes into account the working of God in the inspiration of the books of the Old Testament. If, however, one does not accept the orthodox Christian doctrine of God, it follows that, in the very nature of the case, he will be compelled to reject the high view of the formation of the canon for which we have been contending.

Furthermore, the critical views which we are about to consider are for the most part bound up with attitudes toward the authorship, dates and composition of the individual Old Testament books which are considerably out of harmony with the traditional views upon these subjects. This is not the place in which to enter upon any detailed discussion of the merits of these theories. Suffice it to say that the writer believes that these recent positions are for the most part not in accord with the facts.[6]

[6] For a discussion of the questions of special introduction from a liberal or critical standpoint, the reader is referred to S. R. Driver, *An Introduction to the Literature of the Old Testament* (Edinburgh, 1909); Robert H. Pfeiffer, *Introduction to the Old Testament* (New York, 1941). The question is very capably treated from the standpoint of tradition and consistent Biblical supernaturalism by Oswald T. Allis, *The Five Books of Moses* (Philadelphia, 1943).

According to many scholars, the three divisions of the Old Testament are in reality three separate canons. In order, therefore, properly to understand the formation of the canon, as a whole, we must, they say, first discover how each of the three individual canons came into being.

1. *The Pentateuch*

The Pentateuch, or first five books of the Bible, was, according to many, not written by Moses. Rather, it owes its present form to a process of growth which covered many centuries. In reality, it is not the work of one man at all, but of several men, all unknown, who in many cases lived many centuries apart. It was therefore only when the writings of these different authors were finally edited and combined, to result in approximately the present Pentateuch, that the work was canonized.

When, however, did this canonization take place? For a time it was thought that the final redaction and editing of the Pentateuch was the work of Ezra and his contemporaries. When the Law was read before the assembled multitude in Jerusalem, as is related in Nehemiah 8-10, the Pentateuch was thereby rendered canonical. As a matter of fact, however, there had been, according to many of the supporters of this position, even an earlier canonization. Josiah, the king, it has been claimed, was responsible for the canonization of Deuteronomy. But it was at the public reading by Ezra that the entire Law was first publicly recognized as authoritative.

Such is the view of the canonization of the Pentateuch which has more or less consistently held the field among certain critics of the Old Testament for the past half-century. Indeed, as long as the Pentateuch is regarded as consisting of a number of conflicting documents deriving from different ages and composed by unknown authors, so long will this or some similar low view of its canonization be held.

In his scholarly and valuable introduction to the Old Testament, Dr. Robert H. Pfeiffer broke with the traditional critical account of the canonization of the Pentateuch in at least two respects.

In the first place, he refused to admit that Nehemiah 8-10 is an account of the canonization of the Law of Moses, because he believed that the historicity and chronology of the events recorded therein are too doubtful to support such an interpretation. We do not agree with him in his denial of the historicity of the contents of these chapters, but we do agree that they do not present the account of the canonization of the Law. According to Pfeiffer, the Pentateuch was canonized about 400 B.C. and not when Ezra read the Law to the assembled people. Thus, it would appear that Pfeiffer has taken away the one available incident to which appeal might be made for an evidence of canonization.

In the second place, Pfeiffer has stressed the question of the canonization of Deuteronomy, which earlier critics had also noted, and, as a result, has brought into clearer focus certain difficulties which those who reject the clear Biblical witness to itself must face.

In order to understand these difficulties, it will be necessary to examine cursorily Pfeiffer's theory of the canonization of the Pentateuch. Briefly it is as follows. When, in the eighteenth year of Josiah, the book of the Law was found in the temple, it was regarded as the word of Jehovah and its precepts were immediately enforced. Thus the newly-discovered book of the Law was canonized, and this is the first instance of such canonization in human history. This book, so the theory runs, was Deuteronomy.

There were also already in existence other literary works in ancient Israel. About 650 B.C. these were combined and edited to form a great national epic. Thus Israel, according to the theory which we are now considering, came to have her own national history. However, this national history was not regarded as canonical. About 550 B.C., however, the canonical Deuteronomic Code was inserted into the non-canonical national epic. Apparently, therefore, this transaction imparted canonicity to the national epic. Sometime during the fifth century B.C. there was composed the so-called priestly portion of the Pentateuch which deals with laws, genealogies and the origin of sacred institutions. This portion, however, did not obtain canonical standing until it was later inserted in the already existing combined work of Deuteronomy and the national history. Such an insertion probably took place about 400 B.C. and thus, as soon as this final edition of the Pentateuch was issued, it was received as canonical.

Credit is certainly due to the author of this theory because of his endeavor to construct a satisfying account of the canonization of the Pentateuch. It must be obvious, however, to anyone who has examined it that it cannot stand if Moses were actually the author of the Pentateuch. This is not the place to discuss in any great detail the question of the Mosaic authorship of the first five books of the Bible, but it may be noted that there are compelling reasons for believing in such authorship.

That Moses was the author has been the traditional viewpoint of the Christian church, and there seems to be sufficient evidence for assuming that Christ himself held this opinion. The tradition which asserts Mosaic authorship is, therefore, extremely well-founded. Furthermore, despite whatever difficulties there may be in believing that Moses composed the Pentateuch, the difficulties in any alternate theory of its composition are far more serious.

Pfeiffer proceeds upon the assumption that the original edition of Deuteronomy was written a few years before 621 B.C., and that Deuteronomy was the book discovered in the temple during the reign of Josiah. However, this position is so weak that it is being abandoned today even by some who do not admit that Moses was the author of Deuteronomy. It becomes more and more apparent, if one carefully studies the statements of the Bible itself regarding the book discovered in the temple, that the volume found was not merely Deuteronomy, but a well-known book of law embracing Deuteronomy and far more. Unless the critics can prove otherwise, and they cannot, we may very naturally assume that this book was the Law of Moses, and essentially our present Pentateuch.

Likewise, there is serious objection to the position that a great national epic was edited about 650 B.C., and there is very strong objection also to asserting that the priestly portion of the Pentateuch was composed some time during the fifth century. However, these questions have been discussed thoroughly many times elsewhere. It is another type of objection which we now wish to bring against Pfeiffer's theory, and against most modern views of the canonization of the Pentateuch.

In the first place, Pfeiffer appears to hold a very low view of the meaning of the word "canonical." Apparently his view is that a work may exist for a century and be regarded as merely a human writing and then suddenly become recognized as canonical. Thus, the national epic, it is said, was edited in 650 B.C., but it was not until the insertion of Deuteronomy about a hundred years later that it was actually considered by the people to be canonical. Thus the one who determines the extent of the canon is not God but man. In reality, this makes the canon to be but a list of books which the Jews regarded as sacred. It rules out of the picture the adequate working of God in the inspiration of the Scriptures and also in the inward testimony of his Spirit in the hearts of his people. It asserts that the Jews were led to consider certain books as divine, not because these books actually were divine, but because of mere external reasons. The theory therefore is fallacious because it is too one-sided; it does not take into account all the facts.

Secondly, this viewpoint assumes that the devout Jews of antiquity would incorporate a book which they regarded as canonical into one which hitherto they had looked upon as non-canonical. It also assumes that they would insert a work which they considered to be of mere human origin (*e.g.*, the priestly legislation) into one which they believed to be divine. These assumptions create a tremendous psychological difficulty. Would devout Jewish editors unite a writing which they knew to be non-canonical with a volume which they looked upon as the Word of God? It is almost inconceivable that they should do so. Before them, according to Pfeiffer's theory, lay Deuteronomy. To them it was the very Word of God, and therefore to be obeyed. Before them also lay another book—their national history, a remarkable and praiseworthy writing, but not divinely inspired. Can we possibly conceive of these pious Jewish editors combining the two and from that time on declaring them both to be the Word of God? No! No matter how helpful the national history would be in meeting Israel's religious needs, devout Israelites would never regard it as inspired in the manner in which this theory assumes.

In the last place, this theory would make the unknown authors of the Pentateuch to be guilty of fraud. Thus, when Josiah read the book of the Law, he believed it to be the work of Moses. In this, however, it appears that he erred, for Moses did not write it at all. Rather, it was written by an unknown priest who had been influenced by the prophetic movement and who sought, by using the authority of the name of Moses, to bring about a reformation in religious life. Whether this priest be called sincere, and inspired by noble religious ideals or not is beside the point. The fact remains that he employed a dishonest means to secure his end. When he perceived that Josiah accepted his writing as Mosaic and as the authoritative Word of God, he should, if he had been an honest man, have told Josiah the truth.

In connection with the production of the priestly portions of the Pentateuch also, we cannot escape the fact that fraud was employed, if Pfeiffer's theory be correct. Whether the men of that day believed that what they were doing was wrong or not, is beside the question. As a matter of fact, what they were doing was very wrong. They were using the name of Moses to gain a hearing for their own ideas. They were not merely writing to entertain; they were writing to convince. And when they saw that their own productions were being regarded as divine and authoritative, they should have done something about it. If they actually thought that God was speaking through them, why did they employ the name of Moses?

Thus, on the basis of Pfeiffer's theory and of the theories of many modern critics, the Jews came to accept as canonical a Pentateuch which was produced in a dishonest method. To deny this fraud or dishonesty by talking about the sincerity of the authors or the nobility of their aims and ideals does not change the picture. All honor to Dr. Pfeiffer, who frankly asserted that three of the most influential writings in the Old Testament were technically fraudulent. Would that more critics were as candid as he!

We feel constrained, therefore, because of the tremendous difficulties which it involves, to reject the theory of the canonization of the Pentateuch which was offered by the distinguished professor at Harvard. In fact, if the first five books of the Bible are not essentially the work of Moses, but are a compilation of documents composed by various unknown authors living at widely separated periods of time, the whole question of the canonicity of these books becomes an insoluble mystery and the fact that the Jews ever regarded them as divine one of the greatest enigmas of all time.

2. *The Remaining Books*

In the discussion of Pfeiffer's theory of the canonization of the Pentateuch it was noted that, according to this position, a book might exist for many years before it finally came to be credited with canonicity. This implies that the author of the book had not intended his work to be regarded as sacred and divine and lasting. At first the work was not venerated as inspired Scripture, but in the course of time it did come to receive such veneration.

Not only, however, is the assumption that a book was not intended to be regarded as divine evident in the theory which we have just been considering, it is also particularly apparent in connection with many theories as to the canonization of the remaining books of the Old Testament. It is not always explicitly stated but is clearly implied in the writings of many critics. It is indeed a basic weakness in the critical position, because it raises an unanswerable question. If the books of Scripture were not intended to be regarded as inspired and canonical, what was it that led to their being eventually so regarded? What caused a people, which for years had considered these writings to be uninspired, to change its position and to ascribe to them a canonicity which formerly had been denied? Obviously it could not be the inspiration of the books themselves which produced this change. Rather, the change must have been due, in the very nature of the case, to external causes. What, then, were these external causes which induced the Jewish nation to accept just these particular books and no others? That is the question which critics must answer, and that is precisely the question which critics cannot satisfactorily answer. The reason why no satisfactory answer can be given to this question lies in the fact that the critical theories endeavor to discuss the question of canonicity from an historical standpoint alone. They would rule out of the picture the theological question. Does God exist? Did

God actually inspire the writers of the individual books of the Old Testament? Does the Holy Spirit by his inward testimony produce within the hearts of his people a conviction that he is the author of the Scriptures? These questions are ignored by the critics or are pushed aside as belonging to the realm of "faith" and not to that of historic fact. And it is precisely because of this unconsciously prejudiced attitude that the critic cannot answer the questions which have just been raised.

Any theory which refuses to deal with the theological questions involved is one which refuses to take all of the facts into consideration. The Old Testament books claim to have been spoken by the Lord. Is that claim correct or is it not? To consider that claim one must ask whether there is a Lord and whether he actually spoke to man? This claim permeates practically the entire Old Testament, and yet the critical theories pay little or no attention to it. Did God actually speak these words? That question the critics would either ignore or else by inference deny. Hence the difficulty in which they find themselves.

Let us make no mistake about it. We can never successfully answer the question as to why the Jewish nation recognized these particular books until we deal with all the facts involved. If these books are indeed the Word of the living and true God, as they claim to be, then we may see that in his good providence his people were led to accept those books of which he was truly the author, and the manner in which they came thus to accept them was in its essence very probably that which has already been outlined. If, however, these books of the Old Testament are actually not the Word of God, or if we refuse to consider the question of their inspiration because that question belongs to the realm of "faith," we shall never satisfactorily ascertain why it was that the Jews came to accept precisely these writings.

However, the critics are ready with their answers to the problem, and to these answers we must now devote some attention. It has been asserted that the canon consisted merely of the national literature of the Hebrews. This collection was made so that the second temple, built after the exile, might possess all the advantages of the earlier temple which had been destroyed. Hence, the national literature of Israel was gathered, and thus there came into being the canon of the Old Testament. This explanation, which comes from the heart of German rationalism, has little to commend it, and it possesses a fatal weakness. The Old Testament itself speaks of early Israelitish books, such as the Book of Jashar. Why were not these works also included within the canon, if this explanation be correct? Also, why were those prophetical books included which denounce Israel so strongly? Why should the people desire to perpetuate writings which condemned them so unsparingly?

It has also been maintained that language was the determining principle in the formation of the canon. Books which were written in Hebrew were included, whereas those which were written in Greek or other languages were excluded. However, this assertion is not in accord with the facts, and consequently has been generally rejected. For in Israel there were books composed in Hebrew which have never been recognized as canonical.

Again it has been held that the books which are in

the Old Testament represent the religion of Israel in its greatest purity. This very obviously implies that the Israelites themselves were capable of deciding of which books this was true. The subjective element is surely prominent here. Why also did the Jews include both the prophetical books with their stress upon spiritual religion and books of law with their emphasis upon sacrifice and form? Were not these Israelites as keen in their discernment of "incongruities" as are the modern critics?

Nor can it be successfully maintained that books were accepted only because they agreed with the teaching of the Pentateuch. There is, as a matter of fact, an element of truth in this assertion. The remaining books of the Old Testament do indeed agree with the Law of Moses. They are truly based upon the Pentateuch. However, according to the critics, the Law is in conflict with it-self, being composed by different anonymous authors who lived at widely distant periods. It is this supposed internal conflict which might be called one of the chief axioms of modern Old Testament criticism. If, then, the Law really is what the critics claim, how can we possibly account for the acceptance of Amos, Isaiah and Jeremiah, with their condemnation of sacrifice, or of Ezekiel, who is supposed to be so much at variance with the priestly portion of the Pentateuch? This theory implies that the ancient Jews could perceive in the five books of the Law a unity which the modern critic cannot discover. It in reality becomes, therefore, an argument for the unity of the Pentateuch. Why, too, we may ask in passing, if this theory be correct, was a book such as *Jubilees* omitted from the canon?

Again, it has been urged that the intrinsic worth of

the books, their moral and spiritual quality, led to their acceptance. If by this is meant their inspiration, we can heartily agree, but if, however, there is intended merely the fact that these books are of a superior moral and spiritual quality, we find ourselves once again floundering in difficulty. Why, for example, all other considerations apart, is Esther then included and *First Maccabees* excluded? Also, we today know very little about the quality of other writings in ancient Israel. May there not have been other books of very high quality which, for one reason or another, have perished? Do we today know enough to assert that these books were chosen merely because of their moral and spiritual quality?

Other answers also have been offered. One scholar has suggested that the collection of the prophetical books was due to a desire to secure a weapon against the Samaritans. Another has intimated that possibly the spread of Hellenic culture as a result of Alexander's victories had given the final impetus to the Jewish community to include the prophetical books in its canon. Again, it has been suggested that the idea of a canon arose only in the Greek period when the Jews were compelled to issue a pronouncement which would distinguish authoritative books from apocryphal and other writings. But, if this were the case, how did the nation come to distinguish between authoritative and apocryphal books? What determining principle brought about the exclusion of *First Maccabees*, for example, and the inclusion of Daniel?

It has also been held that the criterion which guided the Jews in the selection of the books was the desire to give to the post-exilic temple the advantages of the earlier temple, or that it was the criterion of language, or that the chosen books represent the religion of Israel in its purest form. Again, it has been held that these books speak of

a covenant between God and man, or they are in agreement
with the Pentateuch, or their authors were prophets, or
the books taught Christ, or the books were chosen because
of their intrinsic worth and merit.

A particular problem faces the critics when they endeavor to account for the inclusion of the historical
books among the prophets. According to some, this inclusion was due to the fact that these books contained
utterances of old prophets such as Samuel and Nathan,
and these utterances gave sanction to the entire historical narrative. However, if this be so, why were not
books such as *The Words of Nathan the Prophet* or
The Visions of Jedo the Seer (see II Chronicles 9:29)
and similar writings included? Nor is it satisfactory to
hold that they were accepted merely because of their
prophetic authorship, because other books of prophetic
authorship have perished. Likewise, if their canonicity
be attributed to their popularity and to their religious
and patriotic significance, we would reply that other
books may have been just as popular and have also had
great religious and patriotic significance. Popularity
alone does not insure the permanent survival of a book.

Why too, we may ask, were the individual books of
the Writings, or third part of the Old Testament, accepted? It is not sufficient to maintain that in mere survival or popularity lies the explanation. Nor can it
consistently be held that anonymity was required. Why
were certain other anonymous books, such as the *Wisdom of Solomon*, excluded?

It must be apparent that these explanations do not
begin to satisfy the requirements of the case. Consequently some of the more thoughtful critics have sought
to discover the answer to the problem not merely in

external circumstances, but have thought that the practical religious life of the Jews compelled them at last to accept these books, and that the Jews did as a matter of fact declare them to be canonical because they considered them to be, to a certain extent at least, divine. However, even with this statement of the case, we cannot rest content. For here, also, theological argument is ignored, and there is assumed the position that the Jews themselves, after the books had already been in existence some time, came to recognize them as canonical. It cannot, as a matter of fact, be too strongly insisted that there is no historical evidence whatsoever that the Jews before the time of Christ ever made any official pronouncement as to the identity of the books which they accepted as canonical. And there certainly is no evidence to support the view that there were three canons, that the Pentateuch was first accepted as canonical, then, at a later time, the Prophets and, finally, the Writings.

It is a hopeful sign that this fact is gradually being realized. A German scholar, Hölscher, has admitted that this almost fundamental dogma of the modern critical school must now be abandoned. In this he has been followed in certain recent popular introductions to the Old Testament. Hölscher has thus shown himself to be a pioneer. His own explanation of the formation of the canon, namely, that the spread of apocalyptic books and ideas caused the idea of a canon to arise, is itself untenable. However, a break has at last been made from what has been a most cherished dogma of certain critics.[7]

[7] G. Hölscher, *Kanonisch und Apokryph* (Naumburg, 1905). By means of the idea of the canon, thinks Hölscher, the Jews

Conclusion

The Old Testament is the Word of the living and true God. It is not merely the national or religious literature of the ancient Hebrews. It is rather the life-giving oracles of God. It speaks of God the Creator, the Almighty One, who by the Word of his power, brought all things into existence. It speaks of man's creation and of man's transgression whereby he was brought into an estate of sin and misery. It speaks of God's promise of deliverance through a Redeemer. It points forward, in its entirety and in its individual parts, to the coming of that one who said, "Search the Scriptures, for in them ye think ye have everlasting life, for they are they which testify of me."

The fact that certain critical scholars choose to refuse to discuss the theological questions involved in the formation of the Old Testament canon need not deter us from so doing. When men endeavor to account for the Old Testament canon upon the basis of historical considerations alone, how unsatisfactory their attempts are! In reality they create more problems than they solve.

The devout Christian need not hesitate boldly to de-

---

were able to combat the influence of apocalyptic literature. Hence, the rabbis considered as canonical only books which they thought were written between the time of Moses and Ezra, the classical period of divine inspiration. Why, however, did the Jews, since their purpose was to combat apocalyptic, accept writings such as Daniel, which they considered to have been the product of the classic period of inspiration? Would not apocalyptic literature, on Hölscher's view, have been dangerous, no matter when it was produced?

clare his belief in the Old Testament as the inspired Word of God. He need not fear to believe that the authority of these Scriptures resides in the fact that God is their author. True, there is difficulty in adopting this position but, apart from it, the Old Testament must ever remain a mystery. Why it has been preserved we can then never know. One man's suggestion is as good as another's. We are left in the hopeless abyss of agnosticism.

THE AUTHORITY OF THE NEW TESTAMENT

By N. B. STONEHOUSE

WHEN men speak today of the authority of the New Testament, radically variant estimates of this volume may be in view. If one shares the distinctively modern approach of C. H. Dodd, for example, the New Testament may be judged to possess "the authority of corporate experience."[1] Such an estimate is frankly far from attributing any objective authority to these writings as a corollary of divine origin. On the other hand, there is the historic use of the designation "authority"— historic because given expression in the great creeds of Christendom—which views authority as the equivalent of "canonicity."[2] It is the latter conception of authority

[1] *The Authority of the Bible* (London, 1938), pp. 131ff. Dodd also speaks of the authority of the Bible as "the authority of the men of religious genius who speak in it" (pp. xv, 31, 193). His own view is set sharply over against the traditional view which has regarded the Bible as "the supreme doctrinal authority in faith and morals, divine in origin and consequently infallible" (p. 8).

[2] The first chapter of the Westminster Confession of Faith would be acknowledged by most historians as presenting the classic Protestant creedal formulation of the doctrine of Scripture. Section 2 lists the sixty-six books of Holy Scripture "or the Word of God written" and refers to them as "given by inspiration of God, to be the rule of faith and life." In Section 3 they are distinguished from the Apocrypha which "not being of divine inspiration, are no part of the canon of Scripture; and therefore are of no authority in the Church of God, nor to be any otherwise approved, or made use of, than other human writings."

which is in view in this discussion, and in the interest of avoiding ambiguity and confusion it must at once be defined and circumscribed as precisely as possible.

To accept the New Testament as canonical is, in a word, to acknowledge the twenty-seven writings in the second part of the Holy Bible as possessing divine authority and as constituting, accordingly, an integral part of the divine rule for faith and life. In attributing divine authority to these writings, the Christian church obviously judges that such authority is to be acknowledged only because these writings are held to possess inherently, that is, by virtue of what they actually are, the right to such a claim. In other words, this authority is conceived of, not as superimposed upon the writings at a time when their true character had become obscured or hidden, but as an authority which the books possessed from the very moment of their origin. There is implicit

---

Section 4 rests the authority of Holy Scripture wholly upon God "the author thereof."

The Council of Trent also affirmed the inspiration and divine authority of the Scriptures, and rested their authority upon divine authorship. However the divine authority of the Scripture is qualified in various respects. Not only are certain traditions preserved in the church accorded a place alongside of the Scriptures, but also the "holy mother church" alone is held to be "the judge of the true sense and interpretation of the holy scriptures." Moreover, in effect the council canonized tradition when it judged that the Vulgate, indeed the Vulgate in current use, was the "authentic" text of Scripture, and "that no one is to dare or to presume to reject it under any pretext whatever." Cf. *Dogmatic Canons and Decrees* (New York, 1912), pp. 7ff. Thus the doctrine of the ultimate authority of the living church takes precedence over the authority of Scripture, and a fundamentally different estimate of the place of authority in religion, and of religion itself, comes to expression in Roman Catholicism.

in the claim of canonicity, therefore, the judgment that divine inspiration has constituted these writings with a quality which sets them apart from all merely human writings. Those who accept this high view of the New Testament, accordingly, do not shrink from identifying it as the Word of God, the infallible and inerrant rule of faith and life.

The canonicity of the New Testament involves more, however, than the divine authority of its constituent parts. The authority of the New Testament attaches not only to the twenty-seven writings *severally* but also to the closed collection considered *as a unit* alongside of the Old Testament. Just as the scriptures of the old covenant form a closed collection, the twenty-seven writings of the new covenant too are received as enjoying a completeness and unity of their own. They are the perfect inscripturated revelation of the new covenant. None is lacking and all belong. There is implicit in this high view of Scripture, therefore, besides the acknowledgment of the authority of the several writings due to their inspiration, the recognition that in the process of their collection into a single volume, to the exclusion of all other writings, there has been a divine control which has governed the formation of the canon.[3] Only thus could the final result, the acknowledgment of the canonicity of the single volume of twenty-seven writings, follow after a period during which the writings came

---

[3] This is not to imply that the idea of a collection, or even of a closed collection, is as fundamental to canonicity as the idea of intrinsic divine authority. As soon as any Christian book was accorded a place of absolute divine authority alongside the Old Testament, there was a concrete expression of the idea of the New Testament canon.

into existence at different times and in different places, and during which they circulated for some time either separately or in smaller groups.

This high view of canonicity must be set over against various current notions which appear to fall short of an adequate estimate of its implications. We regard it as fundamental that canonicity must not be identified merely with sacredness. To evaluate a writing as sacred, even to regard it with "high and reverent esteem,"[4] is not necessarily the same as to acknowledge it as possessing absolute divine authority. A writing might be esteemed reverently because its contents as a whole, or to a considerable extent, were regarded as highly significant for religion, but the essential ingredient of authority as a divine writing might be lacking.

Even the approach of the great Lutheran scholar Zahn suffered from a failure to carry through an unambiguous conception of canonicity. His monumental work has been charged, with a measure of justice, with being a history of the public and private use of writings which came to be accepted as canonical rather than strictly a history of the canon of the New Testament. There is indeed a most intimate connection between the use of Christian writings in public worship and their acceptance as canonical. As the *Muratorian Canon*, for example, shows, decisions as to the right of works to be read in the church, and as to the exclusion of others from that privilege, frequently involved the determination of their divine inspiration and authority. It is held, for example, that the *Shepherd of Hermas* ought to be read privately but, as belonging neither to the prophets nor to the apostles, its public reading to the people in the church is condemned. Nevertheless, the circle of writings regarded as sufficiently edifying to be read, at

[4] *Westminster Confession*, I, 5.

least occasionally, in the services of the church was evidently somewhat larger than the circle of strictly canonical writings.[5]

Other writers fail to draw a sharp line between the canonicity of Scripture and of its revelatory contents. An example may be found in the recently published work of John Knox on the New Testament canon. He is on solid ground when he defines "Scripture" as "a collection of books which have unique authority and value because they are accepted as standing in a unique relation to what is believed to have been a unique revelation of God."[6] But obviously all depends on how that "unique relation" is conceived. If the books are thought of as the inspired inscripturation of the revelation of God, they will no doubt qualify as canonical. Knox, however, seems to fall definitely short of according to the writings an adequate relationship to the revelation to warrant that conclusion. For he affirms that it is "nearness to the revealing events or personalities" that determines canonicity, such nearness that the collection of books is "as unduplicable as the revelation and tends soon to be thought of as being the revelation itself."[7] But *proximity* to a revelation and the *tendency* to become identified with revelation hardly suffice to confer canonicity. The divine authority of inspired Scripture is not adequately grounded in the judgment that it serves in a unique fashion to transmit revelation; its canonicity involves the judgment that it is divinely constituted as Scripture, and thus from the beginning bears the character of divine revelation.

The Issues at Stake

If one concentrates upon the leading issues in dispute

[5] Eusebius reports, *e.g.*, that *I Clement* had from the beginning been read in the church at Corinth (*H.E.* IV 23:11).

[6] *Marcion and the New Testament* (Chicago, 1942), pp. 24f.

[7] P. 25.

among historians of the canon of the New Testament, some progress can perhaps be expected even in a brief discussion of this intricate subject. On certain aspects of the actual course of events, there is a considerable measure of agreement; on other issues the differences are radical and far-reaching.

Few scholars today would maintain that the New Testament stood complete immediately, or almost so, after the last of the twenty-seven writings came into existence. On the understanding that the books possess divine authority because of their origin as inspired scriptures, indeed, the canon was *ideally* complete at that time. The actual collection of the writings into a single volume and their recognition, individually and as a unit, as possessing divine authority alongside of the Old Testament, however, took considerably more than a few years. On this point the expressions of some orthodox scholars seem misleading. Apostolic sanction is regarded as the decisive fact in the history of the New Testament canon, and this is understood as meaning that the apostles imposed the several writings as law upon the churches.[8] In our judgment this view lacks specific confirmation from the available evidence and, moreover, cannot account for the diversity with respect to the limits of the New Testament which prevailed for decades and even for centuries.

If there is today a virtual consensus of belief that the New Testament as a single authoritative volume did

[8] See, *e.g.*, W. M. McPheeters, "Apostolic Origin or Sanction, the Ultimate Test of Canonicity" in *The Presbyterian and Reformed Review*, III (1892), pp. 246ff. and VI (1895), pp. 26ff.; B. B. Warfield, *Revelation and Inspiration* (New York, 1927), p. 451.

not stand ready about the end of the first Christian century, there is likewise a remarkable agreement that only
a century later the great centers of the Christian church
were in conscious possession of a New Testament. Moreover, although some uncertainty still remains about
A.D. 200 as to the right of certain books to a place in the
New Testament, and as to the necessity of excluding
others from it, there is substantial agreement as to its
contents. The New Testament about the year 200 consisted of our four canonical gospels, the Acts, thirteen
epistles of Paul, some of the general epistles, and the
Revelation of John.[9]

It follows, then, that the most acute differences of
judgment among historians relate to developments prior
to the close of the second century. The main question
in dispute, in other words, is how the church about the
end of that century came into possession of the New
Testament. The most radical, and apparently also the
most influential, position is that of which Harnack was
the brilliant exponent. On his understanding of the
second century, the New Testament came into being
suddenly about A.D. 175, so suddenly, in fact, that its
origin may be described as a *creation* of the Old Catholic
Church. Harnack does not suppose that it was a creation
ex nihilo, for he allows, of course, that the individual
books came into existence long before and recognizes,
moreover, that various powerful historical factors prepared the way for a New Testament canon. He maintains, nevertheless, that largely through the impulse and
example provided by the heretic Marcion the church

---

[9] Some scholars would contest the right of the Revelation to
be included here. On its place in the canon of the New Testament see my *The Apocalypse in the Ancient Church,* 1929.

came to a qualitatively new judgment concerning certain writings that had been in circulation in the church for some time. Farthest removed from Harnack's construction is that of historians like Westcott and Zahn who conceive of the process as far more gradual and continuous than sudden and abrupt. Other scholars, like Jülicher and Lietzmann, occupy a position somewhere between these poles, allowing that the events of the latter half of the second century affected the development in decisive fashion, and yet insisting that considerably prior to A.D. 175 certain churches accepted a New Testament canon both in its fundamental idea and in concrete fact.

The study of the authority of the New Testament raises other issues, however—far more profound and divisive issues than those which concern the outward course of the developments within the early centuries of the history of the Christian church. It appears that one cannot discuss the origin of the New Testament without initiating a broad inquiry as to the Christianity in which it came into being, and no discussion concerning the nature of Christianity in its first stages can escape a decision as to the person and purpose of Jesus Christ. And in turn the decision as to the meaning of Jesus Christ is bound up with the most ultimate questions concerning reality—questions concerning God and man, revelation and religion.

It is our conviction that the idea of canonicity has meaning and validity only if Christian theism, the theism of the Bible, is true. Implicit in the idea of a divinely authoritative Scripture is the thought of God as self-existent and self-sufficient, the creator and ruler of the universe. His works necessarily constitute a disclosure of his mind and purpose. And in order that sinful men, darkened in their understanding and at enmity with God, might receive knowledge of their true condition and of the divine remedy for that condition with a view to their glorification of God, it was necessary that God should reveal himself directly in history by word and deed. That special and direct revelation in history, which found its center and goal in the history of Jesus Christ, possesses an objective, final character, of permanent validity and significance for men. The inscripturation of that revelation through the agency of the Holy Spirit was due precisely to the need that a permanent and trustworthy record should be provided of the fact and the meaning of the divine action in history.

The charge is often made that this view of revelation involves a static conception of God, which does not leave him free to act when and how he pleases. The objection might be valid if God were conceived as being or becoming a part of the historical process. But such is not the case. Because the world and history belong to him and are under his control, he can make himself known directly in history. And to set aside that direct revelation as irrelevant is to declare one's own independence from God. The defense of the divine freedom then turns out to be merely an assertion of the autonomy of the human spirit.

The charge that the divine freedom is impaired by this doctrine of Scripture is seen to be unfounded, moreover, in view of the consideration that only Christian theism maintains a true doctrine of transcendence, and this alone allows for the sovereign action of the living

God in contemporaneous history. It is a significant historical phenomenon that John Calvin, who asserted without ambiguity the objective authority of the Scriptures, was "the theologian of the Holy Spirit." A true response to the divine word and deed, made known in his works and in Scripture, is possible, Calvin maintained, only through the inward testimony of the Holy Spirit. This doctrine of the inward witness of the Spirit does not sacrifice the objective authority of the Scriptures, as is often maintained.[10] It does not serve as a means to discover and to distinguish within the Scriptures certain revelatory elements and thus to set aside others as non-revelatory. But it recognizes that man, the sinner, requires a gracious inward action of the divine Spirit in order to receive "the full persuasion and assurance of the infallible truth and divine authority" of Scripture, as he also needs the gracious illumination of the Spirit for its true interpretation. The Reformed doctrine of God is then neither static nor activistic; it neither confines God in his past actions nor restricts his significant acts to the present moment. But God is honored as the God of history and of the present,

---

[10] *Institutes*, Book I, Chapter 8. Among those who have failed to distinguish clearly between the objective authority of the Bible, and its objective witness to its own divinity, on the one hand, and the inward witness of the Spirit in the heart of the believer, on the other hand, and who thus tend to subjectivize the authority of the Bible, and even to set up the subjective witness of the Spirit as the test of canonicity, are C. A. Briggs, *Biblical Study* (Edinburgh, 1884), pp. 108ff., 123; *The Bible, the Church and Reason* (New York, 1892), pp. 55ff.; J. Leipoldt, *Geschichte des neutl. Kanons*, II (Leipzig, 1908), pp. 144f.; C. H. Dodd, *op. cit.*, pp. 296f.

who "was and is and is to come"; his direct, objective disclosures in history and his regenerating activity in the heart of man are both maintained.

It is patent that there are abroad today many notions of the nature of reality and religion which are in conflict with the doctrine that genuine religion finds its foundation in divinely authoritative Scripture. Such hostility is by no means confined to philosophies which are openly anti-theistic. Idealistic philosophy and Mysticism are no less exclusive of such a view of revelation; in both there is a supreme indifference to the sphere of historical phenomena; neither arrives at a true transcendence doctrine, since the human spirit is virtually deified or absolutized.

Other philosophical and religious viewpoints appear less antithetical to the idea of Scripture. Because it postulates the unique significance of the history of Jesus for religion, modern Liberalism might seem to maintain a point of view akin to that of historic Christianity. Actually the differences are thoroughgoing and radical. The distinction between the noumenal and the phenomenal, which it derives from Kant by way of the Ritschlian theology, does not provide a background for the affirmation of the Christian doctrine of revelation. For there inheres in the Kantian dialectic a fundamental agnosticism concerning ultimate reality in combination with a readiness to accord to purely naturalistic phenomena the evaluation of revelation. Thus the personality and teaching of the man Jesus, as a unique manifestation of the human spirit, is accorded a measure of authority. In the nature of the case, however, the authority attached to Jesus is qualitatively different from the objective, divine authority attributed in the confessions to the Scriptures.

This state of affairs becomes abundantly clear from the writings of Harnack, who has enjoyed a signal influence both through his exposition of Liberalism and his interpretation of the rise of the New Testament. It is altogether consistent that the scholar who declared that "The gospel as Jesus proclaimed it has to do with the Father only, and not with the Son"[11] should also have declared that "The New Testament itself, when compared with what Jesus purposed, said, and was, is already a tradition which overlies and obscures."[12] How uncongenial his conception of religion finds the element of Scriptural authority is also evident in his affirmation that through the formation of the canon the Spirit was chased away into a book![13] He could hardly have expressed his antipathy to the idea of a direct historical, objectively valid, revelation in more vigorous terms.

It appears to many today that in the Barthian movement one can find the antithesis and antidote to the Liberalism of Harnack. Barthianism proclaims God as "the wholly Other" and polemicizes against the immanentism of modern Protestantism. It insists that theology must be a theology based upon revelation, the theology of the Word of God. It even maintains that the church may not distinguish between the Word of God and the word of men in the Bible; it must recognize that the canon is finished and that the Scripture as it stands is a witness to the divine revelation. Yet, for all of these apparent affirmations of

[11] *Das Wesen des Christentums* (Leipzig, 1902), p. 91; E. T. *What is Christianity?* (London, 1901), p. 144.

[12] *Die Entstehung des Neuen Testaments* (Leipzig, 1914), p. 31; E. T. *The Origin of the New Testament* (London, 1925), pp. 43f.

[13] *Idem*, p. 25 (E. T., p. 36). Cf. Goodspeed, *Formation of the New Testament* (Chicago, 1926), p. 1: "Christianity began as a religion of the spirit. The primitive believers sought guidance from within, believing that in their own hearts the Spirit of God had taken up its abode, and that it would guide them to the truth. In accepting the authority of a collection of books they sacrificed this early attitude, and seemed to go to the opposite extreme. What occasioned this remarkable change, which concerned something so central in early Christian religious thought?"

orthodoxy, the Barthian theology of the Word is basically as antithetical to the historic Christian doctrine of the canonicity of Scripture as the Ritschlian. In spite of the polemic of Barth against the immanentism and subjectivism of modern thought, his position sustains a far larger measure of continuity with that thought than it does with traditional orthodoxy. This is due no doubt to the essentially Kantian starting point which it shares with Liberalism. Appearances to the contrary, notwithstanding, Barthianism also is fundamentally agnostic; it maintains that God remains wholly hidden in his revelation. The phenomenal world, the world of history, it is held, cannot be the medium in which revelation finds expression (and it cannot because it is not a world which came into being by divine fiat). Revelation is said to cease to be revelation if it is direct in history and objectively valid for all time; to be revelation it must be a momentary, contemporaneous divine act. The Bible is full of blunders and contradictions. Hence it may not be identified with revelation or the Word of God; it is only a witness to the divine revelation. There is accordingly a polemic here, just as there is in Ritschlianism, against the idea of a direct historical, objectively valid, revelation.[14]

I. The Testimony of Scripture

The attestation of the canonicity of the New Testament, in the nature of the case, cannot be provided by Jesus in the manner that his words offer a ratification of the authority of the Old Testament. The writings

[14] *Cf.* Karl Barth, *Die Christliche Dogmatik, Die Lehre vom Wort Gottes*, pp. 38ff., 334ff.; *Die Kirchliche Dogmatik, Die Lehre vom Wort Gottes*, Erster Halbband (Münster, 1932), pp. 101ff., 168ff., 274f.; E. T. (Edinburgh, 1936), pp. 111ff., 184ff., 298f.; Zweiter Halbband (Münster, 1938), pp. 505ff., 524ff.

themselves came into existence after the ascension of our Lord. And their collection and acknowledgment as canonical were not finally accomplished even at the close of the first Christian century. The attestation of the canonicity of the New Testament, in contradistinction from that of the Old Testament, might seem to have to depend exclusively upon an ecclesiastical affirmation. If this were true, it might appear that the New Testament is at a most serious disadvantage, lacking the high sanction that the Old Testament enjoys. As we hope to show later the attestation of the church, as a matter of fact, is exceedingly consequential. The history of the canon is the history of its recognition on the part of the church as divinely authoritative. Nevertheless, back of the attestation provided by the church, there is a witness of the Scriptures themselves, a witness which, on the church's understanding of the relation of the Lord to the Scriptures, provides the New Testament with an attestation from the Lord himself. The manner in which the Lord provides that attestation to the New Testament is, naturally enough, different from his specific affirmations of the authority of the Old Testament. The only concrete form in which that attestation can come, if it is not to be derived from another objective revelation from the Lord of heaven, must be nothing other than the voice of Scripture itself.

A. *The Testimony of the Old Testament Canon*

A good starting point for our argument may be found in the fact of the Old Testament, or, to state the matter more precisely, in the fact of Christianity's acceptance of the divine authority of the Scriptures of Palestinian Judaism of the time of Christ. The preceding chapters have indicated at sufficient length how unequivocal the evidence of the New Testament writings is for this conclusion concerning the fundamental belief of Christianity. We are aware that various attempts have been made in modern times to distinguish between the church's acknowledgment of the canonicity of the Old Testament and a supposedly freer attitude of Jesus himself. With respect to such constructions, suffice it to say here that they achieve their end only by finding the tradition of the teaching of Jesus at variance with itself, and by attributing to Jesus a view which is flatly contradicted by a considerable body of the tradition of his teaching. A sound historical interpretation of the data leads, in our judgment, to the conclusion that Jesus consistently upheld the objective divine authority of the Old Testament.[15]

Christianity's acceptance of the Old Testament is of the greatest conceivable importance for the understanding of Christianity itself, and in particular for the understanding of its fundamental philosophy of the history of revelation, which is basic to the concept of canonicity. One stands amazed that in so many able discussions of primitive Christianity this fact fails to come to its own rights. We have in view here the efforts to find the genius of the earliest Christianity in a narrowly conceived futurist eschatology, which is held to have controlled the church's perspectives and interests in drastic fashion. In particular the claim is often made that the expectation of a momentary return of Christ so dominated the thoughts of the early Christians that they could have had no interest in provisions for the regula-

[15] *Cf.* my discussion in *The Witness of Matthew and Mark to Christ* (Philadelphia, 1944), pp. 193ff.

tion of its historical life in the world. An answer to this charge that is partial and yet sufficient is that an entirely different view of history is involved in the readiness of the church to yield to the authority of the historical Scriptures of the Old Testament.

Implicit in the church's acknowledgment of the Old Testament, then, was the affirmation of the Christian-theistic view of history with its supernaturalistic conception of redemption and revelation. To put the matter in the most concrete and specific terms, Christianity began as a religion of a divine book, as a religion of authority which definitely acknowledged a book as an objective expression of the divine mind and will. Were it not that so many modern writers have approached the study of the New Testament canon with the assumption that Christianity is basically not a religion of authority but a religion of "the spirit," it would hardly seem necessary to emphasize the point that the idea of an inscripturated canon, far from being uncongenial to Christianity, forms an integral element of the Christian faith from the very beginning of its life. One must fly in the face of solid fact, accordingly, to insist that Christianity is fundamentally the religion of man's free, unfetterable, spirit. For the same reason, only at the sacrifice of historical realism can one maintain that the Christian conception of revelation is of a revelation which is momentary, completely contemporaneous, and activistic rather than one that is historical, and, even when completed in the past, remaining objectively valid in the present.

The significance of Christianity's acknowledgment of the divine authority of the Old Testament extends beyond its validation of the fundamental idea of canonicity

of Scripture. The acceptance of the Old Testament
not only is eloquent of Christianity's regard for the past;
it also bears witness to Christianity's interpretation of
itself as the fulfillment of the Old Testament revelation.
The Old Testament itself is characterized by an
eschatological outlook, that is, it looks beyond itself to
a new age which brings consummation and finality.
There was a time when the criticism of the Old Testament was so completely under the domination of an
evolutionary and unmessianic point of view that no
serious place was allowed for eschatology. To some extent at least this fault has been overcome in the approach
of scholars like Gressmann. The conclusion is, in our
judgment, inescapable that the Old Testament history
of revelation looks forward to the establishment of a
new covenant, constituted by new divine action and
speech, and inaugurated by the appearance in history of
one who is described both as the Lord himself and as
the Lord's Anointed.[16] But even if there remained
doubt as to the true interpretation of the Old Testament
itself, it would remain incontrovertible that the Christianity which began with the Old Testament understood it in this messianic sense. And in identifying its
own history with the promised messianic age, Christianity inevitably gave expression to its consciousness of
constituting the new order which was to be brought into
being by new divine action and speech. In short, the
acceptance of the Old Testament itself implied that the
history of the Christ was regarded as a history of new
divine revelation.

If then the Old Testament looked beyond itself to a

[16] See B. B. Warfield, "The Divine Messiah in the Old Testament" in *Christology and Criticism* (New York, 1929), pp. 1ff.

new era of revelation which was to come, and if Christianity regarded itself as constituting that new era, a sufficient answer is provided to the common allegation that Christianity, having begun with the Old Testament canon, would not have felt the need of a new canon of Scripture. It has been maintained that the Old Testament canon was a formidable obstacle in the path of a new canon.[17] Since the Old Testament was accepted as a closed and complete revelation, and since its prophetic teaching provided an authoritative delineation of the Christ, it is held that some significant new development would have had to be forthcoming before the church could think of evaluating other writings in the same manner as the Old Testament. This position breaks down, we believe, because it does not take into account at all adequately the decisive accent upon new divine revelation with which the new movement began, and which was even bound up with its attitude towards the Old Testament. It may not be overlooked, indeed, that the Old Testament was regarded as complete; and the new canon consequently could never have been conceived of merely as a kind of expansion of the Old Testament. Rather it was a philosophy of the history of revelation finding expression in terms of the old and new covenant and rooted in the Old Testament itself, which is basic to the acknowledgment of the canon of the New Testament.

B. *The Testimony of the New Testament*

Our appeal to the fact of the acknowledgment of the Old Testament has proceeded from a distinctly Christian

[17] Harnack, *Die Entstehung des Neuen Testaments*, p. 22 (E. T., p. 31).

position, not from the Old Testament as an isolated fact, and consequently our previous discussion has already taken us into the territory of the New Testament. It is necessary now, however, to approach our subject more directly from the vantage point of the testimony of the writings of the New Testament.

Most simply and at once most comprehensively stated, we may affirm that there is one authority that speaks forth from the New Testament, namely, the authority of the Lord Jesus. The Lord who ratified the authority of the Old Testament speaks with independent and absolute authority alongside of the Old Testament. In a word, the New Testament attests the binding authority of the ancient Scriptures and of the Lord who spoke "as having authority and not as the scribes."

To a point, modern historians agree with this affirmation; they agree that the Christian authorities were "the Scriptures and the Lord." I say there is an agreement to a point only, because in the last analysis profound Christological differences emerge if one probes beneath the surface. Was the lordship of Jesus, in an absolute sense, an integral aspect of the Christian faith from the beginning? Or did the church first acknowledge him as the divine Lord in a Hellenistic environment? And behind such questions relating to the Christology of the early Christian church there press upon us questions as to the Christology of Jesus himself. Was he a mere man who, at the most, claimed a kind of relative spiritual supremacy? Or was there inherent in his claims nothing short of an asseveration of equality with God? On the decisions reached on these issues hang ultimately the final judgments as to the validity of the New Testament canon. If the sovereignty of Jesus is something less than divine, no matter how little less, it is not enough to ground the affirmation of the absolutely binding authority of the New Testament. Only an absolute Lord may occupy the place of absolute authority for faith and life. Only his word may constitute divine revelation.

The New Testament canon presupposes more, however, than the deity of the person of Jesus. While the acknowledgment of his deity provides an adequate conception of authority, it does not serve to place that authority definitely within the structure of history. Only if that authority is viewed in the perspective of the history of revelation will one be able to define the authority of the Lord in relation to that of the Old Testament. Now this want is fulfilled by the consideration that Jesus, the Lord, is the divine Messiah. As the Messiah he occupies a well-defined place in the history of revelation. Only when he is recognized as the divine Messiah can one understand him as standing in solid continuity with the preparatory revelation and yet bringing it to absolute consummation.

The distinctiveness of the historic Christian view of revelation as the revelation of the divine Messiah may be seen in sharper focus if it is set in contrast to the approach of the heretic Marcion, who has frequently been claimed as the real creator of the New Testament canon. In dependence upon Matthew 11:27 (Luke 10:22), which speaks of the absoluteness of the Son's knowledge of the Father and of the sovereignty of his disclosure of the Father, Marcion grasped the truth of the absoluteness and newness of the Christian revelation. But the God whom Jesus proclaimed he held to be an unknown, stranger God. The Old Testament consequently had to be set aside. Now these radical conclu-

sions were bound up with his failure to understand
Jesus in the perspective of history, or, in other words, to
recognize him as the Messiah. It is exactly the concept
of messiahship which demands both continuity with the
old order and its fulfillment. Messiahship is essentially
unintelligible apart from the presupposition of the old
covenant and it remains unrealized unless it ushers in
the new covenant. Hence we see that there emerged in
the case of Marcion an essentially new conception of
Christian revelation, a conception radically at variance
with that which was implicit in the historic acknowledgment of Jesus as the divine Messiah.

If then the messiahship of Jesus, as well as his lordship,
is basic to the final decisions as regards canonicity, it
will appear that the modern debate concerning the historicity of the messianic consciousness of Jesus is an
important aspect of the larger debate as to the essence
of Christianity and the character of true religion. If
Jesus did not think of himself as the Messiah, or if, in
affirming messiahship, he regarded it as merely a formal
or peripheral aspect of his consciousness, or even as uncongenial and burdensome, and thus as not definitely
determinative of his central thought concerning his life,
the follower of Jesus will hardly in any serious fashion
interpret that history as constituting divine revelation.
If, on the other hand, he regarded himself as the Messiah
of the Old Testament (and if he so regarded himself
that conviction must have been so overwhelming and so
all-controlling that it could not have been merely formal), his history, the history of the divine Messiah, immediately and inevitably stands apart from merely
human history. The Liberal holds that "supreme importance" came to be assigned to the history of Jesus,

and especially to his death and resurrection, only in the primitive church. But if the messiahship of Jesus is affirmed and taken seriously, Jesus must himself have attached supreme importance to his own history.

The decision on this great question is in brief the decision as to whether the witness of the Gospels to Jesus is true. There is no real debate today as to whether the Gospels actually represent Jesus as living and dying and rising as the Messiah. The ablest interpreters of the Gospels freely acknowledge that they were written from the point of view of such a belief in Jesus. To mention only one conspicuously pertinent fact, he is represented as one who taught that through his death the new covenant was inaugurated (Luke 22:20; *cf.* Mk. 14:24). The debate is whether we shall accept the evangelical testimony to him or not. Those who have sought to recover an "historical" Jesus—that is, a mere man—behind the figure of the divine Messiah of the New Testament have, we think, not achieved success. No really objective criteria, not excluding the criteria advanced by form-criticism, have been discovered whereby one may remove the supposedly unhistorical accretions of tradition and get back to an original historical stratum of solid fact. The more consistent and thoroughgoing criticism has landed in skepticism.

The divine messiahship of Jesus is then the basic fact behind the formation of the New Testament. But we must freely acknowledge that this fact alone is far from bringing us to the goal of our investigation. The acknowledgment of the presence of the divine Messiah does not carry with it the necessary embodiment of that revelation in a corpus of writings. Jesus left behind no literary productions. The Christian church apparently

for a considerable time was content to rely upon *oral*
tradition for its knowledge of Jesus. A most crucial
phase of our subject is bound up, therefore, with our
judgment as to the factors that served to link the historical career of Jesus with the composition of the New
Testament documents.

According to the New Testament, it was the apostles
who constituted the link between the Lord himself and
the Scriptures of the New Testament. The student of
the early history of the canon likewise will freely con-
cede that there is a close connection between canonicity
and apostolicity. But at once difficult questions emerge
when we try to define that connection precisely. With
our eye upon the origin of the several writings of the
New Testament we may not identify canonicity with
apostolic authorship, for then several writings would
fail to qualify. Nor can we make real progress by de-
fining apostolicity more broadly, as signifying apostolic
sponsorship or apostolic sanction, for, as stated previously, the facts of history do not support such constructions. If then apostolicity will not serve as a touchstone
of canonicity, must we infer that apostolicity is inconse-
quential and irrelevant for our subject? In our judgment
the apostles occupied such a unique place in the life
of the early church that such an inference must be set
aside.

According to the consistent witness of the New Testament, Jesus chose a company of persons who were qualified, both by their personal witness of his life and by
their endowment by the Spirit of Christ, to declare
authoritatively the Christian message.[18] The tradition

18 *Cf., e.g.,* Mark 1:16ff.; 3:13f.; 4:10f.; 6:7ff.; 9:9; Luke 6:12ff.;
Acts 1:1f., 22ff.; John 14:26ff.; 15:26f.; 16:25ff.

which ascribes to the circle of the immediate disciples of Jesus a unique qualification and authority to publish the Christian message has been subjected to severe criticism. Although there may be a readiness on the part of some to acknowledge that there was a small circle of confidants who enjoyed special privileges and for whom Jesus predicted special honors in the kingdom of God, it is widely held that the tradition, in so far as it ascribes to them the right to speak with decisive authority in the church of Christ, reflects a late stage of development in which the apostles had come to be accorded a place of spiritual authority never intended by Jesus. Our answer to this historical skepticism, briefly stated, is that the evangelical delineation of the relation of the apostles to Jesus is as historical as its portrait of Jesus. The conception of the apostolate is really a messianic concept, that is, it has meaning only on the background of Jesus' consciousness of his mission as the Messiah to establish the church.

Now it is clear that Paul, too, claimed the authority of an apostle to declare the Christian gospel. Although he did not accompany Jesus in the days of his flesh, he insisted that, like the others, he was a witness of the resurrection of Jesus and had been otherwise qualified for the apostolic task (I Cor. 9:1; 15:8ff.; II Cor. 12:12). He maintained that his authority as an apostle was quite independent of the authority of the other apostles; it was an apostolic authority immediately derived from the Lord (Gal. 1:1, 11, 17; cf. 4:14). He was not one whit behind the chiefest apostles (II Cor. 11:5; 12:11f.). He implies also that the leaders at Jerusalem recognized the validity of his claims (Gal. 2:8f.). And everywhere his epistles breathe a consciousness of absolute authority to set forth the Lord's mind and will to the churches; he even assumed without argument the right to regulate the exercise of the charismatic gifts of the Christian prophets (I Cor. 14:29ff., 37).

In connection with this estimate of the place occupied by the apostles in early Christianity, we think it of the greatest importance to underscore the observation that the apostolic authority was never conceived of as an authority independent of, or even on a level with, the authority of the Lord. Modern writers often represent the inclusion of the apostolic writings in the canon, even writings like the epistles of Paul, as involving an unforeseen and indefensible exaltation of the apostles to a place alongside of the Lord. Let us hear Harnack as he approaches the question why the New Testament contains other books beside the Gospels, and appears as a compilation of two divisions ("Evangelium" and "Apostolus"):

> "In the New Testament letters which serve momentary and particular needs are set on a level of equal value with the Gospels; what is merely personal with what is of universal import; the Apostles with Christ; their work with His work! In a compilation which is invested with Divine authority we must read: 'Drink a little wine for thy stomach's sake,' and 'my cloak I left at Troas.' Side by side with words of Divine mercy and loving kindness in the Gospels we meet with outbreaks of passionate personal strife in the Epistles; side by side with the stories of the Passion and Resurrection, the dry notes of the diary of a missionary journey!"[19]

[19] *Die Entstehung des Neuen Testaments*, p. 30 (E. T., pp. 42f.). *Cf.* also E. C. Colwell, *The Study of the Bible* (Chicago,

Before the New Testament came to be designated with a name that expressed its unity, it appears indeed that for a time it was spoken of as "Gospel and Apostle." The recognition of that division within the New Testament was natural enough. Yet we are convinced that altogether too much has been made of this twofold division in modern discussions, too much because the fact of the recognition of the single divine authority of the collection tends to be obscured. It is far too simple an analysis of the history of the New Testament canon to imply that the fourfold Gospel canon was accepted because of the absolute authority of the Lord whereas the rest of the New Testament was received because the apostles came in the course of events to be accorded a place on a level with the Lord.

The sharp distinction which is drawn between the Gospels and the Epistles breaks down in at least two ways. In the first place, the Gospels no less than the Epistles were directed to specific historical situations. They too, in a sense, are occasional writings. To recognize them as serving the immediate needs of their time, however, is not to infer that they were not of universal import. The universal import of the Epistles ought to be evident from a consideration of their proclamation and application of the gospel. And it is certainly demonstrated from the use which has been made of them in the history of the church.

In the second place, the apostolic authority which speaks forth in the New Testament is never detached from the authority of the Lord. In the Epistles there is

1937), pp. 3f. and Knox, *op. cit.*, pp. 29ff. For a discussion of the latter work see *The Westminster Theological Journal*, May, 1943, pp. 86ff. and of this point, pp. 93f.

consistent recognition that in the church there is only
one absolute authority, the authority of the Lord himself. Wherever the apostles speak with authority, they
do so as exercising the Lord's authority. Thus, for example, where Paul defends his authority as an apostle,
he bases his claim solely and directly upon his commission by the Lord (Gal. 1 and 2); where he assumes the
right to regulate the life of the church, he claims for
his word the Lord's authority, even when no direct word
of the Lord has been handed down (I Cor. 14:37; cf.
I Cor. 7:10). Nor may it be overlooked that the Gospels
are also apostolic. They were so characterized by the
Christian church of the end of the second century, which
is regarded by Harnack as the creator of the New Testament.[20] And the Gospels themselves, in so far as they
make any explicit claims of authority, appeal to the
apostolic testimony which they contain (Luke 1:1-4;
John 21:24). In spite of the diversity of the contents of
the New Testament, therefore, it does not consist of
"two absolutely disparate entities."[21] The only one who
speaks in the New Testament with an authority that is
underived and self-authenticating is the Lord. Since,
however, his message required to be mediated to the
church through human instrumentalities, it was necessary that those who had been appointed and qualified
by the Lord should become his spokesmen.

Although then the revelation of the new covenant is
apostolic, without ceasing to be the Word of the Lord,
the apostolic origin of that revelation does not as such
constitute the twenty-seven writings of the New Testa-

[20] Cf. Irenaeus, c. Haer. III, 1f.; Tertullian, c. Marc. IV, 2;
Muratorian Canon.
[21] Harnack, ibid.

ment as divine Scripture. If Mark and Luke, for example, are to be judged canonical, their canonicity cannot be made to rest exclusively upon the consideration that they report apostolic tradition, however important that consideration may be for our estimate of their intrinsic character and historical significance. If the writings of Mark and Luke are to be judged canonical, it must be because these evangelists were controlled by the Spirit of the Lord in such a manner that their writings, and not merely the apostolic message which they set forth, are divine. In other words, it is Mark's inspiration (which, to be sure, is not to be isolated from his historical qualifications), and not Peter's inspiration, which provides the finally indispensable ground for the acceptance of that work as canonical.

We necessarily face, therefore, the question whether the witness of the individual writings themselves is of such a character as to justify the high claims that are made for them when they are received as the divinely inspired and authoritative Scriptures of the New Covenant. Now we have no right to insist, if the high judgment of the church concerning these writings is to be vindicated, that the inherent divine authority of the individual writings will have impressed itself upon them in any stereotyped fashion. In the nature of the case a book of history will not bear upon its surface the evidence of its divine origin in the way that prophetic writings necessarily do. The witness of the individual writings, as in the case of the books of the Old Testament canon, varies with the individual character of the writings.

The Revelation of John, the only prophetical book in the New Testament, bears express marks of its claims to inspiration. That which is written is what the Spirit says to the churches (Rev. 1:10f.; 2:1, 7, etc.). The book may be described as constituting the revelation and witness of Jesus Christ and as the Word of God (1:1f.). Consequently, those who hear and keep what is written in it are promised a special blessing, whereas those who presume to add to or to take away from the things that are written come under the divine curse (1:3; 22:18f.).[22]

In the case of the epistles the right to be heard and to be obeyed is made to rest on the personal relation which exists between the writers and their readers, the authority expressed or implied being inherent in the recognized qualifications of the authors. Paul, as noted above, everywhere claims to speak with the authority of the Lord. And he consequently attaches the highest significance to his own writings. He is solicitous for their exchange (Col. 4:16) and intimates, therefore, that he considers them of more than momentary worth. Of more importance, we observe that he considers it so important that his earliest (so most scholars judge) epistle be read to the church that he even *adjures* its recipients to see that this is done (I Thess. 5:27). The extraordinary significance which he attached to obedience to his written word finds striking expression in II Thess. 3:14: "And if any man obeyeth not our word by this epistle, note that man, that ye have no company with him, to the end that he may be ashamed." It is no wonder then that at an early date the epistles of Paul were collected and re-

---

[22] H. Windisch, in an article entitled "Der Apokalyptiker Johannes als Begründer des neutestamentlichen Kanons" (*Zeitschrift für die ntl. Wissenschaft*, X, 1909, p. 159) maintained that the author of the Revelation shows that he was conscious of creating a canonical book.

ceived as worthy of a place alongside of the Old Testament (*cf.* II Peter 3:16).

There are other canonical epistles—the Epistle to the Hebrews, James and Jude—which do not claim specific apostolic origin and authority. They nevertheless in their own way assert their authority in the church. James and Jude speak as servants of Jesus Christ. The author of the Epistle to the Hebrews, while distinguishing himself from the apostolic circle, everywhere speaks as qualified to set forth a true and authoritative expression of the preëminent revelation of the new covenant, a revelation "in a Son" and "spoken through the Lord," and "confirmed unto us by those who heard" (Heb. 2:1-4; *cf.* 1:1ff.; 13:22).

The Gospels assert their authority in still another way. As witnesses to Christ, the evangelists take little or no time to accredit themselves as qualified to publish the gospel with divine authorization. The personality of the evangelists tends to stay so completely in the background that it remains for their messages to authenticate themselves as authoritative proclamations of the gospel. It is true, nevertheless, that the original readers must have known the identity of the writers. Moreover, Luke and John are not, properly speaking, anonymous works. Luke is at pains to set forth at the very beginning his qualifications, method and goal. In particular he informs Theophilus that he is competent to supply a completely trustworthy account of the career of the supernatural figure whom he depicts. He is competent to supply such an account as provided certainty as regards the origins of Christianity. And the evangelist John brings to the attention of his readers the figure of an intimate disciple "whom Jesus loved" evidently in order to exhibit his qualifications to bear witness to Jesus and to supply a written record of that witness (John 13:23f.; 19:26f., 35; 20:2ff.; 21:24; *cf.* 18:15; 1:25, 37, 40). Mark, in spite of its anonymity, claims for itself far more than ordinary significance when in the opening verse it designates itself as "gospel," that is, as the glad tidings of salvation which came to be realized in the history of Jesus Christ.[23] Although Matthew does not contain any similar self-characterization, yet it likewise was evidently written to serve the same fundamental purpose as Mark. The Gospels then, explicitly or implicitly, claim to set forth the gospel of Christ. That gospel as the proclamation of the divine action and word in history is essentially revelatory. And since the revelation is historical, the implication is that it must be published authoritatively by those who stood in intimate connection with the events and could declare their meaning.

The self-evaluation of the records, therefore, is not at variance with the claim of canonicity. We must admit, however, that the later formulations with regard to the character of the writings of the New Testament assume characteristically a specific form not explicit in most of the writings. It does not appear that the church everywhere and at once recognized exactly these writings as divine. And only after some time did the church precisely define the relation of these writings individually and as a unit to the Old Testament. We must inquire more particularly, therefore, as to the nature of the process in which these results were achieved.

[23] See *The Witness of Matthew and Mark to Christ*, pp. 7ff.

II. THE ATTESTATION OF THE CHURCH

In this section we propose to limit ourselves to certain leading phases of the early history of the New Testament canon. We have noted above that historians today are sharply at variance as to many of the decisive facts and factors of the development in the second century; they differ, for example, on the questions whether the New Testament came into being as late as about A.D. 175, whether Marcion's collection affected the course of events in any decisive fashion, whether Justin Martyr gives evidence of a New Testament. The decision on these and other questions is admittedly difficult. One dares not overlook the fact that the history of the New Testament canon is but a part of the complex history of the Christian church. And our search for positive results is often thwarted by the paucity of extant evidence. Nevertheless, even in a few pages it will be possible to examine some of the most pertinent evidence and to gain certain broad perspectives concerning the development as a whole. In order to achieve this end, however, we shall be compelled to limit our discussion to the testimony provided by a few key figures.

The document known as *I Clement,* a letter from the church at Rome to the church at Corinth about A.D. 95, provides one of the most important of the early testimonies. The document indeed has serious limitations for our subject. It provides knowledge of developments in only a small segment of the church, not of the church universal. Moreover, it is not a treatise on canonicity; in fact, what it has to tell us on this subject is told in the most incidental fashion. Nevertheless, its positive statements and its silences contribute significantly to our knowledge of the formation of the New Testament.

The attitude of *I Clement* toward the New Testament writings may be judged on the background of its regard for the Old Testament. It everywhere displays the same high reverence for the Old Testament that is disclosed in the New Testament. There are more than one hundred quotations, and they are frequently introduced with "It is written" or similar formulae. Evidently referring to the Old Testament, the author writes on one occasion: "Ye have studied the sacred scriptures, which are true and given by the Holy Spirit. You know that nothing unjust or counterfeit is written in them" (45:2, 3). Now since this epistle never speaks in similar fashion concerning the writings of the New Testament, it would seem to follow that the New Testament canon had not yet emerged as a concrete reality at the end of the first century in Rome. Still this broad conclusion needs to be qualified. In spite of the secure place which the Old Testament enjoyed as authoritative for the church, this document also affirms, alongside the Old Testament, the authority of "the Lord Jesus" (13:1; 46:7f.). There is also the recognition that the authority of the Lord was mediated by the apostolic proclamation of the gospel and as well by the apostolic appointment of ecclesiastical government (42:1-4; 44:1, 2). Not only the words of the Lord then, but also the apostolic proclamation of the Lord, was regarded as possessing authority.

But how do the writings of the New Testament stand related to the authoritative apostolic proclamation? *I Clement* uses several of these writings, but as we have observed above, the mere use of writings does not establish canonicity. And it is a striking fact that the New

Testament documents are not formally quoted as Scripture. In fact, with a single exception, they are not referred to specifically at all. It knows of the gospel but never speaks of Gospels. So far as the testimony of this witness goes, therefore, the New Testament writings had not yet come to be characterized in terms identical with those applied to the Old Testament. To acknowledge that the church of about the end of the first century had not yet formulated in explicit terms its doctrine of the canonicity of the New Testament is not to admit, however, that the later evaluation was not already implicit in the earliest characterizations. Alongside of the Old Testament, as we have noted, there was an acceptance of the Christian gospel as authoritative because of its provenience from the apostles, who in turn "received the gospel from the Lord Jesus Christ" (42:1). Now it may be acknowledged that as late as the end of the first Christian century the oral tradition of the apostolic proclamation was a highly significant factor in the life of the church. Nevertheless, the written tradition of that proclamation can hardly have been regarded as being at a disadvantage as over against the oral tradition. The use which *I Clement* makes of the written documents is sufficient proof of that. And most eloquent of all is the fact that, although this writer makes specific mention of only one apostolic document, he does so in a manner that makes perfectly clear that certain writings were accorded the highest possible degree of authority. For in referring to I Corinthians he says, "Take up the epistle of the blessed Paul, the apostle. What did he write unto you at the beginning of his preaching? With true inspiration (ἐπ' ἀληθείας πνευματικῶς) he charged you concerning himself and Cephas and Apollos, because even then you had made yourselves partisans" (47:1-3).[24]

If then *I Clement* had spoken specifically of other writings which had come down from the apostles, he could hardly have failed to claim for them also the authority of the Lord and of his Spirit. While then we must recognize that the formulation of the church's estimate of the New Testament writings at this time was far from being what it was about one hundred years later, nevertheless the kernel of the matter is already present. In other words, the explicit recognition of the canonicity of the New Testament does not represent a development sharply at variance with what one might have expected about the year 100; rather, the unique estimate of the authority of the apostles was a guarantee that the specific relation of the apostolic proclamation to the Old Testament would come to be formulated along the line of the church's eventual expression.

About twenty years after the transmission of *I Clement* to Corinth another highly significant witness appeared. Ignatius, bishop of Antioch, passing through Asia Minor on his way to Rome as a condemned man, wrote seven epistles of remarkable originality of thought and expression. If they had been written in the quiet of an episcopal study, they might well have contained many more quotations than they do, and those which appear might

---

[24] The observation might be made that, if *I Clement* bears witness to the inspiration of Paul, he also does so to himself, since he states that he wrote "through the Holy Spirit" (63:2). It is significant, however, that in this immediate context this writer characterizes his writing as an "entreaty" and says "you will give us joy and gladness if you are obedient to the things which we have written." Since, however, this writer merely entreats, there is clearly a qualitative distinction between the inspiration of Paul and his own endowment with the Holy Spirit.

have approximated the literalness characteristic of the quotations in *I Clement*. However, Ignatius was clearly such a vigorous and original personality that we cannot imagine him writing in stereotyped fashion, no matter how academic his surroundings might be. The paucity of specific references to the Old Testament and to apostolic writings is, accordingly, compensated by the freshness of his observations. Ignatius indeed displays a knowledge of many writings of Scripture, and it is meaningful for our understanding of the place which the New Testament writings had come to occupy in the life of the church that, in contrast to the usage of *I Clement*, his letters display a far greater dependence upon the language of the New Testament than upon that of the Old Testament. But again it is not so much the quotation of, or allusion to, language of Scripture that is significant for the study of c nonicity as certain specific reflections upon the history of revelation. Around these passages indeed there has developed a considerable amount of discussion, which cannot be weighed here, and we can only indicate our understanding of some of the more perspicuous passages.

On one occasion the comparison between the two dispensations of revelation takes the following form: "But the gospel has somewhat of preëminence, the coming of the Saviour, our Lord Jesus Christ, his passion, and the resurrection. For the beloved prophets had a message pointing to him, but the gospel is the perfection of incorruption" (*Philadelphians* 9:2). Here the new revelation in Christ is viewed as the fulfillment of the prophetic disclosures. Its preëminence is recognized. It seems clear that the "gospel," as Ignatius refers to it, is not a document or collection of documents, but the *message* of Christianity (*cf.* also *Phil.* 5:1, 2; *Smyrnaeans* 5:1; 7:2).

The very considerable accent which Ignatius puts on the New Testament revelation finds interesting expression in another passage which has been much discussed. A slightly paraphrased rendering of the original which seems to us to express most adequately its meaning follows:

> "But I beseech you to do nothing in factiousness, but after the teaching of Christ. For I heard some men saying, 'If I find it not [the point at issue] in the charters [archives], I do not believe it if it is only in the gospel.' And when I said to them, 'It is written,' they answered me, 'That remains to be settled.' But to me the charters are Jesus Christ, the inviolable charter is his cross, and death, and resurrection, and the faith which is through him. . . ."[25]

The passage clearly implies that certain opponents of Ignatius, apparently of a Judaizing sort, insisted on making the Old Testament Scriptures the touchstone of Christian truth, and Ignatius agrees with them to the extent that he too acknowledges the Old Testament, and on his part he insists that the Christian gospel has received prophetic expression in the ancient scriptures. Nevertheless, he adds that the New Testament revelation does not require the attestation of the Old; it is inherently authoritative. An important and difficult question remains. How did Ignatius conceive of the New Testament revelation? When he refers to the "gospel" in this passage, and particularly when he de-

---

[25] *Philadelphians* 8:2: The Greek text of the difficult conditional sentence follows: ἐὰν μὴ ἐν τοῖς ἀρχείοις εὕρω ἐν τῷ εὐαγγελίῳ οὐ πιστεύω.

scribes Jesus Christ as constituting "the charters" alongside of the "charters" of the Old Testament, does he have
specific Christian writings in mind? So indeed some able
interpreters of Ignatius have judged. My own conclusion
is that the language does not clearly support that interpretation. Here, as in the other passages cited above, the
"gospel" appears to refer to the Christian message, without reflection upon its form, whether oral or written.
And though the term "charters" as applied to the Christian gospel strikingly indicates the parity, and more than
parity, which Ignatius attributed to the distinctive Christian revelation, it seems to be used with reference to
the contents of that revelation rather than to its written
formulation.

There are other data in the epistles of Ignatius, however, which illuminate the question of the specific character of that Christian message. The apostles are accorded a place of unique authority and privilege as pro-
claimers of the gospel; their ordinances possess the same
authority as the Lord (*Phil.* 5:1, 2; *Magnesians* 13:1;
Trallians 12:2; *Ephesians* 11:2). Ignatius himself speaks
with a high measure of authority to the churches to
which he writes, but for all of his claims he is far from
associating himself with the apostles. Writing to the
Romans, for example, he says, "I do not command you
as Peter and Paul; they were apostles, I am a condemned
man" (*Rom.* 4:3; *cf. Trall.* 3:3). The Christian revelation, according to Ignatius, therefore, decidedly is not
a contemporaneous revelation; it is a revelation in the
past which found its embodiment in Jesus Christ and
found authoritative expression in the deliverances of the
apostles. To some extent Ignatius may have depended
upon oral transmission of the apostolic tradition, but
there can be little question that he relied chiefly upon

its written expression. It is generally acknowledged, for example, that he knew and used our canonical Matthew, and though he does not refer specifically to this book or identify it with "the gospel," it must have been to him an expression of the apostolic proclamation of the past which he acknowledged as standing on a level with, and even transcending, the Old Testament Scriptures. So also when he speaks of a collection of epistles of Paul, he evidently regards them as an authoritative expression of the ordinances of the apostles (*Ephesians* 12). The testimony of Ignatius like that of *I Clement,* accordingly, demonstrates that the collection of New Testament writings, and their acknowledgment as authoritative alongside of the Old Testament, were but the concrete realization in history of principles operative in the first decades of the second century.

Our next witness is a voice from Asia Minor. Papias of Hierapolis was the author of a work entitled *Exposition of Oracles of the Lord* which was published within the second quarter of the second century. To our great loss this work is no longer extant, although fortunately a few fragments have been preserved, chiefly by Eusebius. The Eusebian quotations are so meager and isolated that dogmatism with respect to the views of Papias must be eschewed; at the same time they are so significant, as containing some of the earliest traditions concerning the New Testament, that one may not fairly challenge their right to a preëminent place in modern discussions.

A particular reason for including Papias in this brief survey is that he is often held to demonstrate that as late as a time close to the middle of the second century a Christian churchman could be quite indifferent to the canonicity of the New Testament. Quite recently, for example, John Knox has spoken of "Papias' depreciation of written Gospels and his preference for 'the living voice.' "[26] The passage which has been supposed to ground such conclusions is the final sentence of the Eusebian quotation from the preface of Papias' work, in which he says: "For I did not suppose that the things from books would profit me as much as those from a living and abiding voice." The context indeed indicates the interest of Papias in oral tradition, specifically in the tradition handed down from the earliest disciples of the Lord. We must deny, however, the validity of the inference commonly drawn from Papias' statement. Can one seriously allow that Papias depreciated written gospels when one considers his characterization of the Gospel according to Mark? He represents Mark as an accurate and trustworthy account of the things either said or done by the Lord as they had been proclaimed by the apostle Peter. "Of one thing he took forethought," says Papias, "not to omit anything of the things he had heard or to falsify anything in them" (H. E., III 39:15).

Moreover, although this is disputed, we think that Papias is so far from depreciating the gospels that he even characterizes them as being or consisting of "the oracles of the Lord." He implies that Mark carried out what Peter had himself failed to do, namely, to make a composition of oracles of the Lord. And speaking of Matthew he also characterizes his work as a composition of "the oracles," thus indicating that he has a written work in mind. If Papias is using the word "oracles" in the title of his work in this same sense, it follows that his aim was to provide *an exposition of the gospels.* The question remains how then he could express a prefer-

[26] *Op. cit.,* p. 114.

ence for oral tradition as compared with books. It seems commonly to be overlooked that, in the opening sentence of the portion of the preface quoted by Eusebius, Papias sets forth clearly enough the subordinate place to be occupied by oral traditions within the structure of his work, for he says that he will not hesitate *"to append* to the interpretations" the things that had come down to him orally from ancient witnesses. In other words, his exposition or interpretation of the oracles is primary, the recollection of ancient oral tradition is secondary. If then Papias characterizes the gospels as "the oracles of the Lord" in the Marcan passage, and apparently also in the title of his work, we possess a most significant testimony to the reverent regard with which he held the ancient writings. He applies to them a designation which expresses their inspired character; he applies to them the designation which was employed to express the oracular character of the Old Testament.[27]

When we turn from Papias to Justin Martyr we enjoy the great advantage of being able to judge his testimony in the context of writings of considerable length. Justin Martyr wrote in Rome in the sixth decade of the second century, but his earlier contacts with eastern regions of the church make him a witness for a far wider area. The testimony of Justin is most crucial. His testimony and his silences are commonly made the basis for the conclusion that, in the middle of the century, the church had not yet arrived at a New Testament canon. Justin, says Harnack, "is simply crying for a New Testament" but "cannot produce it."[28] It is true, of course, that

[27] *Cf.* esp. Romans 3:2. For the meaning of the term, see the important article of B. B. Warfield, "The Oracles of God," in *Revelation and Inspiration*, pp. 335ff.

[28] *Die Entstehung des Neuen Testaments*, p. 12 (E. T., p. 16). See also Knox, *op. cit.*, p. 24 and especially note 9.

Justin's writings present an extraordinary witness to the secure place which the Christian church accorded to the canonicity of the Old Testament. Moreover, he makes pervasive use of the Old Testament for apologetic purposes: in his apology to the heathen world employing it to establish the antiquity of Christianity, and in his argument with Trypho, the Jew, as providing a common ground for discussion. Admittedly Justin does not use and characterize the apostolic writings in the same fashion. But the question to be kept before the historian in the evaluation of evidence like that of Justin, in our judgment, is not primarily the question whether New Testament writings are appealed to specifically as "Scripture" but whether they are acknowledged as possessing divine authority alongside of the Old Testament. When the question is put in such terms we are convinced that the answer demanded by the testimony of Justin is different from that often provided.

In the first place, we cannot doubt that Justin fully acknowledged the coming of a new era of revelation which found its origin and authority, as well as its central content, in Jesus Christ. Jesus Christ is the authoritative teacher of the Christians and it is his life, the life of the Son of God, which constitutes the fulfillment of the prophetic revelation. Christ is the "new law and the new covenant" (*Dialogue* 11).

In the second place, the new revelation finds expression in Christian documents. It is not confined to the prophetic word of the Old Testament. It is not merely an oral tradition of Christian content. The manner in which Justin speaks of certain Christian documents, and especially of the Gospels, prohibits any other conclusion. In the first *Apology*, perhaps because the stress of his argument falls upon the antiquity of Christianity, there are few definite allusions to the Gospels. In the famous passage in which he describes the worship of the Christians, however—a passage, therefore, in which he is more didactic than apologetic—he accords them the highest place alongside of the Old Testament. In the preceding paragraph, where he has been concerned with the Eucharist, he refers its authority to the apostolic record: "For the apostles in the memoirs which were composed by them, which are called gospels, thus delivered unto us what was commanded them" (I 66). The authority of the apostolic record, an authority ultimately derived from the Lord himself, is here clearly recognized. Now the nature of that authority is most precisely set forth in the passage which treats of the service on the Lord's Day:

> "And on the day called Sunday there is a gathering together to one place of all those who live in cities or in the country, and the memoirs of the apostles or the writings of the prophets are read, as long as time permits. Then when the reader has ceased the president presents admonition and invitation to the imitation of these good things" (I 67).

Here then is reflected not merely the personal slant of Justin but the common Christian practice in Rome and perhaps also in other parts of the Christian world for which Justin could speak. The authority of the apostolic gospels does not fall short of the authority of the prophetic writings; in fact, he mentions the apostolic writings before the others and intimates that they may be read in place of the Old Testament, and not merely along with the Old Testament. It will not be pertinent to retort that public reading is not decisive evidence of canonicity. Our appeal to this passage is not to the effect that the public lection of apostolic writings is evidence of canonical regard, but rather that Justin clearly did not place the Gospels in a category inferior to the Old Testament. He is not speaking, moreover, of an occasional reading of apostolic writings but of their regular use in the church alongside of the Old Testament.

In the *Dialogue* the references to the Gospels accumulate, perhaps because Trypho was well acquainted with them. And it is highly significant that in a number of cases he employs the formula "It is written," or similar language, in introducing quotations from the Gospels (*Dial.* 49, 103, 105, 107). The question arises, however, whether after all we may allow that Justin regarded the Gospels as Scripture in view of his failure ever to characterize them as inspired by the Holy Spirit. If Justin had spoken of the apostolic writings as inspired, we should indeed have reason to regard such testimony as confirmation of our general conclusion. Still the absence of such language does not establish the contrary. The characteristic difference in the designation of prophetic and apostolic writings may be explained from the different evaluation of their place within the total structure of revelation. The significance of the Old Testament was chiefly due to its prophetic character—it was the product of the Spirit of prophecy. The significance of the apostolic memoirs, on the other hand, was that they constituted the historical fulfillment of prophecy, and they are described as the product of the Lord and of the apostles as his instruments. Although the apostles are not described as inspired, they are acknowledged as the spokesmen of the Lord in the new dispensation as the prophets were of the Spirit in the old (*Dial.* 119; *cf.* *Apol.* I, 33, 49, 50, 39).

Accordingly, a New Testament is present both in idea

and fact according to Justin's testimony. We miss a well-rounded statement of the canonicity of the New Testament. Its limits are not defined. But inasmuch as Christian writings are accorded a place of absolute authority alongside of the Old Testament the essence of the matter is present.

A further question must be raised, even though no completely satisfactory answer can be provided. That question is whether the New Testament of Justin contains only Gospels. It is remarkable that he refers only to "the memoirs of the apostles," which evidently are Gospels, in speaking of the Christian public service. It is also noteworthy that he nowhere, in spite of his knowledge of Pauline epistles, appeals to Paul as an authority. We can only wish that Justin had commented expressly on his estimate of the epistles in relation to the Gospels. There are real problems which press for solution. Nevertheless, we think the silence of Justin on these matters is not of sufficient weight to require the definite conclusion that only the Gospels were accepted as authoritative. It may not be forgotten that Justin is not concerned to describe the contents of the New Testament. His references are quite incidental, and there is no doubt that his extensive use of the Gospels was dictated by their significance for his apologetic argument. Moreover, his estimate of the apostles as spokesmen of the Lord, which has been noted above, precludes the judgment that he depreciated them. The Gospels too are accepted as apostolic. And it is significant that he acknowledges the Revelation of John as apostolic and as a divine revelation (*Dial.* 81). It appears therefore that his description of the apostolic writings which were read alongside of the Old Testament was not exhaustive.

The scope of this discussion does not permit or require any detailed examination of the documents which tell of the developments near the close of the second century. In the writings of church fathers like Irenaeus, Tertullian and Clement of Alexandria, and in the *Muratorian Canon,* we are on firm ground. The church is in conscious possession of a New Testament. Some writers speak of it precisely as "the New Testament." It is described as Scripture and as inspired by the Holy Spirit. There is clear indication that it includes, besides the Gospels, the Acts, a considerable collection of epistles, and the Revelation.

It seems to us altogether certain that the struggle with Gnosticism, Marcion and Montanism contributed to the clear-cut formulation of the church's doctrine of Scripture. This contribution has commonly been exaggerated but it may not be ignored. The evidence does not warrant the conclusion that the church about the year 175 came to create a New Testament and thus arrived at an essentially new estimate of the apostolic writings. But in the formulation of the canonicity of the New Testament, as in the formulation of doctrine generally, a definite impulse, not to say compulsion, resulted from the claims made by the heretics. Marcion's rejection of the Old Testament and his distinctive treatment of certain apostolic writings required the church to set forth in explicit terms the view of the apostolic writings which accorded with its own fundamental view of the history of revelation. Similarly the Montanist affirmation of contemporaneous revelation, and of its superiority to the apostolic revelation, demanded that the unique authority of the apostolic disclosure should be unequivocally affirmed. Our general conclusion then is not to the effect that the situation as regards the New Testament canon about the year 200 corresponded exactly with that of the year 100. It is, however, a protest against the current view that the formation of the New Testament was a sudden development late in the second century. There is development in the collection and recognition of the New Testament writings as canonical, but in all the history there is a solid continuity which comprehends not only the second century but the first as well.

That whole development was a complex historical process. We cannot fully explain how exactly the twenty-seven writings of the New Testament, to the exclusion of all others, came to be acknowledged as inspired and authoritative. The development as a matter of fact was by no means complete at the end of the second century. Athanasius of Alexandria, writing in A.D. 367, provides the earliest testimony, so far as our present evidence goes, to a list which corresponds exactly with our present list of New Testament writings. However complex the process was, we may observe various historical factors which were operative. And we regard it as unmistakable that the historical factor of most fundamental significance was the conception that the revelation of the new covenant was essentially an historical revelation, a revelation which found its embodiment in the history of Jesus Christ, and which was mediated to the church through the apostles. The inscripturation of that revelation was not confined to the apostles, nor indeed do we possess evidence of a definite apostolic sanction of the new writings, but the essentially apostolic character of the new revelation is everywhere in view.

Although it is highly important that this historical process be studied and analyzed as a part of our effort to comprehend the implications of the church's doctrine of Scripture, we also insist that the comprehension of the whole development depends on a recognition of divine control of history and of the special guidance of the Spirit of God. Just as the Old Testament church was "intrusted with the oracles of God" (Rom. 3:2), the New Testament church was intrusted with the oracles of the Lord. The acknowledgment of the Old Testament as canonical did not await the ratification which the Lord Jesus Christ provided but, as it were, established itself in the organic life of the people of God. Likewise the Spirit who inspired holy men provided that outward control and inward illumination which guaranteed that exactly the divine writings should be brought together and acknowledged at their true worth.[29]

It will hardly be contested that, according to the New Testament, the church was constituted to be the pillar and ground of the truth, and that the Lord Jesus Christ, its establisher and head, sent forth the Spirit to lead it into all truth. The church is not the creator of the truth but serves to support and exhibit the truth. It receives the truth and is assured a recognition and apprehension of the truth.

As a part of its confession of faith in God the church came to declare that the truth of God committed to it finds concrete expression in the Scriptures. Hence, although the church lacks infallibility, its confession with regard to the Scriptures, represents not mere opinion but

[29] Cf. F. W. Grosheide, *Algemeene Canoniek van het Nieuwe Testament* (Amsterdam, 1935), pp. 122, 132ff., 158, 182f., 204f.; A. Kuyper, *Encyclopaedie der Heilige Godgeleerdheid*[2] (Kampen, 1909), II, p. 415; E. T., *Encyclopedia of Sacred Theology* (New York, 1898), p. 461.

an evaluation which is valid as derived from, and corresponding with, the testimony of the Scriptures to their own character. The basic fact of canonicity remains, then, the testimony which the Scriptures themselves bear to their own authority. But the historian of the canon must recognize the further fact that that intrinsic authority established itself in the history of the church through the government of its divine head.

This reckoning with the divine rule in the formation of the canon does not represent, we contend, an obscurantist flight from reality. Rather this approach to the history of the canon, like the fundamental idea of canonicity itself, as previously observed, is involved in Christian theism. And Christian theism, far from being a philosophy of last resort, constitutes a foundational and all-embracing philosophy of reality. This point of view stands sharply against any view of reality which finds its beginning and end in man, against those views which find the ultimate standard of judgment in the autonomy of man as an individual as also against those whose appeal to the authority of men in their corporate relationships, including even the supposed final authority of the living church. Man must choose whom he will serve: God or man. To choose a philosophy which makes man ultimate is, in our judgment, to commit intellectual and moral suicide. To acknowledge the final authority of the God of Christian theism, the God of the Bible, is, however, to guarantee intellectual and moral integrity. True religion, as involving a right relationship to the living God, must accept God and him alone as the infallible rule of faith and life. His Word must necessarily bear witness to its intrinsic divine character and must establish its authority in history.

THE TRANSMISSION OF THE SCRIPTURES

By JOHN H. SKILTON

"The Old Testament in Hebrew (which was the native language of the people of God of old), and the New Testament in Greek (which, at the time of the writing of it, was most generally known to the nations), being immediately inspired by God, and, by His singular care and providence, kept pure in all ages, are therefore authentical; so as, in all controversies of religion, the Church is finally to appeal unto them."

—*The Westminster Confession of Faith*, I. viii.

"WE WILL never be able to attain the sacred writings as they gladdened the eyes of those who first saw them, and rejoiced the hearts of those who first heard them. If the external words of the original were inspired, it does not profit us. We are cut off from them forever. Interposed between us and them is the tradition of centuries and even millenniums." These strange words are taken from a remarkably confused passage in an article written many years ago by Dr. C. A. Briggs.[1]

Dr. Briggs further asserts in the same passage:

Doubtless by God's "singular care and Providence they [the Scriptures] have been kept pure in all ages, and are therefore authentical." (Conf. of Faith, I. viii.) Doubtless throughout the whole work of the authors "the Holy Spirit

[1] C. A. Briggs, "Critical Theories of the Sacred Scriptures in Relation to their Inspiration," *The Presbyterian Review*, II (1881), 573f.

141

was present, causing His energies to flow into the spontaneous exercises of the writers' faculties, elevating and directing where need be, and everywhere securing the errorless expression in language of the thought designed by God" (Art. "Inspiration," PRES. REV. II. 231), but we cannot in the symbolical or historical use of the term call this providential care of His word or superintendence over its external production—Inspiration.[2]

Conservative scholars, whatever their disagreements with Dr. Briggs may be, will readily grant that we cannot in the technical use of the term call God's providential care of his Word "inspiration." Their viewpoint in this matter is that which is reflected in the Westminster Confession of Faith. According to the Confession, the canonical books were given by inspiration of God (I. ii). The Old Testament in the Hebrew and the New Testament in the Greek—the Scriptures in the languages in which they were given—were immediately inspired by God (I. viii). Quite distinct from the inspiration of the original manuscripts have been the care and providence whereby the Scriptures have been kept pure. It is by virtue of these two separate considerations—the immediate inspiration of the sacred writings in their original form *and* the singular divine care and providence—that the Old Testament in Hebrew and the New Testament in Greek are to be regarded as authentical (I. viii). Indeed, far from confusing these two matters, conservative scholars would insist on making a very sharp distinction between them.

If then we do not call God's care and providence by the name of inspiration, must we grant that the centuries have cut us off forever from the words of the

[2] *Ibid.,* p. 574.

original and that there is now no profit for us if those words were inspired? We can grant no such things. We will grant that God's care and providence, singular though they have been, have not preserved for us any of the original manuscripts either of the Old Testament or of the New Testament. We will furthermore grant that God did not keep from error those who copied the Scriptures during the long period in which the sacred text was transmitted in copies written by hand. But we must maintain that the God who gave the Scriptures, who works all things after the counsel of his will, has exercised a remarkable care over his Word, has preserved it in all ages in a state of essential purity, and has enabled it to accomplish the purpose for which he gave it. It is inconceivable that the sovereign God who was pleased to give his Word as a vital and necessary instrument in the salvation of his people would permit his Word to become completely marred in its transmission and unable to accomplish its ordained end. Rather, as surely as that he is God, we would expect to find him exercising a singular care in the preservation of his written revelation.

That God has preserved the Scriptures in such a condition of essential purity as we would expect is manifestly the case. The Hebrew text of the Old Testament has survived the millenniums in a substantially and remarkably pure form. Among the extant manuscripts of the Hebrew Bible from the Christian era there is an extraordinary agreement. Kennicott in his edition of the Hebrew Bible with variant readings deals with consonantal variants in more than six hundred manuscripts.[3] Dr. Robert Dick Wilson has pointed out that there are about 284,000,000 letters in the manuscripts considered by Kennicott and that among these manuscripts there are about 900,000 variants, approximately 750,000 of which are the quite trivial variation of *w* and *y*.[4] There is, Dr. Wilson remarks, only about one variant for 316 letters and apart from the insignificant *w* and *y* variation only about one variant for 1580 letters. The variants for the most part are supported by only one or by only a few of the manuscripts. Dr. Wilson has elsewhere said that there are hardly any variant readings in these manuscripts with the support of more than one out of the 200 to 400 manuscripts in which each book is found, except in the full and defective writing of the vowels, a matter which has no bearing on either the pronunciation or the meaning of the text.[5]

The agreement which exists among the extant manuscripts of the Hebrew Old Testament which date from the Christian era is a sign of the extraordinary care exercised in the transmission of the text by the Jews. It is true that the oldest of these witnesses are relatively late. Among the earliest are the Leningrad Manuscript of the Prophets, which has been dated A.D. 916, and a manuscript of the Pentateuch in the British Museum,

---

[3] B. Kennicott, *Vetus Testamentum Hebraicum, cum variis lectionibus,* 2 vols. (Oxford, 1776, 1780).

[4] Robert Dick Wilson, "The Textual Criticism of the Old Testament," *The Princeton Theological Review,* XXVII (1929). See pp. 40f.

[5] *A Scientific Investigation of the Old Testament* (Chicago, [1959]), pp. 61f. Used by permission, Moody Press, Moody Bible Institute of Chicago.

which has been thought to date back to the ninth century or earlier.[6]

It was the practice of the Jews to place worn manuscripts in a receptacle called the "Geniza" and to use newer copies, which had been made with incredible care.[7] In natural course the discarded manuscripts perished.[8] But though our extant manuscripts of the Hebrew Old Testament from the Christian era are rather late, the text which they contain can be traced to a considerably earlier time.

The text of our Hebrew Bible goes back, first of all, to the Masoretes, a succession of Jewish scholars, notably connected with a school at Tiberias, whose painstaking work on the text began about A.D. 600 or before. The Masoretes introduced into the text an intricate system of accent and vowel notations. Since the Hebrew alphabet was entirely consonantal and since in earlier times no full-fledged system of vowel notation had been employed in the manuscripts, readers had been required to supply vowels to the text. The Masoretes also provided notes on the text, notes of such abundance and detail that from them alone it is possible to a considerable extent to reconstruct the text.[9] They mentioned even what they regarded as unusual accents, vowel points, and spelling. They recorded a number of variant readings—on the average of about one to a page

[6] Frederic Kenyon, *Our Bible and the Ancient Manuscripts*, (4th ed. New York, 1940), p. 44.

[7] *Ibid.*, pp. 38f.

[8] *Ibid.*, pp. 42f.

[9] William Henry Green, *General Introduction to the Old Testament — The Text* (New York, 1899), pp. 153, 165.

of a printed Hebrew Old Testament[10]—and they made reference to eighteen corrections attributed to the scribes before them.[11] But the Masoretes did not originate the Hebrew traditional text.[12] They received from their predecessors a text already traditional which they treated with great reverence. Their high regard for the text that had come down to them is evidenced by their placing in the margin readings which they believed to be correct and leaving the text itself unaltered.

The Masoretes were heirs of the text in use when the Talmud was written, a text which, as is clear from the Talmud itself, had previously been in a relatively fixed condition. The Aramaic versions or paraphrases (the Targums), the Syriac Peshitto version, the Latin Vulgate version of the Old Testament, and quotations

[10] Wilson, *op. cit.*, p. 62; Robert H. Pfeiffer, *Introduction to the Old Testament* (New York and London, 1941), pp. 93ff.

[11] Pfeiffer, *ibid.*, pp. 84f.; Green, *op. cit.*, p. 151. Green remarks that "according to Buxtorf they are passages in which one might suppose from the connection that the writers meant to express themselves differently from the way in which they actually did; but in which the scribes adhere to the correct reading." In a footnote, he says: "The passages in question are Gen. xviii.22; Num. xi.15, xii.12; 1 Sam. iii.13; 2 Sam. xvi.12, xx.1; 1 Kings xii.16; 2 Chron. x.16; Jer. ii.11; Ezek. viii.17; Hos. iv.7; Hab. i.12; Zech. ii.12; Mal. i.13; Ps. cvi.20; Job vii.20, xxxii.3; Lam. iii.20. As specimens it is said that in Gen. xviii.22 they changed 'The Lord stood yet before Abraham' to 'Abraham stood yet before the Lord'; 2 Sam. xx.i, 'Every man to his gods' (אלהיו) to 'Every man to his tents' (אהליו); Hos. iv.7, 'They have changed my glory into shame' to 'I will change their glory into shame.' All which looks like frivolous punning upon the text by ingenious alterations of its meaning, and casts no suspicion upon the correctness of the received text" (pp. 151f.)

[12] Pfeiffer, *op. cit.*, p. 89.

of the Old Testament in the writings of Jerome and Origen, and the Hexapla of Origen, with its Hebrew text and Greek versions, bear witness, like the Talmud, to the existence of a Hebrew text for several centuries before the time of the Masoretes which closely resembled their text. Rabbi Akiba, who died about A.D. 132, had a high regard for exactness and fixity of text, and has been credited with inspiring measures toward the settling of the text in the early second century.[13] The view of P. de Lagarde that after A.D. 130 all manuscripts of the Hebrew Bible were closely fashioned after one archetype which had been decided on not long before that date has not been accepted by all; but it is at least the case that a type of text basically that of the Masoretes existed around A.D. 100 and that this text subsequently overcame whatever competitors it had. Biblical texts which have been discovered recently at Wady el-Muraba'at in southern Palestine, which have been dated in the second century A.D., are in notable agreement with the Masoretic text.[14] Kenyon thinks that since the end of the first century A.D. the text has not been altered in any material way.[15]

Tracing the investigation still further back, Dr. Wilson maintains that citations of the Old Testament

13 Ibid., pp. 76ff.

14 Ibid., pp. 78f.; Otto Eissfeldt, The Old Testament: An Introduction, tr. Peter R. Ackroyd (New York and Evanston, [1965]), p. 684; Edward J. Young in Robert Dick Wilson, A Scientific Investigation of the Old Testament (Chicago, [1959]), p. 178; Charles F. Pfeiffer, The Dead Sea Scrolls (Grand Rapids, 1962), pp. 16, 92f.

15 Op. cit., p. 35.

found in the New Testament, in the writings of Josephus and of Philo, and in the Zadokite Fragments bear witness to the existence of a text quite similar to the Masoretic from A.D. 40 to 100.[16]

The state of the text of the Hebrew Bible about the time of Christ and somewhat earlier has been illumined in the last two decades by the discovery of a great many manuscripts in the area of the Dead Sea. A particularly significant scroll, containing the entire book of Isaiah, in all probability dates from 100 B.C. or earlier. Here is a Hebrew text of substantial length which is about a millennium older than the manuscripts dating from the Christian era mentioned above — and it gives striking support in the main to the Masoretic text. Another scroll, which contains portions of the Hebrew text of Isaiah and which dates from perhaps 50 B.C., gives even stronger support to the traditional text. A commentary on Habakkuk, dating probably from the first century B.C., contains a text closely akin to the Masoretic. Fragments of Leviticus, which go back at least to the second century B.C., provide a firm witness to the traditional text. Certain fragments among the scrolls, however, have some significant agreements with types of texts which diverge to some extent from the traditional or Masoretic, such as those of the Samaritan Pentateuch and of the Septuagint. Texts somewhat out of the main line of transmission can, of course, contribute

---

[16] *Op. cit.*, pp. 62f. Wilson maintains: "These citations show those who used them had our present text with but slight variations. The numerous citations in the Hebrew of the Zadokite Fragments are especially valuable as a confirmation of the Hebrew text of Amos and other books cited" *(ibid.)*.

to our knowledge of the history of transmission and when carefully studied and utilized may at times make important contributions to our knowledge of the nature of the original text itself.

Mention might also be made of an ancient manuscript of the Hebrew text which was discovered before the Dead Sea scrolls came to light and which gives support to the traditional text. This witness is the Nash Papyrus, which was written perhaps around 50 or 100 B.C. and which contains portions of the text of Exodus 20 and of Deuteronomy 6.

W. F. Albright has held it to be certain—and recent discoveries give support to his position — that the Hebrew text between *c.* 150 and *c.* 50 B.C. was already fixed and that the variations between it and our Hebrew Bibles today are rarely of significance.[17]

Studies of the textual situation in the centuries just before Christ must take careful account of the Septuagint, a translation of the Old Testament into Greek, which was made up of a number of distinct translations of different books or sections made at different times. The Pentateuch, the oldest section of the Septuagint, dates back to about 250 B.C. Although agreeing in the main with our received Hebrew text, the Septuagint does contain differences worthy of study which are of importance to the textual critic. There is a danger in magnifying these differences and in drawing false inferences from their presence. When the Septuagint translation of the Old Testament was made, the

17 "The Old Testament and the Archaeology of Palestine," in *The Old Testament and Modern Study*, ed. H. H. Rowley (Oxford, 1951), pp. 24f.

Hebrew text used was, of course, not marked with the vowel points which the Masoretes later placed in their text. And it is to be observed that the great majority of the variations between the Septuagint and the Masoretic text arise from the fact that the translators supplied different vowels to the consonantal text from those which the Masoretes employed. In numerous other instances the translators had before them the same text as that of the Masoretes, but mistook it, misunderstood it, or interpreted it differently. At times it is clear that the translators were not at all sure what the Hebrew text before them meant and it is quite possible that at some other times, when they did feel sure of the meaning of the text, they were mistaken. Furthermore on some occasions they attempted to throw light on the original by the addition of material. Comparative Semitic philology has shown that numerous supposed variations in the Septuagint from the Masoretic text do not represent any difference at all in the basic text.[18]

18 Wilson says: "The differences between the Hebrew Masoretic text and the Greek Septuagint are often grossly exaggerated. The vast majority of them arise merely from a difference of pointing of the same consonantal text. The real variants arose from errors of sight such as those between r and d, k and b, y and w, or from errors of sound such as between gutturals, labials, palatals, sibilants, and dentals, or from different interpretations of abbreviations. There is a goodly number of transpositions, some dittographies, many additions or omissions, sometimes of significant consonants, but almost all in unimportant words and phrases. Most of the additions seem to have been for elucidation of the original" (op. cit., p. 63). See also R. D. Wilson, "The Textual Criticism of the Old Testament," The Princeton Theological Review, XXVII (1929), 49-59; D. Winton

Dr. Green calls attention to the fact that Origen and Jerome place on translators or transcribers of the Septuagint the responsibility for the variations of the Septuagint from the Hebrew text known to them and do not entertain any belief that the Hebrew text had been altered.[19] Pfeiffer expresses the opinion that Origen was misled by reason of a virtual fixation of the Hebrew text which had occurred before his time and by reason of the notable agreement among the available Hebrew manuscripts.[20] But it is nevertheless important to observe that neither Origen nor Jerome nor any other early writer evidences any suspicion that a real revision or a fixation of the Hebrew text had occurred after the time of the Septuagint. Dr. Green does not deny the possibility that the Septuagint may have been made from a Hebrew text considerably, if not substantially, different from the text in use in Origen's day. He thinks it quite possible that there may have been some inferior manuscripts of the Old Testament in use, especially among Jews outside of Palestine; but he holds that, even if this were the case, it would not follow that no authoritative text then existed and that there were no standard copies from which the traditional text has descended. He states a truth quite important in this connection that "reverence for the Scriptures and regard for the purity of the sacred text did not first originate after the fall of Jerusalem."[21] Although conceding the possibility that the Septuagint

Thomas, "The Textual Criticism of the Old Testament," in ed. H. H. Rowley, *op. cit.,* pp. 242f.

19 *Op. cit.,* pp. 172f.

20 *Op. cit.,* p. 108.

21 *Op. cit.,* p. 173.

was made from a text considerably different from the
traditional text, he thinks that the differences between
the Septuagint and the received Hebrew text are more
satisfactorily explained if attributed to the translators.[22]
The distinctive readings of the Septuagint at times
prove superior to readings which have come down in
the Masoretic text, and are naturally of importance for
textual criticism, as has been mentioned; but they do

[22] *Ibid.*, pp. 173f. Green says in this passage: "The same
causes which lead to a modification of the text in transcription
would be operative in a translation in an aggravated form. A
freedom might be used in rendering the Scriptures into another
language which would not be thought of in transcribing the
original. A measure of discretion must be allowed in a translator
for which a copyist has no occasion, and which would not be
permissible in him. And in this first attempt at making a work
of such magnitude intelligible to those of a different tongue,. no
such rigorous rendering could be expected as would be demanded
from a modern translator. The sacredness and authority of the
original would not attach to an uninspired version. Accordingly,
accurate precision was not aimed at so much as conveying the
general sense, and in this the translators allowed themselves a
large measure of liberty. When to this is added an imperfect
knowledge of Hebrew, conjectural renderings or paraphrases of
words and passages not understood, slips arising from want of
care and the like, it is easy to understand how the general correctness of the Septuagint might consist with very considerable de-
viations from the original text." See Edward J. Young in Wilson,
Scientific Investigation, pp. 180f. on the willingness of the
Alexandrian Jews and the Samaritans, who did not adhere to a
strict Judaism, to introduce minor modifications in the text. For
a discussion of the Dead Sea manuscripts on Septuagint studies
and on the transmission of the Hebrew text, see Patrick W.
Skehan, "The Biblical Scrolls from Qumran and the Text of the
Old Testament," *The Biblical Archaeologist* XXVIII (1965),
87-105.

not indicate that the Hebrew text underlying the Septuagint was basically superior to the traditional text or even radically different from it. Wilson holds that in the Septuagint and also in the citations found in Ecclesiasticus, the Book of Jubilees, and other writings, we can find evidence of the existence of a text substantially the same as our Masoretic text back as far as about 300 B.C.[23] He would trace the Hebrew text to a yet earlier date through the evidence which he believes is furnished by the Samaritan Pentateuch.[24]

There is furthermore much in favor of the view that the Hebrew text was faithfully transmitted from the time of the collection of the canon in the days of Ezra and Nehemiah. The scribes undoubtedly watched care-

[23] *Op. cit.*, p. 63.

[24] *Ibid.*, pp. 63f. Wilson holds that the Samaritan Pentateuch carries the evidence for our Pentateuchal text back to at least 400 B.C. The text of the Samaritan Pentateuch varies from the Masoretic text in about 6,000 instances. In 1900 of these variants the Samaritan text agrees with the Septuagint (Pfeiffer, *op. cit.*, p. 101; Green, *op. cit.*, pp. 134f; and see Green, pp. 139ff. for a helpful treatment of the significance of the agreements of the Samaritan Pentateuch and the Septuagint). A great many of the variants in the Samaritan text are quite unimportant and do not modify the meaning. The extant manuscripts have not been copied so carefully as those produced by the Jews and vary considerably among themselves. None of them has been shown to be earlier than the tenth century A.D. The Samaritans at Nablus have claimed that a roll of the Pentateuch in their possession dates back to the thirteenth year after the conquest of Canaan; but the roll has not been made available for proper study (Kenyon, *op. cit.*, pp. 51f). Gesenius has maintained that with few exceptions the distinctive readings of the Samaritan text are intentional modifications. On the literature concerning the Samaritan Pentateuch, see Eissfeldt, *op. cit.*, pp. 694f.

fully over the text.[25] The high regard in which the sacred books were held called for accuracy in copying. Dr. Green places in the period between Ezra and the Masoretes the counting of the letters, words, verses, and sections in all the books, the noting of the location of the middle letters and words of every book, and the marking of them at times by a letter of abnormal size. He remarks that the Talmud regards all this as old and as performed by the early scribes. He holds that some exacting rules designed to guard the text from error in transmission were formed and followed in this period.[26]

We may be confident, according to Albright, that the consonantal text of the Hebrew Bible has been transmitted with remarkable accuracy.[27] He maintains that the Masoretic text of the earlier books of the Bible can be followed back to the Babylonian Exile, when he believes they were edited. After the Exile, he holds, these fixed texts were taken back to Palestine. There the consonantal text was copied and transmitted with exceptional fidelity.[28]

In the period from the writing of the earliest books

[25] Green, *op. cit.*, pp. 146f. On the work of the Sopherim, 400 B.C. to A.D. 200, in the transmission of a standard text, see Gleason L. Archer, Jr., *A Survey of Old Testament Introduction* (Chicago, [1964]), pp. 36, 54f.

[26] Green, *op. cit.*, pp. 146ff.

[27] *Op. cit.*, p. 25.

[28] *Recent Discoveries in Bible Lands* (New York, [1955]), pp. 133f. On the question of early recensions of the Old Testament see W. F. Albright, "New Light on Early Recensions of the Hebrew Bible," *Bulletin of the American Schools of Oriental Research*, 140 (1955), 27-33, and Frank Moore Cross, Jr., *The Ancient Library of Qumran and Modern Biblical Studies* (Garden City, 1959), pp. 124-45.

to the collection of the canon, some scribal errors undoubtedly were made;[29] nevertheless a study of the text which has come down to us will bring forth much to support the belief that it has been preserved from the very beginning with exceptional accuracy and faithfulness. Some evidence to the contrary might be thought to be found in parallel passages, especially in variations of names and numbers. But many of the variations in these passages may not be due to scribal errors. For one reason or another, these passages may not originally have been identical.[30] We should also guard against

29 Green, *op. cit.*, p. 144. Green maintains that "the veneration with which the sacred writings were regarded as the product of inspiration and invested with divine authority, has effectually operated in preserving them from destruction . . . and it doubtless led to special care in their transcription, though it is probable that the excessive scrupulosity of later times was not brought into requisition until actual experience of the existence of divergent copies had demonstrated its necessity."

30 *Ibid.*, pp. 145f. Green thinks that some variations in duplicate passages may "be explained otherwise than as errors of transcription. Villages may be included in the lists which are not counted as cities in the enumeration; or cities which subsequently grew up in the districts described, may have been inserted to complete the lists without a corresponding change of the numbers. The differences occurring in the duplicate Psalms, such as Ps. xviii. compared with 2 Sam. xxii., may be in part attributable to the mistakes of copyists, but in the main they are better explained as the result of a revision by the author himself or by others, or as Ps. xiv. and liii., an adaptation to another occasion. The inference sometimes drawn from such passages of a lack of care in transcribing the sacred books during this period is wholly unwarranted." Green further says: "An improper use has been made of duplicate passages on the assumption that they must originally have been identical in every word and phrase, and that every

erroneous conclusions drawn from the failure of the text at times to meet the reader's expectations as to structure and from its refusal to satisfy the requirements of some artificial theories.[31]

Dr. Wilson in *A Scientific Investigation of the Old Testament* mentions a number of considerations which clearly evidence the noteworthy reliability of the tra-

---

deviation of one from the other is a textual error requiring correction. Thus Num. xxiv. 17b,

וּמָחַץ פַּאֲתֵי מוֹאָב וְקַרְקַר כָּל־בְּנֵי שֵׁת,

'shall smite through the corners of Moab and break down all the sons of tumult,' is repeated with variations in Jer. xlviii. 45b,

וַתֹּאכַל פְּאַת מוֹאָב וְקָדְקֹד בְּנֵי שָׁאוֹן

'hath devoured the corner of Moab and the crown of the head of the sons of tumult'; but these variations are not errors of transcription. One inspired writer in adopting the language of another did not feel bound to repeat it verbatim, but in the confidence of his equal inspiration modified the form at pleasure to suit his immediate purpose. So the Psalms that occur more than once with some change in the expressions by no means warrant the conclusion that only one of them has been accurately preserved, or that neither has, and the true original must be elicited by a comparison and correction of both. Both copies are authentic; and their very discrepancies are proof of their careful preservation, and the conscientious pains both of the collectors of the Canon and of subsequent transcribers in retaining each in its integrity and keeping them from being assimilated to each other. Ps. liii. is not an erroneous copy of Ps. xiv., nor *vice versa;* but an adaptation of an earlier Psalm to a new situation. As Delitzsch correctly remarks, 'a later poet, perhaps in the time of Jehoshaphat or Hezekiah, has given to David's Psalm a reference to the most recently experienced catastrophe of judgment.' Ps. xviii. and 2 Sam. xxii. are two different forms of the same Psalm, the former as it was sung in the sanctuary, the latter most probably as it was current in the mouths of the people when the Books of Samuel were written" (pp. 175f.).

[31] *Ibid.,* pp. 176f.

ditional text. He calls attention, for example, to some important instances of its demonstrable accuracy in difficult transmission. In its correct spelling of the names of numerous kings of foreign nations, the Hebrew text, as it has been transmitted, is almost unbelievably accurate. The spelling of the names of twenty-six or more foreign kings in our Hebrew text can be compared with the spelling on the monuments of the kings and in documents of their own times. In no case is the spelling in our Hebrew text demonstrably wrong; rather in practically every case it is demonstrably right. Likewise the names of many of the kings of Israel and Judah are found spelled in Assyrian contemporary documents agreeably to the fashion in which they are spelled in our Hebrew Bibles. Wilson observes that "in 143 cases of transliteration from Egyptian, Assyrian, Babylonian and Moabite into Hebrew and in 40 cases of the opposite, or 184 in all, the evidence shows that for 2300 to 3900 years the text of the proper names in the Hebrew Bible has been transmitted with the most minute accuracy. That the original scribes should have written them with such close conformity to correct philological principles is a wonderful proof of their thorough care and scholarship; further, that the Hebrew text should have been transmitted by copyists through so many centuries is a phenomenon unequalled in the history of literature."[32] He reasons further that since it can be shown that the text of other ancient documents has been reliably transmitted and that the text of the Old Testament has been accurately transmitted for the past

[32] *Op. cit.*, p. 71. For other evidences of the accurate transmission of the text see pp. 74-86.

2,000 years, we may rightly suppose that the text of the Old Testament has been accurately transmitted from the very beginning.[33]

On the basis of varied evidence Wilson concludes: The proof that the copies of the original documents have been handed down with substantial[34] correctness for more than 2,000 years cannot be denied. That the copies in existence 2,000 years ago had been in like manner handed down from the originals is not merely possible, but, as we have shown, is rendered probable by the analogies of Babylonian documents now existing of which we have both originals and copies, thousands of years apart, and of scores of papyri which show when compared with our modern editions of the classics that only minor changes of the text have taken place in more than 2,000 years and especially by the scientific and demonstrable accuracy with which the proper spelling of the names of kings and of the numerous foreign terms embedded in the Hebrew text has been transmitted to us.[35]

It does appear that we may rightfully say that the

[33] Ibid., pp. 79-82.

[34] Ibid., p. 84. Wilson explains that by "substantial" he means "that the text of the Old Testament and of the other documents have been changed only in respect to those accidental matters which necessarily accompany the transmission of all texts where originals have not been preserved and which consequently exist merely in copies or copies of copies. Such changes may be called *minor* in that they do not seriously affect the doctrines of the documents nor the general impression and evident veracity of their statements as to geography, chronology, and other historical matters."

[35] Ibid., p. 84. On the bearing of the Lachish ostraca on the general reliability of the Masoretic text, see D. Winton Thomas, op. cit., pp. 239f.; and for further evidence of the "essential accuracy" of that text see the Appendixes by Edward J. Young in Wilson, op. cit., pp. 164-84.

singular care and providence of God has kept the text of our Old Testament in an essentially and remarkably pure condition. We may agree with Green that no other work of ancient times has been transmitted as accurately as the Old Testament has been.[36] And we can be grateful that, along with our Hebrew texts, the care and providence of God have provided versions and other aids for the important and necessary work of textual criticism.

The text of the New Testament has also been preserved in a reliable form. There are vastly more manuscripts of the Greek New Testament than there are of the Hebrew Old Testament or of any other ancient work, and some of them were written not a great while after the time of the originals. We have about 5,000 manuscripts containing portions or the whole of the New Testament in Greek, whether of the continuous text or of selections for reading in church. The available papyrus manuscripts number about eighty. Although most of them are quite fragmentary, some of the Bodmer Papyri and the Chester Beatty Papyri, written in the third century or earlier, contain very large portions of the text.[37] The oldest of the papyrus manuscripts, a fragment of the Fourth Gospel, containing John 18:31-33, 37, 38, survives from the early second century. It was written perhaps within fifty years of

[36] Op. cit., p. 181.

[37] On the papyri and other Greek manuscripts of the New Testament, see Bruce M. Metzger, The Text of the New Testament (New York and London, 1964), pp. 31-67, 247-256, and Kurt Aland, Kurzgefasste Liste der griechischen Handschriften des Neuen Testaments: I (Berlin, 1963).

the time when John composed his Gospel.[38] There are over 260 manuscripts written on vellum in large, separate letters called uncials. Two of the oldest and best known of these manuscripts, the Codex Vaticanus and the Codex Sinaiticus, date back to the fourth century.[39] A large number of manuscripts—more than 2,700 —called cursives or minuscules, were written in a smaller, running style. They date from the ninth century to the sixteenth. There are also about 2,100 lectionaries, containing selections from the Greek New Testament for use in church services, and a number of ostraca and amulets. In addition to all these Greek witnesses, we have the testimony of manuscripts of the numerous ancient versions of the New Testament.[40] The manuscripts of the Latin Vulgate alone have been estimated as at least 8,000 in number. Furthermore, we have a vast number of citations of the New Testament in early church writers, many of which are in Greek.[41]

The New Testament is preeminent among ancient transmitted works in the number and variety of the witnesses to its text and in the proximity in date of the earliest extant manuscripts to the time when its

[38] Kenyon, op. cit., p. 128.

[39] Ibid., pp. 101f. Under the heading, Transmission from First to Fifteenth Century, Kenyon furnishes a helpful treatment of the dates of the uncial manuscripts. See also Metzger, op. cit., pp. 42-61.

[40] See Kenyon, Handbook to the Textual Criticism of the New Testament, (2nd ed.; London, 1912), p. 4. Used by permission of the Wm. B. Eerdmans Publishing Co.

[41] Burgon's index gives the number of citations in Irenaeus as 1,819, in Clement of Alexandria as 2,406, in Origen as 17,922, in Tertullian as 7,258, in Hippolytus as 1,378, in Eusebius as 5,176. See Kenyon, ibid., p. 264.

books were written.[42] By virtue of the abundance of material for the text of the Gospels, Streeter thinks that "the degree of security that, in its broad outlines, the text has been handed down to us in a reliable form is *prima facie* very high."[43] Surely if scholars justly feel that they have essentially the original text of classical works, which have comparatively few manuscript witnesses, may we not feel certain that in the vast and varied company of extant witnesses to the New Testament text (among which different early textual traditions are represented), the original text in practically every detail has been transmitted to us? Kenyon thinks that "it is practically certain that the true reading of every doubtful passage is preserved in some one or other of these ancient authorities" and that "this can be said of no other ancient book in the world."[44]

There are many variant readings in the extant manuscripts of the New Testament. Although these variants are very helpful in textual criticism, in enabling us to form judgments about relationships among documents and about the merit of different individual manuscripts, and of groups and families of manuscripts, the great majority of them are trivial. Dr. F. J. A. Hort, who with Bishop Brooke Foss Westcott published an excellent

[42] See *ibid.*, pp. 3ff., and Kenyon, *Recent Developments in the Textual Criticism of the Greek Bible* (London, 1933), pp. 74ff. Hort says that "in the variety and fullness of the evidence on which it rests the text of the New Testament stands absolutely and unapproachably alone among ancient prose writings" (*The New Testament in the Original Greek*, New York, 1881, Text Volume, p. 561).

[43] Burnett Hillman Streeter, *The Four Gospels*, (4th imp., rev.; London, 1930), p. 33.

[44] Kenyon, *Our Bible and the Ancient Manuscripts*, p. 23.

reconstruction of the original text of the Greek New Testament in 1881 and who prepared for their edition the most important treatise on textual criticism that has ever appeared,[45] says of our New Testament text in that treatise that "the proportion of words virtually accepted on all hands as raised above doubt is very great, not less, on a rough computation, than seven eighths of the whole. The remaining eighth therefore, formed in great part by changes of order and other comparative trivialities, constitutes the whole area of criticism."[46] Hort is of the opinion that "the amount of what can in any sense be called substantial variation ... can hardly form more than a thousandth part of the entire text."[47] Dr. Benjamin B. Warfield has said:

... if we compare the present state of the New Testament text with that of any other ancient writing, we must ... declare it to be marvellously correct. Such has been the care with which the New Testament has been copied, —a care which has doubtless grown out of true reverence for its holy words,—such has been the providence of God in preserving for His Church in each and every age a competently exact text of the Scriptures, that not only is the New Testament unrivalled among ancient writings in the purity of its text as actually transmitted and kept in use, but also in the abundance of testimony which has come down to us for castigating its comparatively infrequent blemishes.[48]

[45] Alexander Souter calls their introduction "an achievement never surpassed in the scholarship of any country." *The Text and Canon of the New Testament* (New York, 1913), p. 103.

[46] *The New Testament in the Original Greek* (New York, 1882), Introduction, p. 2.

[47] *Ibid.*

[48] *An Introduction to the Textual Criticism of the New Testament*, 7th ed. (London, 1907), pp. 12f.

Warfield calls attention to Ezra Abbott's view that nineteen-twentieths of the variations in the New Testament text "have so little support that, although they are various readings, no one would think of them as rival readings; and nineteen-twentieths of the remainder are of so little importance that their adoption or rejection would cause no appreciable difference in the sense of the passages where they occur."[49] Warfield feels justified by the facts in saying that "the great mass of the New Testament . . . has been transmitted to us with no, or next to no, variation; and even in the most corrupt form in which it has ever appeared, to use the oft-quoted words of Richard Bentley, 'the real text of the sacred writers is competently exact; . . . nor is one article of faith or moral precept either perverted or lost . . . choose as awkwardly as you will, choose the worst by design, out of the whole lump of readings.' "[50]

The text of the New Testament, then, like that of the Old, has been preserved for us in a remarkably pure form. The traditional text of the Hebrew Bible has been guarded against error by copying of the most painstaking type and by scholarly work of a very high order, such as that of the Masoretes. Versions and other materials have come down to us which aid us in our effort to ascertain the original text. The text of the New Testament has survived in an extraordinary abundance and variety of witnesses, some of which are quite early. Kenyon feels justified in saying, "The Christian can take

49 *Ibid.*, p. 14. See pp. 13f. on how the variants are reckoned.
50 *Ibid.*, p. 14. *Cf.* the objection made by Edward F. Hills to this claim in John W. Burgon, *The Last Twelve Verses of the Gospel according to Mark* (The Sovereign Grace Book Club, 1959), pp. 33-38.

the whole Bible in his hand and say without fear or hesitation that he holds in it the true Word of God, handed down without essential loss from generation to generation throughout the centuries."[51]

If, then, the Scriptures have been singularly well preserved throughout the centuries or even throughout millenniums, if they have been kept pure in all ages, we must recognize that the singular care and providence of God have really been operative in their behalf. It seemed reasonable to us at the beginning of our study to suppose that the God who is sovereign over all and who works all things after the counsel of his will would preserve his Word in a state of essential purity. We have since observed that God's Word has been preserved throughout the ages in an essentially and remarkably pure form. It is incumbent on us to acknowledge that the praise for the preservation of the Scriptures belongs to God. We are not to attribute the preservation of the Scriptures in a pure form ultimately to circumstance or to the will of man. We are to attribute it ultimately to the design and the working of him whose kingdom ruleth over all.

To give the praise to God in the matter of the preservation of the Scriptures and to acknowledge that we are heirs of the working of a divine providence is of course not to deny that God has used circumstances and men in accomplishing his purpose. One way in which he has brought about his design has been through the regard he has caused his people to have for his Word. In the case of the Old Testament, as Dr. Green would counsel us, that regard early had a bearing upon the

[51] Kenyon, *Our Bible and the Ancient Manuscripts*, p. 23.

manner in which the Scriptures were transmitted.[52] As for the New Testament, Dr. Warfield has been heard saying that the care with which it has been copied has undoubtedly sprung from reverence for its words. And for the New Testament also that reverence was early in its rise. The inspired apostolic writings were not regarded by either their authors or by the church in the first century as unauthoritative. Paul could write, "If any man think himself to be a prophet, or spiritual, let him take knowledge of the things which I write unto you, that they are the commandment of the Lord" (I Cor. 14:37). Peter ranked the epistles of Paul with the *other* Scriptures (II Pet. 3:16). John solemnly writes, "I testify unto every man that heareth the words of the prophecy of this book, If any man shall add unto them, God shall add unto him the plagues which are written in this book: and if any man shall take away from the words of the book of this prophecy, God shall take away his part from the tree of life, and out of the holy city, which are written in this book" (Rev. 22: 18, 19). Such statements as these, along with the whole tenor of the New Testament writings, called forth reverence from believers in the earliest days of the church.

Although it is to be acknowledged that men have exercised care in the transmission of the Scriptures, it must not be forgotten that men have not exercised such care or displayed such skill as to preserve the Scriptures in all copies without variation. Despite the phenomenal care taken with the copying of the Masoretic text, He-

---

52 Green, *op. cit.*, p. 144. On minor changes introduced by those somewhat out of line with strict Judaism, see Edward J. Young in Wilson, *op. cit.*, pp. 180f.

brew manuscripts of that text vary among themselves. Men make mistakes no matter how high their regard for the text which they are copying. In the case of the New Testament, variations may be attributable also in some measure to such special factors as untrained copyists in the early days, the wide geographical extent of the church, the unavailability or loss of the original manuscripts or of standard copies of them for comparison, attempts at harmonization, including Tatian's Diatessaron, and the survival in early times of authentic information not given in the Scriptures which men might be moved to record in the margins of their manuscripts as glosses and which copyists of those manuscripts might by a very natural misunderstanding include in the text of their new documents.

Dr. Ernest Cadman Colwell thinks that the Greek and Roman Churches did not take such extraordinary care of the text of the New Testament as the synagogue did of that of the Old because they did not ascribe to their Bible the exclusive religious authority which the Jews attributed to theirs. He thinks that the Christian Bible met with a rivalry for authority from hierarchy and creed, from clergy and dogma, which adversely affected men's zeal for the preservation of the exact text.[53] Of course, true creeds properly used and church order agreeable to the Scriptures should foster regard for the Bible and its text. But there can be no question that in the course of time the unique authority of the Bible has not everywhere been recognized, that in the Roman Catholic Church the Bible has not been given its right-

[53] Ernest Cadman Colwell, *The Study of the Bible* (Chicago, 1937), pp. 47ff.

ful place, and that want of the proper regard for the Scriptures may at times, if not always, produce relative indifference to questions of text. When we commend the care that has been exercised by men in the transmission of the text of the Bible, we do not mean to imply that the care could not have been improved. If the care of men had been greater, the variant readings in our manuscripts would have been even fewer than they are. And when we commend the purity of the text of the Bible as transmitted to us, we are not claiming that any one manuscript offers us a full and unblemished text. Although all our witnesses are substantially correct, all are nevertheless, to varying degrees, imperfect or incorrect. We are required to make choices among the readings which they offer. It is our task to attempt to reconstruct from all the witnesses available to us the text essentially preserved in all, but perfectly and completely preserved in none. It is necessary for us, in God's providence, according to his appointment, to strive to ascertain the true, the original, text, to obtain by faithful study of all the pertinent materials available and by the application of correct principles, a text which is better than the best found in any manuscript. We must, in other words, engage in what is called textual criticism of the Bible.[54]

54 Green writes of textual criticism that "its function is to determine by a careful examination of all the evidence bearing upon the case the condition of the sacred text, the measure of its correspondence with or divergence from the exact language of the inspired penmen, and by means of all available helps to remove the errors which may have gained admission to it from whatever cause, and to restore the text to its pristine purity as it came from the hands of the original writers" (op. cit., p. 162).

Textual criticism, along with the study of grammar and lexicography, is to be placed in the category of lower criticism—a science which lays the foundations for literary, historical, exegetical, and theological study of the Scriptures and which is preparatory for what is called higher criticism. The latter concerns itself with such matters as the genuineness, integrity, and reliability of the Scriptures and need not be governed by a naturalistic bias, but can be employed by conservatives to the edification of the church.[55] In his "criticism" of a textual sort, the conservative scholar will be moved by his regard for the worth of the original text which he is attempting to reconstruct. He will engage in his textual studies not in spite of his view of the Bible, but because of it. Believing that every word of the original manuscripts was breathed by the Holy Spirit, the consistent Christian scholar will be eager to recover every word of those originals. Although recognizing that no doctrine rises or falls with a disputed reading and that most variations are relatively unimportant, the conservative will nevertheless realize that not one jot or tittle of the law of God is actually unimportant (Matt. 5:18) and that our Lord held that even with regard to a brief statement in the Old Testament the Scripture cannot be broken (John 10:34, 35). Accordingly the Christian scholar will strive to recover the exact form of words and phrases used in the original. Variations such as that between short and long "o," at Romans 5:1, will not seem to him of no consequence. He will be eager to ascertain whether Paul wrote "we

[55] See Robert Dick Wilson, *The Lower Criticism of the Old Testament as a Preparation for the Higher Criticism* (Princeton, 1901). See also Green, *op. cit.*, pp. 160ff.

have" or "let us have," ἔχομεν or ἔχωμεν. And, of course, he will be greatly concerned to know what view to adopt with regard to the larger variant readings. He will wish to know whether the Gospel of Mark should end at the eighth verse of the sixteenth chapter or not, whether the so-called "heavenly witnesses" statement in I John 5:7, 8 appeared in the epistle in its original form, and whether the passage concerning the woman taken in adultery, found at the beginning of the eighth chapter of John in some manuscripts, belongs in the Scriptures or not. The conservative scholar, then, in his use of textual criticism will be moved by reverence for the written Word of God. He will not be seeking to tear the Scriptures apart after the fashion of some naturalistic critics, but will be endeavoring to ascertain what the infallible Scripture, which he regards as inviolable, actually is. And his reverence for the Scripture and his labors on the text will be used by God in the preservation and transmission of his Word.

Textual criticism, in God's providence, is the means provided for ascertaining the true text of the Bible. Its fruits cannot be obtained from any other tree. Most clearly it has been the design of God to require us to labor to know his Word in its original form. No valid appeal can be made to the doctrine of providence to escape the necessity for a thoroughgoing enlightened scientific criticism. God's special care and providence cannot be expected to guarantee that the type of text used most widely in the past and for the longest time is, in every respect, the best text. All types of text in use in the past were essentially pure: but God, of course, did not grant to men in former times who followed erroneous principles of criticism the fruits of the use of correct principles. And it would be utterly wrong for us to permit our textual criticism to be shackled by the mistakes of the past. It would be absurd for us to expect the past ages, which, whatever their virtues, certainly had manifest limitations, to place the best possible text in our hands and to make textual criticism relatively unnecessary for us.

It should be evident also that we cannot remove the necessity for textual criticism through an appeal to the inward testimony of the Holy Spirit. The witness of the Holy Spirit to the Bible does not involve the direct communication of facts. As Dr. C. Wistar Hodge has said, the witness of the Holy Spirit to the Word "is not the mystical communication of a truth, nor the causing to emerge in consciousness of a blind and unfounded faith. Hence it does not witness to questions which are to be determined by exegetical and historical considerations."[56] We must look for such grounds for the acceptance or rejection of variant readings as God has provided and seek to glorify him by arriving at the truth

[56] C. Wistar Hodge, "The Witness of the Holy Spirit to the Bible," *The Princeton Theological Review*, XI (1913), 71. Dr. Hodge also says: "The Witness of the Holy Spirit to the Bible, then, is not objective in the sense of being the mystical communication to the mind of a truth or proposition, nor is it a subjective inference from Christian experience. It is simply the saving work of the Holy Spirit on the heart removing the spiritual blindness produced by sin, so that the marks of God's hand in the Bible can be clearly seen and appreciated. . . . Those who are born of the Spirit have their minds and hearts enlightened so that they are enabled and persuaded to accept the objective testimony which God gives to the Bible, and to recognize immediately or behold intuitively the marks of God's hand in the Scripture" (pp. 63f.).

in the manner which he has made available to us. By the grace of God we may recognize the validity of the claims of certain readings and may make right decisions, we may receive benefits from the working of the Holy Spirit in us, but we ought not to expect that the necessity for consecrated scientific investigation will be removed.

We will, furthermore, not find any infallible solution to textual problems in the deliverances of popes and church councils. The Scriptures do not confer on popes infallibility in determining textual questions, and they certainly do not promise to any men or councils inerrancy in decisions regarding the text. The Church of Rome has had some unenviable experiences with papal ventures in the sphere of textual criticism. Pope Sixtus V, in 1590, published an edition of the Latin Vulgate, with a revised text, which he sought to make authoritative. He prefaced his edition with a bull in which he declared:

In this our perpetually valid constitution . . . we resolve and declare from our certain knowledge and from the plenitude of apostolical authority that that Vulgate Latin edition of the sacred page of the Old and New Testament, which was received as authentic by the Council of Trent is without any doubt or controversy to be reckoned that very one which we now publish, corrected as best may be, and printed in the printing office of the Vatican, to be read in the universal republic of Christendom and in all the Churches of the Christian world, decreeing that it, approved as it is, first by the universal consent of the holy Church and of the holy fathers, then by the decree of the general Council of Trent, and now also by the apostolical authority delivered to us by the Lord, is to be received and held as true, legitimate, authentic, and undoubted in all public and private controversies, readings, preachings, and expositions.[57]

Variant readings, according to Sixtus' proscription, were not to be printed in the margin in subsequent editions and the edition then issued was not to be modified. The major excommunication was to be visited upon violators and absolution was to be received from the pope alone.[58]

Sixtus V died soon after the appearance of his edition of the Vulgate, and his authoritative edition came on evil days. As early as September 5, 1590, according to Dr. Steinmueller, the sale of Sixtus' Bible was forbidden and the available copies were destroyed.[59] Pope Gregory XIV, in 1591, appointed a commission to revise the Sistine Vulgate, and the principles supported by the revision committee were quite drastic.[60] The revision was completed on June 23, 1591, and in 1592, Clement VIII, who had become pope in that year, gave his approval to the work of Gregory's commission, and the newly revised text was published under the name of the late Sixtus V. This edition, which differed from the Sistine Vulgate in some few thousand readings, was supported by a bull, *Cum sacrorum*. Although it was admitted in the Preface that the new edition was not perfect, any changes in it or marginal insertions of variant readings were forbidden by the bull. The effect of this bull was

[57] Green, *op. cit.*, pp. 127f.

[58] A Roman Catholic writer, John E. Steinmueller, in *A Companion to Scripture Studies* (New York, 1941), I, 192, says that this bull "today is commonly recognized as not having been properly and canonically promulgated."

[59] *Ibid.*

[60] See *ibid.*, p. 193.

to hinder for centuries the advance of textual criticism of the Vulgate in the Church of Rome. At long last in our day a critical edition of the Vulgate is being provided under church auspices.[61]

It appears, then, that we cannot rightly expect providence to place the best possible text of the Scriptures in our hands, or the Holy Spirit to communicate to us information as to which readings are correct, or some ecclesiastical authority to settle infallibly for us questions of text. We must engage in consecrated scientific labor, the method of God's appointment for us.

In the exercise of the textual criticism necessary for us, we should seek to make use, as already indicated, of all the important materials available as witnesses to the text of the Bible. These include not only manuscripts in the original languages of Scripture, whether of the continuous text or of selected portions of it for use in church services, but also the ancient versions, paraphrases, and citations of the Scriptures.[62]

Versions, of course, offer many a difficulty to the textual critic. There is a problem of textual criticism for the versions themselves. If we are to use them wisely in our effort to ascertain the original text of the Bible, we must first endeavor to determine what their own original texts were. In the case of the Latin Vulgate, for example, with its thousands of manuscripts, it can be seen that this task of criticism calls for considerable knowledge and sagacity.[63]

[61] Publication began in 1926 with the appearance of the revised text of Genesis.

[62] In the case of the Old Testament it is well to consider medieval quotations of manuscripts not extant now.

[63] The Wordsworth-White critical edition of the New Testament text began appearing at Oxford in 1889, when the first part,

A great amount of work yet needs to be done on the text of the Septuagint.[64]

Once we have arrived at a competent reconstruction of the original text of a version, we must then seek to ascertain what was the Hebrew or Greek text from which it was made (if indeed it was not a secondary translation). Again we have a task of no little difficulty on our hands. One language is not always able to reflect accurately or unambiguously the expressions of another; translators for one cause or another may render the original inaccurately; translations vary in literalness among themselves and even within themselves; some translators take great liberties with the original. If we were to attempt to translate back into Hebrew or Greek some of the free "translations" of the Scriptures made in our times, we might arrive at a text astonishingly different from the original. Further, we ourselves may err in our interpretation of the translation and in our effort to reconstruct the text on which it was based. Unquestionably the difficulty we meet in our attempt to determine the text on which a version was based should encourage carefulness and restraint on our part.

However, despite such problems as we encounter in our use of versions and our consequent caution, we will find versions witnessing clearly at times to the text on which they were based and providing an important testimony to the existence of that text at the time and place of their emergence—a witness of exceptional value to the textual critic. In the case of the Old Testament, as we have seen, the Septuagint translation gives testimony to a Hebrew text in existence long before the time of the Masoretes; and important early witnesses to its own text are extant.

the Gospel of Matthew, was published. An *Editio Minor* of the entire New Testament appeared in 1911.

[64] For literature on the Septuagint and texts see Eissfeldt, *op. cit.*, pp. 701ff.

The Chester Beatty Papyri of the Septuagint belong to the second to fourth centuries A.D. The John Rylands Library Papyrus Greek 458 and Papyrus Fuad 266, containing portions of Deuteronomy, probably go back to the mid-second century B.C. Other early manuscripts have been found in the area of the Dead Sea. In the case of the New Testament the first of the Syriac, Latin, and Egyptian versions were made as early as the latter part of the second century or the beginning of the third.

It is likewise important in textual criticism, as has been indicated, to consider the quotations of Scripture found in early writings. As with versions, a work of textual criticism has to be performed on the writings whose witness is being examined. Then we must inquire whether the writers quoted accurately or not. In early times, because of the difficulty and real inconvenience in locating passages in manuscripts and perhaps because manuscripts may not always have been readily available for consultation, there was a great temptation to quote from memory. If the citations are in some other language than that of the original, we have, again as with the versions, a retranslation problem on our hands. But the fruits of study of the early citations are very valuable. They help to date and localize certain readings. Of great interest to the student of the New Testament text are the citations found in the writings of Justin Martyr, Tatian, Irenaeus, Clement of Alexandria, Hippolytus, Origen, Tertullian, Cyprian, Eusebius, and Chrysostom.

Once we have given requisite attention to the varied available witnesses to the sacred text, we must attempt to make an intelligent selection among the variant readings which they contain. Our choice should be made not in any haphazard fashion, but in accordance with carefully weighed principles. In determining our text we shall hardly be inclined to follow the method by which the texts of the earliest of the printed Greek New Testaments were formed. The first to be published was that of Erasmus. Froben, a publisher in Basel, Switzerland, who had probably learned of the effort being made in Spain to publish a Polyglot Bible (the Complutensian Polyglot), including a text of the Greek New Testament, urged Erasmus to prepare a Greek text of the New Testament for publication. The Complutensian New Testament had been printed by January 10, 1514; but failed to receive papal approval for its publication until March 22, 1520, and apparently was not actually published until about 1522. Erasmus came to Basel for the undertaking. He consulted only a few minuscule manuscripts, none of which contained the entire New Testament, and adopted in the main a text of inferior quality. He used only one manuscript of Revelation and that lacked the last six verses of the book. To supply this defect and to make up for other deficiences he translated from the Latin Vulgate back into Greek, except for Revelation 22:20, where he made use of Laurentius Valla's translation. On March 1, 1516, less than a year after he had come to Basel for the undertaking, his Greek Testament was published. The first two editions of his Greek Testament did not contain the poorly attested passage, I John 5:7, 8; but he rashly promised to place this reading in his text if it could be found in any Greek manuscript. A manuscript of the sixteenth century containing this passage was produced, and Erasmus admitted the reading to his third edition in 1522.[65] It was accepted in the Greek text received for centuries thereafter.

[65] Caspar René Gregory says of the manuscript brought to

Other early editions of the Greek New Testament do not radically differ in merit of text from those of Erasmus. The second edition of the Elzevirs, publishers at Leiden, in 1633, contained in its preface the words, "Textum ergo habes, nunc ab omnibus receptum: in quo nihil immutatum aut corruptum damus."[66] From this statement, of course, the words familiar in the history of the textual criticism of the New Testament have come—the *textus receptus* or the "received text."[67] The text of the Elzevir edition of 1624 and the quite similar third edition published by Robert Estienne of Paris in 1550 dominated the text used for more than two hundred years, the former on the Continent, the latter in England. This inferior but long dominant type of text was based, as Souter says, "on Erasmus' last edition, the Complutensian Polyglot, and a handful of manuscripts—in fact, on something like a hundredth part of the Greek evidence now at our disposal, not to speak of versions and citations."[68] Kenyon grants slight critical value to the received text:

The number of MSS. consulted for its production, in all the century from Erasmus to Elzevir, is very small; few of these were of early date, and they were but slightly used; in the main, the text rested upon a few late minuscule

Erasmus' attention that "there is every reason to believe that this manuscript was written, with the words added, to compel Erasmus to add them, as he then did, 'for his oath's sake,' like Herod, to his text" (*Canon and Text of the New Testament*, New York, 1907, p. 374).

[66] These words have been translated, "Therefore thou hast the text now received by all: in which we give nothing altered or corrupt."

[67] See Gregory, *op. cit.*, p. 444.

[68] Souter, *op cit.*, pp. 96f.

MSS. which happened to be accessible to the editors. It must be plain, therefore, that so far as human agency is concerned, the received text (which of course formed the basis of our Authorized Version ...) has no commanding claims upon our acceptance, and, indeed, that it would be contrary to all the ordinary canons of textual criticism if it did *not* need considerable correction by the use of earlier and better authorities.[69]

In the two centuries that followed the establishment of the "received text," much work was done in the study of the materials of textual criticism and some progress was made in the theory of criticism. Bengel, Semler, Griesbach and Scholz attempted the classification of authorities for the text into groups or families. A notable advance was made by Karl Lachmann (1793-1851) and a new period in the history of the textual criticism of the New Testament was introduced in 1831 with his publication of an edition of the New Testament in Greek which deserted the *textus receptus* and in which he offered a text which he had endeavored to form by critical selection. Constantin Tischendorf (1815-1874) edited and published the text of many ancient manuscripts, among them the highly meritorious fourth-century Codex Sinaiticus, which he discovered at the monastery of St. Catherine on Mt. Sinai. In the eighth edition of his Greek New Testament, an edition with an admirably full critical apparatus, he gave much weight to readings found in this manuscript. In fact his eighth edition contains more than 3,000 modifications of his seventh edition, which was published before he discovered this codex. Influential, scholarly opposi-

[69] Kenyon, *Handbook to the Textual Criticism of the New Testament*, p. 272.

tion to the received text was furnished in Great Britain by Samuel P. Tregelles (1813-75).

The greatest contribution to the textual criticism of the New Testament that has yet been made, however, is that of Brooke Foss Westcott (1825-1901), and F. J. A. Hort (1828-92), whose edition of the New Testament has already been mentioned. The principles which they enunciated and followed (and which are to some extent set forth and interpreted below) have exercised a great influence since their day and some of their most important conclusions have received general acceptance. Their work has provided the basis for subsequent developments.

It may be asked whether conservatives can rightly join with scholars of other schools in the adoption of certain principles of criticism. Conservatives, of course, have an all-embracing life- and world-view, a Christian philosophy, which renders all their conceptions and activities distinctive. Liberals and radicals likewise have distinctive philosophies, and, whether they are aware of it or not, make basic assumptions which color all their thinking. But even unbelievers, by reason of creation in the image of God and by reason of common grace, are enabled to recognize facts and principles of benefit to all. Their prejudices will naturally color those facts and principles, their interpretations of them may be quite faulty; but they are enabled to obtain knowledge of a formal sort which the Christian may adapt and interpret to his own good and to the glory of God. In exegetical work, for example (and sound exegesis is important to textual criticism), the basic viewpoint of the interpreter will be very important; but the Christian exegete can derive benefit from the grammatical and historical studies of non-Christian scholars. He will indeed transmute all that he finds: but he will make use of much that others employ. He will be able to express a formal agreement in various matters with those of other schools of thought, with whom he is in a thoroughgoing, fundamental disagreement.

In considering principles of criticism, Hort deals first with what he regards as the most rudimentary form of criticism of variants—that which concerns itself with each instance of variation separately and independently of all others, which seeks to weigh the internal evidence for each reading and adopts immediately the reading which appears most probable. The textual critic asks which of the variant readings the author would have been most likely to write and also—the entirely distinct question—which of the variants scribes would have been most likely to introduce. In dealing with the first of these questions, with what the author would have been most likely to write (with what is technically called "intrinsic probability"), we must endeavor to put ourselves, so far as possible, in the author's place. We should make a careful study of the immediate and the broader context, obtain a competent knowledge of our author's thought, style, times, the circumstances of composition, and whatever other matters may have a significant bearing on the question. In attempts to answer this first question, there can be no substitutes for enlightened exegetical precision and for what Warfield calls "a fine candour and an incorruptible mental honesty."[70] In dealing with the second of these questions, we ask which of the variant readings scribes would have been most likely to introduce—we attempt to determine what is technically called "transcriptional probability." We ask ourselves the question, "From which reading, if original, would the others have been most likely to have been derived by

[70] *Op. cit.*, p. 85.

scribal error?" Much is known about the types of variation, unintentional and intentional, introduced by scribes, and the reasons why they introduced them, and on the basis of such knowledge it is possible to formulate some general rules that are, when applied judiciously, often helpful.[71]

When both intrinsic probability and transcriptional probability concur, we may form a judgment of no little importance as to the merit of rival readings. If a conflict between the two exists, we may be able to resolve it on further study or the voice of intrinsic probability may be so strong as to be decisive. But obviously in cases in which we can come to no decision as between conflicting intrinsic and transcriptional probability and in other cases in which we can arrive at no clear judgment as to which variant is favored by internal evidence of readings, we must look elsewhere for help. And even if we did feel clear about the internal evidence of readings, it would be advisable for us to gather as much other evidence as is available to aid us in arriving at our final decision. Too large an element of the subjective is liable to enter into our judgments regarding intrinsic and transcriptional probability—and in our textual criticism we should attempt to reduce the area of the subjective as much as possible. Greater security is to be sought than that which attaches to single, isolated judgments. We take a step in advance of internal evidence of readings when we enter the field of external evidence. In this field we deal with the merit of documents, of groups of documents, of classes or families of documents, and with the history of the text of the New Testament.

It is obviously important to consider the merit of the documents which furnish our variants. Hort is right in holding that "knowledge of documents should precede final judgment upon readings."[72] We shall wish to know some-

[71] See *ibid.*, pp. 93-108.
[72] Hort, *op. cit.*, Introduction, p. 31.

thing about the date of a manuscript and about other matters of an external sort with reference to it; we shall wish to know the date of the text furnished by the manuscript; but, above all, we will wish to ascertain the merit of that text. We shall have to consider the internal evidence offered by the documents themselves as to the value of their text. The texts of two manuscripts may be evaluated relatively by a study of the merits of their rival readings. It is therefore possible to form a conception of the relative value of all our witnesses to the text of the New Testament by a study of the variants which they contain.

The information furnished us by a study of individual documents is very helpful. It may, for example, aid us in deciding cases in which the internal evidence of readings was not clear. But it by no means solves all our problems. If we were to find one particular document always right and all other documents invariably wrong when they disagree with it, we might satisfy ourselves with the adoption of the text of that document. But we find no such thing. The manuscript which contains the best text, the Codex Vaticanus, is not free from error. We may accord preeminent weight to its testimony among the manuscripts. To say that it favors a reading may, on the whole, be to state a presumption in favor of that reading; but it will not be to decide for that reading. When the best manuscripts favor the same reading, there will be a strong presumption in its favor, but when they favor different readings, decision will not be easy. Furthermore, some manuscripts vary in merit in different sections of the New Testament and within the sections themselves. Scribes did not always copy from one manuscript alone.

It will be helpful, as has been said, to ascertain the relative merit of individual manuscripts. We make progress when we do so. But still further progress is possible for us. We can attempt to isolate the various elements found within the documents. We can attempt to weigh the merits of groups of documents. Hort, it is true, for good reasons takes up the matter of internal evidence of groups of documents after he has dealt with classes or families of documents, with what he calls genealogical evidence; but he recognizes that in a sense it is intermediate between internal evidence of documents and genealogical evidence. Manuscripts group themselves in support of given readings. In so doing they bear witness, at least in general, to the readings of a common ancestor. Usually it is true that "community of reading implies community of origin." If all the manuscripts of the New Testament agree on a certain reading, the presumption is that the reading is traceable to an ancestor common to them all, and was found in the original text. If the manuscripts of the New Testament divide into two camps at a given point, we may assume that those on one side bear witness to a reading found in one ancestor and those on the other side to a reading found in another. We must inquire as to the relative merits of the various groups formed by our documents. In doing so, we shall of course be attempting to ascertain the merit of the common ancestors to which they bear witness. We will be desirous of learning the value of the readings contained in the groups formed by our manuscripts in each section of the New Testament. By investigating internal evidence of groups, we shall obtain helpful information, sometimes of very great importance. We shall be able to discern and evaluate different elements of our documents.[73]

By considering the internal evidence of documents and of groups of documents, we have advanced beyond the internal evidence of readings. But there is yet an important, even a decisively important, step to take, a step which

[73] *Ibid.,* pp. 61f. Hort says, "The value of Internal Evidence of Groups in cases of mixture depends, it will be seen, on the fact that by its very nature it enables us to deal separately with the different elements of a document of mixed ancestry" (p. 61).

will make possible a large measure of assurance and objectivity in our solution of textual problems. The remaining step takes us to the heart of Hort's principles of criticism. In dealing with groups of manuscripts, although we have considered strictly internal evidences, we have been required to anticipate the genealogical method. Agreement in readings has been held generally to represent community of origin. Two manuscripts unite in readings—at least generally—because some common ancestor contained those readings. It will be observed that the New Testament documents form certain marked combinations of different merit. What is the reason, we may ask, for these combinations? The explanation is to be found in the genealogy of the manuscripts. Each manuscript has a certain place on the family tree of the New Testament text. It is rightly maintained, therefore, by Westcott and Hort that *"all trustworthy restoration of corrupted texts is founded on the study of their history, that is, of the relations of descent or affinity which connect the several documents."*[74] They maintain with good reason that "the importance of genealogy in textual criticism is at once shown by the considerations that no multiplication of copies, or of copies of copies, can give their joint testimony any higher authority than that of the single document from which they sprang, and that one early document may have left a single descendant, another a hundred or a thousand. Since then identical numerical relations among existing documents are compatible with the utmost dissimilarity in the numerical relations among their ancestors, and *vice versa*, no available presumptions whatever as to text can be obtained from number alone, that is, from number not as yet interpreted by descent."[75]

It is possible, then, and indeed requisite, for us to arrange

[74] *Ibid.,* Text volume, p. 544.
[75] *Ibid.*

our New Testament witnesses in a genealogical scheme. On doing so, according to Westcott and Hort, we can distinguish four important classes or families, containing different types of text. One of the four types of text which they distinguished, which they called "Syrian"—the text found in the bulk of the manuscripts of the New Testament—they held, on very good grounds, to be the latest of the four and of inferior merit. They found no sure instances of the use of this type of text by any church writer before Chrysostom's time; they observed in the Syrian text manifest combinations of conflicting readings in earlier types of text; and found that the distinctive Syrian readings characteristically bore marks of inferiority and posteriority. They regarded the Syrian type of text as the result of a revision which took place in two stages and they placed its emergence at Antioch. They believed that the Syrian revisers drew upon all of the three earlier texts and not infrequently introduced modifications of their own making. The goal of the Syrian revisers was apparently clarity, smoothness, and fullness. They tended to include, unless inclusion seemed to produce conflict.

The other three types of text which Westcott and Hort distinguish may be evaluated by considering internal evidence of classes or families, by weighing the relative merits of their distinctive readings. They regard the text which they call "Neutral," notably found at Alexandria, as preeminent, as representing the pure textual line, and as free from conspicuous defects. A second type of pre-Syrian text, according to their view, is the "Alexandrian." Formed, apparently, they think, in Alexandria in the opening years of the third century or perhaps a long time before, it did not obtain a wide early distribution. It is marked by modifications designed to improve the language and style of the original, and at times engages in some paraphrase and what Hort calls "inventive interpolation."

The most widely distributed of the pre-Syrian texts, according to Westcott and Hort, was that which they call "Western." They believe that the "Western" text is marked by paraphrase, by alterations, additions, assimilation, and in general by striking freedom in dealing with the original text, but at times where it omits readings found elsewhere they would give it preference.

According, then, to the theory of Westcott and Hort, the true apostolic text in the second century was most securely established at Alexandria. But early in the second century the Western text strayed farther and farther from the original. At Alexandria, before the middle of the third century, changes were introduced into the apostolic text, changes not so serious as those introduced in the Western text. Not a great while after, it would seem, an effort was made at Antioch to correct the developing confusion in readings by a revision which united readings from the three main texts and by the introduction of further altera-tions. This Antiochian revision was itself later revised and became dominant.[76]

It would follow from Westcott and Hort's theory of the history of the text that any reading found exclusively in the Syrian text may confidently be rejected. If there are two or more readings with pre-Syrian attestation, an effort must be made to determine to what specific types of text those readings belong. Since considered as wholes, the Western and Alexandrian texts are aberrant, Hort main-tains, "where there are but two readings, the Non-Western approves itself to be more original than the Western, the Non-Alexandrian than the Alexandrian: where there are three readings, the neutral reading, if supported by such documents as stand most frequently on both the Non-Western and the Non-Alexandrian sides in the preceding cases, approves itself more original than either the Western

[76] See *ibid.*, Introduction, pp. 145f., for Westcott and Hort's recapitulation of the history of the text.

or the Alexandrian."[77] Exceptions to these conclusions are to be observed in some readings, but in the main they hold.

In arriving at a final decision on readings Westcott and Hort do not wish to neglect any type of evidence, including internal evidence of readings. Hort writes:

"The aim of sound textual criticism must always be to take account of every class of textual facts, and to assign to the evidence supplied by each class its proper use and rank. When once it is clearly understood that, by the very nature of textual transmission, all existing documents are more or less closely related to each other, and that these relations of descent and affinity have been the determining causes of nearly all their readings, the historical investigation of general and partial genealogy becomes the necessary starting-point of criticism. Genealogical results, taken in combination with the internal character of the chief ancient texts or of the texts of extant documentary groups, supply the presumptions, stronger or weaker as the case may be, which constitute the primary and often the virtually decisive evidence for one reading as against another. Before however the decision as to any variation is finally made, it is always prudent, and often necessary, to take into consideration the internal evidence specially affecting it, both intrinsic and transcriptional. If it points to a result different from that which the documentary evidence suggested, a second and closer inspection will usually detect some hitherto overlooked characteristic of the best attested reading which might naturally lead to its alteration; while sometimes on the other hand reexamination brings to light an ambiguity in the attestation. No definite rule can be given in the comparatively few cases in which the apparent conflict remains, more especially where the documentary evidence is scanty on one side or obscure. The ultimate determination must evidently be here left to personal

[77] *Ibid.*, Text volume, p. 553.

judgment on a comprehensive review of the whole evidence. But in a text so richly attested as that of the New Testament it is dangerous to reject a reading clearly commended by documentary evidence genealogically interpreted, though it is by no means always safe to reject the rival reading.[78]

This rather long quotation will give a clear impression of the way in which Westcott and Hort would apply their theories to the actual practice of textual criticism. And surely the consistent application of such principles as they advocate will make a good measure of justifiable assurance possible in many of our decisions.

In some few cases recourse may be had to conjectural emendation to remove what would seem to be errors in the best text at which we can otherwise arrive. Some errors entered the stream of transmission at a very early date and are found or reflected in all our extant documents. Such conjectural corrections as are made should be able to claim strong support from intrinsic and transcriptional evidence.[79]

[78] *Ibid.*, pp. 559f. See also the Introduction, pp. 62-66, for Hort's "Recapitulation of Methods in Relation to Each Other."

[79] See *ibid.*, pp. 66-72; A. T. Robertson, *An Introduction to the Textual Criticism of the New Testament* (2nd edition, Garden City and New York, 1928), pp. 237-241; Warfield, *op. cit.*, pp. 205-210; and for the Old Testament, Green, *op. cit.*, p. 177. Warfield states two sensible rules for conjectural emendation: "(1) Critical conjecture is not to be employed in settling the text of the New Testament until all the methods of criticism have been exhausted, and unless clear occasion for its use can be shown in each instance. (2) No conjecture can be accepted unless it perfectly fulfil all the requirements of the passage as they are interpreted by intrinsic evidence, and also perfectly fulfil all the requirements of transcriptional evidence in accounting for the actual reading, and if variants exist also for them (either directly or mediately through one of their number). The dangers of the process are so great that these rules are entirely reasonable, and

The views of Westcott and Hort met with strong opposition from John William Burgon, dean of Chichester, and Edward Miller, Wykehamical prebendary of Chichester, who argued, on unsatisfactory grounds, for the received text.[80] Some modifications of their views of the pre-Syrian types of text have been suggested by later scholars in the light of new information, but the text which they considered best is highly esteemed today. The scope of this paper prohibits any extensive treatment of the developments in the textual criticism of the New Testament since their time. It should be remarked, however, that advances have been made in the discovery of manuscripts, the publication and study of texts, and that much attention has been given by scholars to the theory of textual criticism. Among manuscripts discovered or brought to the attention of the world of scholarship since Hort's day are the Sinaitic Manuscript of the Old Syriac Version, the Washing-

---

indeed necessary. The only test of a successful conjecture is that it shall approve itself as inevitable. Lacking inevitableness, it remains doubtful" (p. 209).

Westcott and Hort think that "the history of the text of the New Testament shows the meeting-point of the extant lines of transmission to have been so near the autographs that complete freedom from primitive corruption would not be antecedently improbable. As far as we are able to judge, the purity of the best transmitted text does in all essential points receive satisfactory confirmation from internal evidence" (*op. cit.*, Text volume, p. 560).

[80] For criticisms of their arguments see Kenyon, *Handbook to the Textual Criticism of the New Testament*, pp. 315-23; Warfield, *Critical Reviews* (New York, 1932), pp. 36f.; Metzger, *op. cit.*, pp. 135f. For a recent defense of the Syrian or Byzantine text, see Edward F. Hills, *The King James Version Defended!* (Des Moines, 1956) and in John W. Burgon, *op. cit.*, pp. 17-67.

ton Manuscript of the Gospels, the Washington Manuscript of the Pauline Epistles, the Koredethi Codex, and the papyri manuscripts, among them the Chester Beatty and the Bodmer Papyri, which have previously been mentioned. Much attention has been given to the text which Hort called Western; the question of its merit as compared with the Neutral text has been debated, and its claim to homogeneousness has been tested. Professor Kirsopp Lake has done much in the distinguishing of an important family, to which Canon B. H. Streeter, who has also made a valuable contribution to the study of the subject, gave the name "Caesarean."[81] Streeter has given a clear statement of his views on the text in *The Four Gospels*. He holds that at an early time distinctive texts were to be found in various localities, texts which later gave way to the Byzantine standard text (Hort's Syrian). He believes that the Codex Vaticanus and the Codex Sinaiticus are representatives of the text of Alexandria. He would apply the term "Alexandrian" to that local text and drop the term "Neutral." He breaks up the Western family of Hort into an Eastern class and a Western class with subdivisions in each, with the Caesarean text forming a subdivision of the Eastern class. In some points of theory he is not in full agreement with Hort, as when he asserts that the "eclectic principle of deciding in each separate case on grounds of 'internal probability' what appears to be the best reading is, in spite of its subjectivity, *theoretically* sounder than the almost slavish

---

[81] On the Caesarean text of the Gospels, see Bruce M. Metzger, *Chapters in the History of New Testament Textual Criticism (New Testament Tools and Studies*, IV) (Grand Rapids, 1963), pp. 42-72.

following of a single text which Hort preferred."[82] and when he maintains that "the authorities available for determining the text are more numerous and more independent of one another" than Hort realized and that "though on minor points of reading absolute certainty may often be unobtainable, a text of the Gospels can be reached, the freedom of which from serious modification or interpolation is guaranteed by the concurrence of different lines of ancient and independent evidence."[83] But despite his differences with Hort, Streeter believes that a critical text of the Gospels (though not of Acts) will be based in the main on his Alexandrian type of text as found in the Codex Vaticanus and the Codex Sinaiticus, that the Alexandrian text (which is similar, of course, to Hort's Neutral) is the best of the local texts, and that the *textus receptus* is to be rejected. He acknowledges that "due weight must be given to Hort's principle that the authority of a MS., which in a majority of cases supports what is clearly the right reading, counts for more than that of others in cases where decision is more difficult,"[84] and believes that the text of Westcott and Hort is satisfactory for most purposes.

Streeter's endorsement of an eclectic principle in textual criticism by no means stands alone in the period since Westcott and Hort. G. D. Kilpatrick for one has called for a "rigorous eclecticism."[85] Those who

[82] *Op. cit.*, p. 145.
[83] *Ibid.*, p. 148.
[84] *Ibid.*, p. 146.
[85] See "Western Text and Original Text in the Gospels and Acts," *The Journal of Theological Studies*, XLIV (1943), 24-36,

chose the basic text for the *Revised Standard Version* of the New Testament followed an eclectic method.[86] The Greek text which underlies the *New English Bible: New Testament* was likewise eclectically determined.[87] The employment of eclectic or "rational" criticism will naturally differ with different scholars, but fundamentally it would give more weight to what Westcott and Hort called "internal evidence of readings" than to external evidence. In its most extreme form it would ignore external evidence completely.[88]

The eclectic method, although still vulnerable to such criticism as Westcott and Hort leveled against it, need not, when carefully employed, yield results radically different from those which Westcott and Hort themselves obtained. Thus Frederick C. Grant, a member of the revision committee which prepared the *Revised Standard Version* of the New Testament says: "... it is really extraordinary how often, with the fuller apparatus of variant readings at our disposal, and with the eclectic principle now more widely accepted, we have concurred in following Westcott and Hort. Not that we agreed in advance in favor of Hort — quite the

---

and "Western Text and Original Text in the Epistles," *ibid.*, XLV (1944), 60-65.

[86] See Frederick C. Grant, "The Greek Text of the New Testament," in *An Introduction to the Revised Standard Version of the New Testament* (The International Council of Religious Education, [1946]), pp. 37-43.

[87] R. V. G. Tasker, *The Greek New Testament* (Oxford University Press; Cambridge University Press, 1964), pp. vii ff.; *The New English Bible: New Testament* (Oxford University Press; Cambridge University Press, 1961), pp. vii f.

[88] On eclecticism and its advocates see Metzger, *The Text of the New Testament*, pp. 175-79.

contrary, there was no such unanimity; our agreement is really a tribute to Westcott-Hort, which is still the great classical edition of modern times."[89] Indeed the general reliability of much in the approach of Westcott and Hort has not been lacking in support and recognition since their time.[90]

We have occupied ourselves in the main with illustrating principles of textual criticism in their application to the text of the New Testament. The same principles valid in the criticism of the New Testament text will be valid in the criticism of the text of any other ancient work, the Old Testament included. Of course, in the case of the Old Testament it is not very difficult to ascertain the text used by the Masoretes. A major problem, however, has to do with the extent to which the Septuagint is to be followed in the reconstruction of the original text. Dr. Green, would accept the reading of the Septuagint when it differs from the received

[89] *Op. cit.,* p. 41.

[90] See Vincent Taylor, *The Text of the New Testament* (2nd ed.; London, 1963), p. 54; Metzger, *op. cit.,* pp. 135, 137, and Ernest Cadman Colwell, "Scribal Habits in Early Papyri: A Study in the Corruption of the Text," *The Bible in Modern Scholarship,* ed. J. Philip Hyatt (Nashville; New York, [1965]), pp. 370ff. See also Colwell's critique of the genealogical method in "Genealogical Method: Its Achievements and its Limitations," *Journal of Biblical Literature,* LXVI (1947), 109-33. On the subject of the light shed by the papyri on the date and character of the Neutral type of text, see Calvin L. Porter, "Papyrus Bodmer XV (P 75) and the Text of Codex Vaticanus," *Journal of Biblical Literature,* LXXXI (1962), 363-76, and Carlo M. Martini, *Il problema della recensionalità del codice B alla luce del papiro Bodmer XIV* ("Analecta Biblica," 26) (Rome, 1966).

Hebrew text only if the Hebrew text were subject to doubt on other grounds.[91]

It should be apparent that with the aid of textual criticism we can obtain a text nearer to the original than that preserved in any one manuscript. In God's providence men may glorify him by textual studies and may aid in the preservation of his Word in a form of exceptional purity. Warfield expressed the conviction that in the Greek Testament of Westcott and Hort we have "substantially the autographic text" and that probably future criticism would not cast doubt on more than one word of it in a thousand.[92] Further advances in the field of textual criticism should, of course, be made whether one accepts Warfield's judgment completely or not; but we may take a considerable amount of sat-

[91] *Op. cit.*, p. 174. Dr. Green holds that "there is a general agreement among careful scholars that, while this version is to be highly esteemed for its antiquity, and the general testimony which it renders to the integrity of the exsiting text, and the aid which it furnishes in the rendering of obscure and doubtful passages, the Masoretic text is on the whole vastly superior to it, and should not be corrected by it, except where there are stringent reasons for so doing; and that in the great majority of cases where a divergence exists, the presumption is strongly in favor of the Hebrew and against the Septuagint. Neither the original character of the latter, nor the history of its preservation, nor the present state of its text entitles it to the precedence. Only in cases where there are independent reasons for suspecting the accuracy of the Hebrew, can emendations by the Septuagint be reasonably admitted." On the textual criticism of the Old Testament, see Archer, *op. cit.*, pp. 47-58; Ernst Würthwein, *The Text of the Old Testament*, tr. Peter R. Ackroyd (Oxford, 1957); Eissfeldt, *op. cit.*, pp. 669-721.

[92] "The Greek Testament of Westcott and Hort," *The Presbyterian Review*, III (1882), 356.

isfaction in the results that have already been achieved and in the promise which future studies offer. Warfield has rightly said: "If, then, we undertake the textual criticism of the New Testament under a sense of duty, we may bring it to a conclusion under the inspiration of hope. The autographic text of the New Testament is distinctly within the reach of criticism in so immensely the greater part of the volume, that we cannot despair of restoring to ourselves and the Church of God, His Book, word for word, as He gave it by inspiration to men."[93]

In view of the reasonable assurance that we may have with regard to the reliability and purity of the text of the Scriptures at which we are able to arrive, the statement made by Dr. Briggs which was quoted at the beginning of this chapter seems strange indeed: "If the external words of the original were inspired, it does not profit us. We are cut off from them forever. Interposed between us and them is the tradition of centuries and even millenniums." God in his singular care and providence has manifestly caused his Word to triumph over the hazards of time. Even if further progress is possible for us in textual criticism, even if at present some very small proportion of the words of the original may yet have to be established, words which affect no doctrine of the Scriptures, we should neither ignore nor despise the results which, in the providence of God, have been achieved. It is a matter of first importance that words of preeminent value, words inspired by God, have survived the ages and can address themselves to us today as they did to men centuries or even millenniums ago.

[93] *An Introduction to the Textual Criticism of the New Testament,* pp. 14f.

THE RELEVANCY OF SCRIPTURE

By PAUL WOOLLEY

THE most poignant longing of the average human heart is for authoritative guidance. A disheartening indication of this truth is the continued popularity of astrological books and pamphlets, the meddling with horoscopes, that still goes on. Related to it is the green, purple and yellow array of fortune tellers' parlors that decorates the business streets of the less well-to-do sections of American cities. These things point to an unsatisfied longing of human nature. That longing is justified, and there are proper ways of satisfying it.

Reasons have already been presented in this symposium for concluding that the Bible is a trustworthy source of knowledge. The question that now demands an answer is this: What particular needs for knowledge does the Bible satisfy? Obviously the Bible is not a compendium of all possible knowledge. There are a great many truths of, shall we say, chemistry, for example, which are not to be found in the Old and New Testaments. For what knowledge, in particular, can one turn to the Bible?

There are three types of need which the Bible satisfies: the need for conceptual knowledge of God and the principles which control the relationship between himself and the created universe; the need for directional knowledge as to matters of experience and conduct; the need for a knowledge of the basis for devotional meditation upon the nature of God, his relationship to man, and the meaning of the universe.

The realm of conceptual knowledge with which the Scripture deals is concerned with such matters as the being and nature of God and his activity in connection with matters external to himself, past, present and future. The nature of the physical universe, of man, and all creatures is within this sphere.

The realm of directional knowledge cannot be artificially divorced from the previous field. But it has to do with the more intimate human concerns of a way of dealing with the power and consequences of sin. What means are available for relieving the guilt of sin, what guidance can be found to mark a pathway through life, what authority is there for making the decisions of living? Can credence be given to the demands of reason, of instinct, of intuition, of irrational faith? Is there a way to secure divine guidance for human living?

Lastly, a basis of fact is provided for meditation upon the divine being, for determining the nature, limits, and possibilities of human communion with the divine, and for determining how the validity of supposed communion may be tested and assessed.

Scripture thus meets the greatest instinctive needs of the human spirit, the needs for knowledge, authority, guidance, communion, and sympathy.

But there are no divisions in Scripture over which these words stand as captions. The Bible is not systematically divided among these subjects. It is not either an encyclopedia or a handbook of technical practice. On the contrary it meets these needs by furnishing a history of God's dealings with mankind and in particular his provision for reconciliation between God and fallen man. The apostle John indicates this with reference to his Gospel when he says, "Many other signs therefore did Jesus in the presence of the disciples, which are not written in this book: but these are written, that ye may believe that Jesus is the Christ, the Son of God; and that believing ye may have life in his name. . . . And there are also many other things which Jesus did, the which if they should be written every one, I suppose that even the world itself would not contain the books that should be written" (John 20:30f.; 21:25). The same general purpose animates not only the Gospel of John but the Bible as a whole.

The Bible, then, should not be approached with a view to finding it a comprehensive treatise on, for example, natural science. A great many statements in the realm of natural science are to be found in the Bible and they are true statements. But the Bible offers no information as to the validity of the various modern theories concerning the nature of matter and the constitution of the physical world. There is nothing in the Bible with which to test the theories of relativity. The Bible has some very definite statements to make about the creation of the universe, for the history of creation is the foundation of the understanding of all of God's dealings with man. But the Bible gives us no information about the biological history of animal forms between the time of their creation and the time contemporary with the Biblical writers. There is history concerned with the preservation of animal life when the flood occurred but not history about how the animals of that day compared in structure and habits with the animals of other ages. One could not write a biological textbook from the Bible alone.

There are other matters more immediately connected with the church about which the Bible gives such information as is necessary to ensure that the church shall carry out its mission as the body of Christ's elect, but which are not set forth in closely delineated detail. The officers of the church are named in Scripture. The functions of the elder and of the deacon are made clear. But the number of church courts is not specifically prescribed, and nothing is said about what dress the officers shall wear. God has ensured that the essential elements of the church may be found in Scripture; the non-essentials are within the realm of liberty.

Similarly, in the realm of public worship the Bible mentions the essential elements, but it makes no attempt to impose a limitation upon the methods of praise, for example. Saved men should worship God. There are certain appropriate avenues for the expression of that worship. The Bible sets them forth. It does not declare the exact forms in which these avenues shall be walked.

It is of the utmost importance, then, that when Scripture is read its purpose should be kept in mind and no attempt made to draw final conclusions from it concerning matters about which it does not speak. On the other hand, for the purposes which it is designed in the plan of God to serve, it is sufficient and it is clear. Its infallibility in its original manuscripts was perfect, and the principles which it sets forth are applicable to the whole of life.

What, more specifically, is meant by its sufficiency? For one thing, Scripture contains all the information which a man needs in order to set forth the way of salvation. Further, the Bible contains all the guidance which is needed for the continuous living of the Christian life.

It is completely sufficient at this point. If there are absolute rules which must be followed, the Bible states them. In the absence of such rules the Christian is at liberty to follow a course or courses which accord with the general principles presented in Scripture.

There is one very important consequence of this fact. God does not today guide people directly without using the Scriptures. There are no divinely given "hunches." God does not give people direct mental impressions to do this or that. People do not hear God's voice speaking within them. There is no immediate and direct unwritten communication between God and the individual human being. If the Scriptures are actually sufficient, such communication is unnecessary. On the other hand, if such communications were actually being made, every Christian would be a potential author of Scripture. We would only need to write down accurately what God said to us, and we would be legitimately adding to the Bible, for such writings would be the Word of God. Many people have thought they were writing new Bibles. Many more people have thought that God spoke to them directly. But when these supposed revelations are examined, what a strange mass of nonsense, contradiction and triviality this so-called Word of God proves to be. Many of my readers could construct a pot-pourri of such supposed revelations from the accounts which they have heard themselves—and what a sorry mess they would make!

That people have "hunches" is obvious; that many of them work out very well and others quite poorly is also obvious. It is probable that they involve the use of some means or source of communication with which science is as yet very imperfectly acquainted. But that they come directly from God is no more to be supposed than it is that the waves that bring sounds to our radios come immediately from God.

Scripture is not only sufficient to direct Christians in every respect in which they must have guidance, but it is also clear. Its clarity, like its sufficiency, is with respect to its particular purposes.

Clarity, however, should not be confused with superficiality or with simplicity. The Bible is deep. Skimming will not exhaust its contents. The themes with which the Bible deals would hardly begin to be touched if the Bible were to speak only in simple terms. There is, then, complexity in the Bible, and study is of the greatest value. It is here that we who live in the twentieth century have a great advantage over our predecessors. The longer the study of the Bible is pursued, the more truth may be gathered from its pages. Those who disregard the labors of past generations and feel themselves sufficient for the task of understanding the Bible practically assure themselves that they will be limited in their appreciation of Biblical truth. Study, then, enhances the clarity of the Scriptures and adds new knowledge to that which has been more quickly gained.

"The natural man receiveth not the things of the Spirit of God: for they are foolishness unto him; and he cannot know them, because they are spiritually judged" (I Cor. 2:14). The essential point for our purpose in this quotation from Paul is that there is a difference of viewpoint between the Christian and the non-Christian, between the man who has been renewed by the Spirit of God and the man who has not. That difference in viewpoint has a vital bearing upon the question of the clarity of the Scriptures. The spiritual man has, through his regeneration, a basis for comprehension which the natural man lacks. Given equal mental gifts and powers, therefore, the spiritual man has a key, as it were, which the other lacks to unlock the meaning of Biblical statements.

The characteristic of infallibility which the Scripture possesses has been set forth elsewhere in this volume by one of my colleagues (*cf.* chapter 1) and needs no further comment at this particular point.

It should be noted now, however, that there is no realm of life which is exempt from the applicability of Scripture. As God is the sovereign of the whole universe, so his Word has meaning throughout that universe. The details and particularities of application will vary tremendously, but the principles are the same wherever God is God and humanity human.

One of the greatest, perhaps the greatest, obstacle to the proper use and understanding of Scripture is a series of misunderstandings which are commonly diffused throughout Christendom and which interfere in the most serious way with the acceptance by modern men of the Bible as the authoritative Word of God. I propose to devote attention to a series of these and to endeavor to remove them.

1. One of the more surprising of them, one which is widely found, however, is that the Bible is not only a unique book but a magical book. People use the Bible to find out the will of God by turning to it at random when a problem arises and seeking the answer to their difficulties in the first section that they read. Sometimes they even let the Bible fall open "at will" and then start reading; or they let it fall open and then blindly put their finger on a verse and, having read it, force it into

a plausible meaning for their particular difficulty. It may sound peculiar to some of my readers, but very good men have attempted this type of magic. For such purely mechanical systems are of the essence of magic.

But Christianity is not a religion of magic. Magicians and sorcerers are condemned throughout both the Old and New Testaments (see, for example, Mal. 3:5 and Rev. 22:15). The command of God is, "be ye not foolish, but understand what the will of the Lord is" (Eph. 5:17). Reference to a concordance to the Bible will easily show the reader how frequently our Lord's emphasis dwelt upon understanding the truth, but he does not so much as suggest methods for pursuing magical arts in order to determine God's will. Rather the New Testament tells us to give diligence to present ourselves approved unto God, workmen who need not to be ashamed, handling aright the word of truth (II Tim. 2:15).

The only way of ascertaining the will of God, as well as the truth of God, is to learn it by zealous application as students of the revelation of that will contained in the Scriptures. Such short cuts as pulling verses out of boxes, getting guidance by daily motto books, and letting the Bible fall open like a casting of dice are not only useless; they are deceptive.

2. A more serious misapprehension concerning the Scripture is that the Holy Spirit so inspired the writers as to cause them to use modern scientific canons in their use of language. For example, it is argued that, when the inspired writer said, "it is he that sitteth above the circle of the earth" (Isa. 40:22), there is in this form of statement a reference to the sphericity of the earth. Such an interpretation is mistaken for several reasons. a) Revelation came to an inspired writer for a specific purpose.

Scripture was not written by mechanical dictation and God did not reveal to its writers truths quite irrelevant to the purpose in hand. The prophet at this particular point had no need of a revelation concerning the shape of the earth. b) The writer often, as we shall see, did not understand the entire import of his writing but he was not writing what were to himself obscure conundrums, and the interpreter of Scripture must not read into it meanings of an entirely different genus from those of the writer. The author here doubtless had in mind the rough circle visible to an observer from a point elevated above the earth's surface. He was not talking about astronomical truth at all. c) Figurative forms of expression, when they appear in the Bible, are to be recognized as such and not interpreted as natural science.

3. If the writers of the Bible were not inspired to use modern scientific canons, neither were they enabled to use modern historical canons. They employed popular forms of speech, without regard for the meticulous reservations as to approximations, probabilities and definitions which often encumber, as well as assist, a modern historian. When the historian who wrote the First Book of Kings stated that Solomon "made silver to be in Jerusalem as stones" (I Kings 10:27), this is obviously not to be taken as a crass literalism. It is a popular way of expressing the simple truth that silver had become commonplace.

4. The writers of Scripture were under the necessity of using words in the common meaning attached to them at the time. It is true that there may have been a fuller meaning within the purview of the Spirit of God but the Bible was written to be intelligible to contemporaries.

It was not something essentially esoteric which could have no immediate usefulness to the people of the times when its various parts were being written. That means that we cannot without question apply to terms used in the Scriptural writings their current modern meaning. An example of this is found in Luke 2:1, where it is stated that "there went out a decree from Caesar Augustus that all the world should be enrolled." Does this mean that the Eskimos of Greenland were to be included in this census? Obviously not. It did not even mean that all the peoples of the then known world were included. There were many peoples within the knowledge of the Roman world but outside of the scope of this taxation—in Mesopotamia, in Arabia, in India, for example. Similarly the statement that "all the earth sought the presence of Solomon to hear his wisdom" (I Kings 10:24) is obviously not to be understood in a meticulously literal sense. A meaning natural to the times, sometimes even a colloquial meaning, is to be sought for words when we are reading the Bible.

5. In the interpretation of Scripture the meaning will only be apparent if a due regard is had to the form of literary expression the writer is employing. The difference between the imagery of poetry and the more sober diction of prose is often apparent. But is it always recognized that the description of Leviathan in the book of Job (ch. 41) is poetical not only in form but in content? It should not be interpreted as a pedestrian recital of biological data.

The poetry of the Bible is full of non-literal images such as "his [Jehovah's] eyelids try the children of men" (Psa. 11:4). But such figures are not confined to poetry. It is in prose that John is told that the seven heads of the woman whom he had seen "are seven mountains, on which the woman sitteth" (Rev. 17:9), where one symbol is interpreted by another. Such an example obviously teaches caution in interpretation.

The parables of Christ are, of course, works of fiction, composed to point a lesson and make vivid a particular truth. They are not accounts of actual happenings, nor does every detail of them have a meaning or a lesson. The details are there to lend point to the main thrust. The story of the Good Samaritan (Luke 10:30-35) is likewise most probably a piece of fiction, told by our Lord to illustrate a point. There are other examples of this in the Scriptures. Symbolism and story are to be recognized as such.

6. The Bible is the Word of God, but it is not identical with what it would be were it possible to imagine that God had written it without human intervention or operation. An indication of this is the variety of style, vocabulary, grammatical construction and manner of treatment which characterize the various books. It is, of course, impossible to conceive of the Bible being written without mediation of some sort, but it is also impossible to maintain that that mediation was without effect upon the finished product.

One result of this is that while the Bible is without error in the original manuscripts, its statements are not to be interpreted as though they were the statements of omniscient masters who knew *all* truth concerning the subject in hand. They are true statements but they are not always complete statements. The entire Bible is, of course, an illustration of this point, but perhaps it may be clarified by a reference to the fact that there are four Gospels, not one. It is the fact of human mediation which makes four separate Gospels appropriate. Each one supplements the other and serves to amplify and complete the picture. The three accounts of healing the blind in the vicinity of Jericho in the synoptic Gospels (Matt. 20:29ff.; Mark 10:46ff.; Luke 18:35ff.) need not at all be understood as contradictory to one another. It is quite possible to harmonize them. But each one supplements the other and makes the picture more complete.

When this principle is applied to details, it means that the Bible is not to be understood as always giving such a balanced, well-rounded, all-comprehensive account of an event, or enunciation of a truth, as one might, may I say, anticipate from omniscience. On the contrary the Bible is written by men, preserved from error, but not given the perceptive faculties of God.

7. Another reason why Biblical accounts are not always entirely comprehensive, however, is that such completeness was not necessary for the purpose which the writers had in mind. An example may be found in the omission from the Gospels of any appreciable amount of information on the years of Jesus' life which intervene between the visit to Jerusalem at the age of twelve and his baptism by John the Baptist. Such information would doubtless have been satisfying to human curiosity, as is indicated by the popularity in the early church of non-canonical gospels which purported, at least, to supply this lack. But there was no need for it in order to accomplish the purposes of the Holy Spirit and of the Gospel writers, which were centered particularly upon preserving a record of the events and words which were of especial, universal significance.

8. It is not to be thought, however, that the writers of

Scripture always understood the full meaning or the full application of their statements. They were, of course, as has been said above, not writing nonsense in their own eyes. They understood *a* meaning of what they wrote. But that was not necessarily the entire meaning which subsequent readers were rightly to draw from the passage. The most obvious examples of this are probably to be found in connection with predictive prophecy. There is no reason to suppose, for example, that Jeremiah, when he wrote, "Thus saith Jehovah: A voice is heard in Ramah, lamentation, and bitter weeping, Rachel weeping for her children; she refuseth to be comforted for her children, because they are not" (Jer. 31:15), had any notion that this would find a fulfillment in connection with a royally authorized murder of the children of Bethlehem in an effort to kill the infant king of the Jews. But the same principle applies in less obvious cases. The apostle Paul did not know that there would ever be such things as motion pictures which would be made the subject of ecclesiastical ordinances when he wrote, "If ye died with Christ from the rudiments of the world, why, as though living in the world, do ye subject yourselves to ordinances, Handle not, nor taste, nor touch (all which things are to perish with the using), after the precepts and doctrines of men? Which things have indeed a show of wisdom in will-worship, and humility, and severity to the body; but are not of any value against the indulgence of the flesh" (Col. 2:20-23). But the principle he set forth applies to motion pictures as much as to the interests of his own day.

9. A related principle is the truth that although the writers of Scripture were kept from error in their inspired writing, they often had wrong notions in their

heads. They certainly, for example, did not all know of the rotation of the earth. Not only that, but they, at times, had wrong views as to the implications of what they wrote. Hosea gives no evidence of understanding that "I will say to them that were not my people, Thou art my people; and they shall say, Thou art my God" (Hosea 2:23) was to apply to any one but the Jews. Yet Paul makes it clear that the statement has application to Gentiles (Rom. 9:25).

10. The question of the use of source materials by inspired writers also arises in this connection. When a writer of Scripture incorporates a passage from another source into his work, does that source bear the same character as the context? Obviously not in every sense. Its style, for instance, is different. There may be cited as an example the poetical passage in Joshua 10:12, 13 which appears to be a quotation from the book of Jashar.

Was the writer of any particular source inspired in the same sense in which the immediate Biblical writer was? It would be rash and without warrant to affirm that he was. The inspiration of the Biblical writer doubtless extended to his selecting activity in choosing the material to be incorporated. For statements beyond that, there probably is no warrant.

11. Another pitfall to avoid is that of applying a scriptural precept to conditions other than those to which it is truly applicable. The decision in cases of this type is one which must be left to the individual reader and student. It is often a difficult one to make. Yet it is part of the responsibility of the individual Christian. The Roman Catholic Church has undertaken to provide infallible guidance in the interpretation of Scripture on the basis of its doctrine of the authority of the

Church. The Church does not always undertake a pronouncement upon any given question, but if it does do so, its decision is final and the responsibility of the individual is limited to the acceptance of that decision. There is no actual evidence, however, to show that God has designed to endow his church or any branch of it with such authority. Evidence for the authority of Scripture, from the lips of our Lord and otherwise, is multiform but not for that of the church. The individual Christian must, therefore, undertake the task of interpretation for himself. He may, and should, secure all of the assistance possible from other scholars and sources of learning, but the final decision must lie with himself.

An example of a decision of this sort is that which must be made with reference to Paul's statement that he desired that women should not adorn themselves "with braided hair, and gold or pearls" (I Tim. 2:9). Since the First Epistle to Timothy is inspired Scripture, how is this statement to be understood by Christian women in America in the twentieth century? It is an expression of a desire of Paul. Can it, for that reason, be held to be nothing more than a personal pious wish of the apostle? I think not. The statement occurs in the middle of a series of exhortations directed by Paul to Timothy under the inspiration of the Holy Spirit. If one exhortation is authoritative, all are. The series, which covers the first three chapters of the epistle, is concluded by the statement, "These things write I unto thee, . . . that thou mayest know how men ought to behave themselves in the house of God, which is the church of the living God, the pillar and ground of the truth" (I Tim. 3:14, 15). The exhortations are all parts of a series designed for the authoritative guidance of Christian people. Should one, therefore, conclude that a Christian woman today may not braid her hair or wear any ornament made of gold or including pearls?

Some Christians have so decided. There are many of them to be found among members of Mennonite congregations. I think, however, that their decision is erroneous. This opinion is based upon the fact that the use of braided hair, of gold, and of pearls was much less common in the first century A.D. than it is now. Such usage therefore was more conspicuous. Gold and pearls were proportionately more expensive. Their use then marked the wearer as one who gave considerable attention and money to personal adornment. The purpose of Paul, judging from the immediate, and the remote, context was to exhort women to personal inconspicuousness and a balanced outlay of effort and money. In his day braided hair, gold, and pearls were incompatible with this end. Today in America they are not. The use of braided hair, of gold, and of pearls is, therefore, not always to be avoided today as it was then.

Another example of this type of problem is raised by Jesus' washing of the feet of his disciples and concluding with the statement, "If I then, the Lord and the Teacher, have washed your feet, ye also ought to wash one another's feet" (John 13:14). Should Christians today wash one another's feet? Many members of the Church of the Brethren so believe.

But foot washing was a constant practice in first century Palestine. It was customary whenever one came in from a walk on the dusty roads. It was similar to our modern hand washing. But in the case of the feet it was a service more easily performed by another than by oneself. Christ was teaching that Christians should perform humble, ordinary services for one another. Foot washing was such a service then. It is quite inappropriate now, and to give the commandment of our Lord a binding literal interpretation is out of place.

12. It is not only the alteration of physical conditions in the external world by distance, by time, or by place which changes the application of Scripture. There are injunctions which are simultaneously appropriate to certain undertakings and circumstances and not to others. At the Last Supper Christ said to his disciples, "But now . . . he that hath none [purse and wallet], let him sell his cloak, and buy a sword" (Luke 22:36). A few hours later in the Garden of Gethsemane Jesus said to one of his company, "Put up again thy sword into its place: for all they that take the sword shall perish with the sword" (Matt. 26:52). Was the first injunction abrogated a few hours later by the second? Not at all. The first statement was for later immediate application than the second, and is still just as true as the other. Proper equipment, even to weapons for defense if needed, is always the Christian's responsibility. It is, also, always true that violence will provoke violence. A given Biblical text cannot be applied as a universal plaster for any conceivable condition. Its use depends upon its specific applicability.

Karl Barth has propounded a doctrine which, superficially, has some resemblance to this truth. It is his contention that the Bible is not always the Word of God. Any given portion of it may be the Word of God for a particular person at a particular time. The *character* of the Scripture, says he, is dependent upon the circumstance of mind and environment. But, in fact, it is the *applicability* of the Word, not its character, which is affected by the circumstance. And, most important, that applicability, if effective, is the same for all Christians. It is not dependent, as Barth contends, upon the character or state of the individual Christian.

13. There is one broad rule which goes far to obviate the several types of difficulty which we have recently been discussing. All Scriptural statements must be understood and applied in the light of the conditions and circumstances which they were intended to describe or under which they were originally written. The *truth* of the statements, in the strict sense, is not dependent upon those circumstances but the *meaning* frequently is, and the truth can only be understood if the meaning is understood. That cannot be determined apart from a knowledge of the circumstances. An obvious example is the fact that the impact of the first two plagues imposed upon Egypt would not be apparent without a knowledge of the importance of the river Nile in the life of the country. Turning the waters of the river into blood and making the river swarm with frogs meant far more in Egypt than in a country which was not exclusively dependent for its existence upon the river.

A more important example is the case of the speeches of Job's so-called "comforters." These speeches are true because they are accurate representations of the points of view and positions of the different individuals. But these individuals were, of course, not always speaking absolute truth with reference to any external or objective standard of reference. What they said may have been false but the account of their saying it is accurate.

A still more important example of this type of reporting is the book of Ecclesiastes. It is a presentation of the scene of human life, and man in the midst of the scene, from a humanly self-determined point of view. It does not represent the wisdom of God, but the experience of man. At the conclusion of his series of ventures, the author, doubtless a regenerated man, presents a picture of life as it appears to one who has tried all that human experience has to offer. The record is viewed·under the inspiration of the Spirit of God, but the report is of human experience. It is set forth with divine authority as a warning against reliance upon man's unaided powers.

14. The last principle is of such outstanding importance that it is unique and deserves not only the final place but, logically, a category of its own. This is the principle that Scripture is to be interpreted as a whole, in the light of all of its parts. It is set forth in the *Westminster Confession* in the words, "The infallible rule of interpretation of Scripture is the Scripture itself: and therefore, when there is a question about the true and full sense of any Scripture (which is not manifold, but one) it must be searched and known by other places that speak more clearly" (I, 9). Excellent examples of the truth of this are to be found within the Sermon on the Mount. Christ assures us, "Think not that I came to destroy the law or the prophets: I came not to destroy, but to fulfil" (Matt. 5:17), and later declares, "Ye have heard that it was said, An eye for an eye, and a tooth for a tooth: but I say unto you, Resist not him that is evil: but whosoever smiteth thee on thy right cheek, turn to him the other also. And if any man would go to law with thee, and take away thy coat, let him have thy cloak also" (Matt. 5:38-40). The one passage illuminates the meaning of the other.

Often the interpretation of a statement is to be found

not in the immediate context but at a point at considerable distance. The meaning of Old Testament prophecy
is best illustrated by the examples of its fulfillment given
in the New. The command of Christ, "Judge not, that
ye be not judged. For with what judgment ye judge, ye
shall be judged" (Matt. 7:1), is to be understood in the
light of Paul's questions, "Dare any of you, having a
matter against his neighbor, go to law before the un-
righteous, and not before the saints? Or know ye not
that the saints shall judge the world? and if the world
is judged by you, are ye unworthy to judge the smallest
matters?" (I Cor. 6:1, 2).

The application of each passage for the Christian
believer is limited and explained by the other. The
original writer, as indicated above, may not in every case
have known as much concerning the divinely-intended
meaning as does the modern Christian who can compare
Scripture passage with Scripture passage and thus reach
a unified conception of the divine intention. The teaching of Scripture for the Christian is the sum of all its
parts. No single passage should be used as the basis for
moral action without asking whether other passages
throw additional light upon the teaching on the subject
in hand.

If Scripture is read and applied by Christians today
in the light of these considerations, they will ever approach more nearly to a valid understanding of God's
revelation to men. Viewed in accordance with these
principles, the Bible will shine forth as a great, many-
faceted jewel, sparkling with an internal divine fire and
giving a clear and adequate light to every pilgrim upon
his pathway to the Celestial City.

SCRIPTURAL PREACHING

By R. B. KUIPER

OF THE many attempts made by writers on Homiletics
to define *Christian preaching* comparatively few have
done justice to the apostolic conception of preaching
as "ministry of the Word"[1] or to Paul's solemn charge
to Timothy: "I charge thee in the sight of God and of
Jesus Christ, who shall judge the living and the dead,
and by his appearing and his kingdom: preach the
Word. . . ."[2]

A few definitions from the not too distant past may
serve as examples. Phillips Brooks described preaching
as "the communication of truth by man to men."[3] In
his undiscriminating book *Preaching from the Bible*,
Andrew W. Blackwood permits this definition to go un-
challenged.[4] And yet, how wide open it lies to criticism.
The English liberal Andrew E. Garvie finds fault with
it for not stating the "final cause" of preaching and he
expands it to read: "Preaching is the communication of
divine truth through human personality for eternal
life."[5] But this revision still has serious defects. It says
nothing, for instance, of the Scriptural teaching that
Christ has assigned preaching to that office in his church
which represents him as prophet and that, therefore,

[1] Acts 6:4.
[2] II Timothy 4:1, 2.
[3] *Lectures on Preaching*, New York, 1877, p. 5.
[4] Nashville, 1941, p. 35.
[5] *The Christian Preacher*, New York, 1921, p. 9.

preaching is an official task. Its greatest fault, however, remains to be named. Brooks makes no attempt to define "truth," which preaching is to communicate, and even Garvie's "divine truth" is far from unambiguous, for all truth is divine. What must be stated unequivocally in any definition of preaching is that it is proclamation of truth revealed in Holy Scripture, the supernaturally inspired Word of God.

The principle that Christian preaching is proclamation of the Word must obviously be determinative of the content of the sermon, but it can also be shown that this principle makes demands as to the method of constructing the sermon. What follows is intended as an elaboration, within certain limits, of these two propositions.

I. THE CONTENT OF SCRIPTURAL PREACHING

The content of Scriptural preaching is accurately described by the phrases *Scriptura sola* and *Scriptura tota*. The Christian preacher must proclaim only the Word of God, and he must declare the whole Word of God.

Only the Word of God

That the modernist preacher has no scruples about going beyond the bounds of Holy Scripture in his search for a message is to be expected, for he denies the supernatural inspiration of the Bible and, hence, the unique character of Scriptural revelation. True, even he will usually introduce a sermon by the reading of a Biblical text, but neither he nor his audience ordinarily expects the sermon to be determined by the text. It is distinctly disappointing, however, to find the professor of Homiletics in Princeton Theological Seminary per-

fectly willing to grant that not all preaching need be
from the Bible and to recognize as "master preachers"
men "who seem not to have relied chiefly upon the
Scriptures as the basis of their pulpit work."[6]

Surely, when outspoken Modernists and an avowedly
Reformed teacher of Homiletics agree that the Christian
minister does not need to preach the Word only, it is
high time that the *Scriptura sola* principle be stressed.

That the preacher must *interpret* Scripture goes without saying, and that in interpreting Scripture he is subject to error none will care to dispute. It is clear that
only when he interprets Scripture correctly is he really
proclaiming the Word of God. Therefore it behooves
him to exercise extreme care in exegeting his text. Anything but the most painstaking exegesis is unworthy of
Christian preaching. It also follows that he has no right
to be apodictic when presenting exegesis the correctness
of which is not beyond reasonable doubt. But it does not
follow by any manner of means that what he preaches
may never be said to be the Word of God. Granted that
human language is an imperfect vehicle of truth, yet it
is an extremely valuable and altogether usable vehicle.
After all, words do have meanings. Stones are not bread,
nor is killing synonymous with bringing to life. And so,
when Scripture says that God created heaven and earth,
this surely means that the universe did not come into
existence independently of him. Or, when the Bible
tells its readers that there is but one God, it most as-
suredly rules out polytheism. Here let it be said that
the difference between orthodoxy and religious liberalism is not primarily one of difference of interpreta-

[6] Andrew W. Blackwood, *Preaching from the Bible,* p. 15.
Quoted by permission of Abingdon-Cokesbury Press.

tion of Scripture. Their evaluations of Scripture differ radically. The one regards it as the very Word of God, the other does not. The one accepts every one of its teachings as truth, the other does not. That, rather than exegetical differences, drives them apart. The conclusion is amply warranted that explanation of Holy Scripture may very well be declaration of the Word of God. Correct explanation always is just that.

That the *Scriptura sola* principle does not exclude the use of extra-Biblical illustrative material need hardly be said. He who was incomparably the greatest preacher ever to tread the earth used it profusely. The underlying assumption of Christ's parables and allegories is that the natural and the spiritual are analogous. As both are divine creations revealing the Creator, they could hardly help being analogous. Even after nature has been blighted in consequence of man's sin, it remains true that "the heavens declare the glory of God, and the firmament showeth his handiwork."[7] Therefore, to quote one of Henry Drummond's titles, there is "natural law in the spiritual world." More precisely, there is spiritual law in the natural world, for the natural was patterned after the spiritual, not *vice versa*. The very fact that God intended nature to reveal him attests this truth. For one example, God is the eternal Father, and human fathers remotely resemble him. And did not Jesus say: "I am the true vine,"[8] meaning that he is the original and that the vine in nature no more than faintly reflects some of his virtues?

If there is room in the sermon for material drawn from general revelation, the question arises with what right

[7] Psalm 19:1.
[8] John 15:1.

it may be asserted that preaching should be exclusively on special revelation. The answer is simple. General revelation is to be introduced by way of illustration only, and that which it illustrates must be special revelation. The minister who observes this rule will be preaching special revelation, no matter how much use he may make of general revelation in his sermons. When Jesus likened the kingdom of heaven to a grain of mustard seed or to leaven, he was, of course, not preaching on mustard seed or leaven, but on the kingdom of God.

Perhaps the suggestion is permissible that ministers might to advantage make much more use than is ordinarily made of illustrative material drawn from the Bible. Ignorance of Scripture on the part of the average church-member of our day, to say nothing of the average preacher, approaches the abysmal. The minister who makes abundant use of Biblical illustrations is grasping a God-given opportunity to acquaint himself and his hearers with the content of Holy Writ. However, this suggestion may not be interpreted as even a mild deprecation of the use of extra-Biblical illustrations in preaching.

Again, the principle that the Christian minister is to preach only the Word of God most certainly does not forbid him to apply the teaching of Holy Writ to the specific needs of his hearers and the peculiar conditions of his day. Application, as well as explanation, is of the essence of preaching. It may even be said that, in preaching, the exegesis of Scripture must itself be applicatory. P. Biesterveld has said of Calvin's preaching: "The exegesis in his sermons is always genuinely homiletic exegesis. He explains in the pulpit not in order to explain. It is ministry of the Word: explanation and application together. . . . No *exegesis scholastica,* which belongs in academic circles, but genuine *exegesis popularis. . . ."*[9]

May it be said, for example, that the minister who militates from the pulpit against the rampant state totalitarianism of this second quarter of the twentieth century is preaching the Word of God? To answer that question is not difficult. If he is conscious of being *Verbi Divini Minister,* he will not deal with this phenomenon from the viewpoint of political science, but he will be content to view it in the light of Holy Scripture. But if he does that, he is certainly preaching the Word. Nor may it be thought that the Scriptures shed no light on such a matter. From the Scriptural teaching that the individual, the family, the church and the state are all of them divine creations it follows by good and necessary inference that they are severally sovereign in their own spheres and that not one of them may impinge upon the rightful authority of another. And in the Scriptural avowal that Christ is "head over all things"[10] it is unmistakably implicit that the state is not head over all things. When God inspired holy men of old to write his Word, he had in mind, and made provision for, all the moral and religious exigencies that would arise in future centuries to the end of time. The Bible is the Word of God for all ages. As such it is ageless. A lecturer of high repute once advised a gathering of ministers to turn from the preaching of the Word to the preaching of the world. That was wretched advice. The minister should preach the Word, and only the Word. But this

[9] The quotation is taken from T. Hoekstra, *Gereformeerde Homiletiek,* Wageningen, pp. 162f.
[10] Ephesians 1:22.

does not at all mean that he must ignore the world. It is his business to declare what the Word has to say about the world. To do that is, beyond cavil, to preach the Word.

What are some of the things excluded from preaching by the *Scriptura sola* principle?

Man is indebted to revelation for whatever knowledge he has. Without divine revelation he would be in total ignorance of truth. Now God has revealed truth to man in two books, so to speak. One is the book of general revelation, comprising nature and history. The other is the Bible, the book of special revelation. Making due allowance for some overlapping of the two, one may say that, if the minister is to preach only special revelation, he may not preach general revelation.

It follows that a review of *The Hope of a New World* by Archbishop Temple, or of Lloyd C. Douglas' best seller *The Robe,* or of any other book of mere human authorship, can never deserve to be named a sermon. It also follows that sermons so called on such famous Americans as George Washington, Thomas Jefferson, Abraham Lincoln, Theodore Roosevelt and Woodrow Wilson are not really sermons at all. Precisely the same judgment must be passed on discourses on noted churchmen as, for example, Athanasius, Augustine, Anselm, Aquinas, Luther and Calvin. And again the conclusion is unavoidable that Garvie was in error when he wrote with reference to social problems: "However reluctantly and modestly, the Christian preacher must already make the venture to offer to others such solutions as many of the best minds concerned with these problems have agreed upon."[11] The Christian preacher must indeed

[11] *The Preachers of the Church,* London, 1926, p. 198.

offer solutions for certain social problems, but not the solutions of sociologists and economists, however generously the common grace of God may have endowed them with the light of nature. He may present only those solutions which God himself has given in his supernaturally inspired Word. This is not to say that he should not welcome whatever help Christian sociologists and economists may be able to lend in the discovery of these Scriptural solutions. But beyond Scripture he may not go.

In the second half of the eighteenth century preaching in Germany by and large fell under the spell of prevalent rationalism. It was the age of *die Aufklärung*. Scriptural teachings that were thought not to square with human reason, such as the doctrines of original sin, the atonement and justification by faith, were banished from the pulpit. Such doctrines as that of the Holy Trinity and the two natures of Christ were pronounced purely speculative and, hence, futile. The content of preaching was restricted to the trilogy of God, morality and immortality. Christ was preached only as a great teacher and exemplar. In a word, revealed religion was practically swallowed up by natural religion. From this rationalism the beginning of the nineteenth century brought a reaction under the leadership of the famous F. W. Schleiermacher, and this reaction has ever since been exerting a mighty influence on preaching, not only in Germany, but throughout Christendom.

Schleiermacher did indeed react from the rationalism of his day, but, sad to say, he reacted all too feebly. He could hardly do more, for his reaction was conditioned by his faulty view of Scripture. He regarded the Bible, not as a record of God's objective revelation of himself to man, but as a record of the subjective religious experience of certain outstanding saints. Consequently, according to his *Theorie der religiösen Rede*, the content of preaching must be derived from the religious consciousness of the preacher, which is to be identified with the religious consciousness of the congregation and nourished by the reading of Scripture, particularly of the New Testament. Preaching according to Schleiermacher is not the explanation and application of Holy Scripture, but "the real thing in the religious discourse is an imparting of the religious consciousness."[12] Accordingly, he barred systematic theology from the pulpit and posited as the aim of preaching, not indoctrination, but Christian living.[13] Thus Schleiermacher agreed with rationalism that the content of preaching is to be obtained subjectively, but in distinction from rationalism he took as his starting point not the rational but the religious subject.

The flood of works on Homiletics that since Schleiermacher has issued from the religious press of many countries bears witness to his widespread influence. To be sure, more than a negligible number of these take the firm position that preaching must be declaration of the Word of God; yet they constitute a minority. A great many English and American books on the subject, under the negative influence of Schleiermacher, stress method out of all proportion to content and consequently excel in superficiality. The impression is left that it does not matter a great deal what is said in the pulpit, provided it is said nicely. But there are also a

---

[12] *Praktische Theologie*, 1850, p. 213. The first part of Schleiermacher's *Praktische Theologie* deals with public worship, and his *Theorie der religiösen Rede* is a subdivision under that head.

[13] "nicht Belehrung sondern Belebung."

considerable number of ably written works on Homiletics which side outspokenly with Schleiermacher in substituting subjective religious experience, whether of the individual or of the race, for the objective revelation of the Bible as the content of the sermon. That may be said to be the characteristic position of prevalent present-day Modernism.

A few examples will bear out the truth of that statement. In *The Preacher and His Sermon,* published in 1922, J. Paterson-Smyth of England advises his students to correct "those old false views about the Bible and verbal inspiration,"[14] and he informs them that, if they are fit for the high office of the ministry, God will inspire and train them as he inspired and trained the writers of the Bible.[15] In 1924 Harry Emerson Fosdick delivered the Yale Lectures on Preaching and the / were published under the title, *The Modern Use of the Bible.* The main thrust of the book is stated thus:

"To-day there are two parties in the churches. They are in active controversy now, and every day their consciousness of difference becomes more sharp and clear. The crux of their conflict lies at this point: one party thinks that the essence of Christianity is its original mental frameworks; the other party is convinced that the essence of Christianity is its abiding experiences. To one party a mental category once worked out and expressed in Scripture is final. . . . To the other party nothing in human history seems so changeable as mental categories. They are transient phrasings of permanent convictions and experiences."[16]

The question aside whether or not Fosdick has ade-

14 P. 56.
15 P. 17.
16 Pp. 102f.

226 THE INFALLIBLE WORD

quately stated the orthodox position, concerning his own
position he leaves no doubt. The Scriptural doctrine of
the essential deity of Jesus Christ he emasculates by
these fine-sounding phrases: "This Gospel of God revealed in Christ, released from literal bondage to old
categories and set free to do its work in modern terms
of thought and speech, ought to be the central affirmation of our preaching. . . . The men of the New Testament were not primarily philosophers, metaphysicians,
theologians. They were primarily men of profound religious life endeavoring to get their vital experiences
conveyed to others in such terms as were at hand. I
believe that they would have agreed with George Eliot's
Adam Bede: 'I look at it as if the doctrine was like finding names for your feelings.' The doctrine of the divinity
of Jesus was thus the expression in current terms of the
central experience of the Christian life—finding God in
Christ."[17] In his *Preaching and the Mind of Today*, a
1934 publication and an eloquent plea for the virtue
of actuality in preaching, Gaius Glenn Atkins ascribes a
timeless authority to the great creeds because, in the
words of George Eliot, they are "the massive and ardent
spiritual experience of humanity."[18] And after speaking
of the minister's training, he says: "Nearer still to every
sermon is the preacher's life experience. . . . I do not
know what other sources, shot through with immediate
power and passion, the preacher can draw on compara-
ble with the drama of his own soul. It will all depend
upon the range and veracity of his own experience and
the extent to which it is humanly representative."[19]

[17] P. 261.
[18] P. 193.
[19] P. 196.

To make the religious consciousness or experience of the minister the theme of preaching is to violate flagrantly the *Scriptura sola* principle of preaching. And to contend that the preacher's religious consciousness and experience may well coincide with the religious consciousness and experience of the human authors of the Bible does not render this violation a whit less flagrant. For the Bible is not a record of what certain saintly but fallible men of old felt and thought concerning God. By its own claim it is the inerrant record, written by supernaturally inspired men of God, of what God has revealed to mankind concerning himself.

A warning would seem to be in order against quite another violation of the principle that Christian preaching is proclamation of the Word of God alone. In certain orthodox churches it is not unusual for ministers to base sermons more or less directly on portions of one or another of the great creeds of Christendom. There is at least one denomination in America which requires of its ministers that they ordinarily preach one sermon of this kind each Sunday.[20] Now this type of preaching, however excellently intended, is in at least some danger of running afoul of the *Scriptura sola* principle.

Not that "catechismal preaching" is to be condemned. On the contrary, if it be performed properly, it deserves the warmest approbation. Doctrinal preaching of the right kind is one of the most crying needs of our day.

---

[20] Article 68 of the Church Order of the Christian Reformed Church reads: "The ministers shall on Sunday explain briefly the sum of Christian doctrine comprehended in the Heidelberg Catechism so that as much as possible the explanation shall be annually completed, according to the division of the Catechism itself, for that purpose."

What is truth? always has been and ever will be the most basic question of religion. Yet many ministers keep repeating the trite and utterly false prattle that Christianity is not a doctrine but a life, and they preach accordingly. In consequence, their audiences, with no way of discerning between truth and falsehood, are completely indifferent to matters of doctrine. A story which has enjoyed much popularity concerns the man who under the influence of liquor inquired of a well-known preacher concerning the difference between Modernism and Fundamentalism, and, on being promised an answer when he should have become sober, rejoined that then he would no longer care to know. Such indifference accounts in large measure for the complacent capitulation of almost all American churches to theological liberalism. It is hardly an exaggeration to say that the Protestant ministry is today working as hard at keeping the laity in doctrinal darkness as was the Roman Catholic clergy before the dawn of the Reformation. The Christian church has no greater present need than that of systematic doctrinal preaching.

But doctrinal preaching, like all preaching, must be based upon the Word of God, and that is a way of saying that it may not be based upon the creeds. Protestantism from the beginning rejected the Roman Catholic teaching of an infallible church and, therefore, has always been scrupulously careful not to place the creeds on a par with Scripture. The greatest creeds of Christendom are but fallible interpretations of Holy Writ. It does not follow that they cannot perform valuable service for preaching. They can indeed do that, for, although fallible, they are precious products of the illumination of the historic church by the Holy Spirit. Christ's promise to the apostles that the Spirit of truth would guide them into all the truth[21] was intended for the church of all ages, and Scripture describes the generic church as "the pillar and ground of the truth."[22] Therefore, for the minister of the gospel to stress his right of private interpretation to the practical exclusion of the illumination of the historic church deserves to be described as boundless conceit. Nevertheless, the church's interpretation of Scripture is fallible, and so its confessions of faith and catechisms can do no more than serve as helpful guides in preaching. Never may they be regarded as the source of doctrine or the touchstone of truth. Those distinctions belong to the Bible alone. And he who makes use of the creeds in preaching is in sacred duty bound to keep that fact unmistakably clear.

The Whole Word of God

That the Word of God is in the Bible is a half-truth which frequently implies a falsehood. The truth of the matter is that the Bible is the Word of God. That being the case, the preacher does not do full justice to the Biblical injunction to preach the Word unless he proclaims the whole of Scripture.

The error that not all of Holy Writ is the Word of God has in the course of history assumed a great variety of forms. In recent decades it has appeared in somewhat subtle form in the dialectic theology, popularly known as Barthianism.

Karl Barth and his fellow dialecticians, among whom are such distinguished theologians as Emil Brunner and Karl Heim, take a definite stand against the liberal view

[21] John 16:13.
[22] I Timothy 3:15.

that the Bible is merely a record of human experience, and not of divine revelation. It has been intimated that their view of Scripture coincides with that of the sixteenth century reformers. John McConnachie, an ardent admirer of Barthianism, says: "For God's Word Barth goes back to the Scriptures. He takes his stand on Calvin's central doctrine of the Word of God."[23] But that statement is extremely misleading. The fact is that Barthianism, under the influence of German higher criticism, teaches that there are numerous errors in Scripture. It is said that God did indeed speak to the prophets, for instance; but Scripture is, strictly speaking, not a record of what God actually spoke; rather is it a record of what the prophets, fallible human beings, thought God said. The perfect Word of God is the personal living Word, the Christ, but the Barthian holds that it is not correct to identify him with what the fallible writers of the New Testament recorded conerning him. Consequently, the Bible contains both the Word of God and the word of man. And, when the minister proclaims Scripture, he is not necessarily preaching the Word of God. Nor does he who listens to genuinely Scriptural preaching in every instance hear the Word of God. Only when it pleases God to reveal himself through Scripture to a given individual at a given moment does the Word of God actually come to him.

Brunner has said: "The Christian Church can never afford to forsake its base: the Scriptures—and the Scriptures alone are God's Word." But he goes on to say:

"What I said of God incarnate is true of the revelation

[23] *The Significance of Karl Barth*, New York, 1931, p. 94.

in the Bible; to be a real revelation it must be veiled. The Word of God in the Scriptures is as little to be identified with the words of the Scriptures as the Christ according to the flesh is to be identified with the Christ according to the spirit. The words of the Scriptures are human; that is, God makes use of human and, therefore, frail and fallible words of men who are liable to err. But men and their words are the means through which God speaks to men and in men. Only through a serious misunderstanding will genuine faith find satisfaction in the theory of verbal inspiration of the Bible. In fact, this misrepresents what true faith conceives the Bible to be. He who identifies the letters and words of the Scriptures with the Word of God has never truly understood the Word of God; he does not know what constitutes revelation."[24]

Karl Heim, who has gained considerable fame as a preacher, has said: "The historical form of the Bible is a part of the 'form of a servant' which God took upon Himself in order to help us, thereby deliberately laying Himself open to the criticism of men. . . . What we have to bring to the world, therefore, is not the wonder of an infallible book. We bring the living personality who stands behind the book. . . . The apostles did not bring to the world any dogmas or rules or ethics. The aim of their teaching was only this: to bring men into touch with Christ Himself, to lead them to the inexhaustible Spring. They knew that, if a man or a nation is brought to this Spring, the Spirit of Christ will lead them into all truth and they will find in this way the solution of all their personal and national problems."[25]

[24] *The Theology of Crisis,* New York, 1929, p. 19.
[25] "The Gospel Which Commands Us" in *The Jerusalem Meeting of the International Missionary Council, March 24-April 8, 1928,* New York, 1928, vol. VIII, p. 84.

That Barthianism's conception of the Bible is not that of historic orthodoxy is evident. Calvin identified the Scriptures with the Word of God when he said:

"Since we are not favored with daily oracles from heaven, and since it is only in the Scriptures that God has been pleased to preserve his truth in perpetual remembrance, it obtains the same complete credit and authority with believers, when they are satisfied of its divine origin, as if they had heard the very words pronounced by God himself."[26]

And the Westminster divines made the same identification when they declared:

"The authority of the Holy Scripture, for which it ought to be believed and obeyed, dependeth not upon the testimony of any man or church, but wholly upon God, (who is truth itself,) the author thereof; and therefore it is to be received, because it is the Word of God."[27]

It is equally evident that Barthianism destroys the very foundation of Christian preaching. If Holy Scripture is not the very Word of God, how is the preacher to know whether what he preaches is the Word of God? To that question there is no objective answer, nor can there be. It is no wonder that John McConnachie, after saying that "Barth defines preaching as the declaring of the *Word of God*," proceeds:

"Preaching is not only a difficult, it is an impossible task. As preachers we are called to preach the Word of God, but we are human and we cannot speak it. 'Ah, Lord God, behold! I cannot speak,' ought to be the confession of every

[26] *Institutes of the Christian Religion*, I, vii, 1.
[27] *The Westminster Confession of Faith*, I, iv.

preacher. All we can hope is to bear an imperfect 'witness' and give God the glory."[28]

That the *Scriptura tota* principle of preaching leaves room for textual criticism goes without saying. The men who throughout the centuries copied Holy Scripture were, for all their remarkable accuracy, fallible. It is altogether likely, for one example, that I John 5:7 of our Authorized Version does not belong in the text. In order to make certain that he is preaching the Word of God, the minister will even find textual criticism necessary. That a given minister need not attempt in course of time to preach on every verse of Scripture may likewise be set down as a truism. If Scripture contained a million distinct words of God teaching as many truths, each minister should presumably try to cover all this ground. The fact that Scripture is the Word of God setting forth truth in a self-consistent system renders insistence on such procedure absurd. Again, even the blind may see that the principle that the preacher must proclaim the whole Word of God does not rule out the elementary distinction between historical and normative authority. Every statement in Scripture has historical authority, but not every statement taken by itself is a rule for faith and life. Job's friends said all that the Bible tells us they said, but not all the sentiments they uttered were divine truth. God himself expressed disapproval of many of them.

What are some of the positive requirements of the *Scriptura tota* principle of preaching?

Preaching should be based on both the Old Testament and the New, for both are the Word of God. The two

[28] *The Significance of Karl Barth*, p. 169.

constitute an indissoluble organism. Augustine's well-known aphorism, "The New Testament is latent in the Old, the Old is patent in the New," is as true as it is pointed.

Yet a great many preachers have neglected the Old Testament. That Modernists regard it as of far less value than the New Testament is common knowledge. Schleiermacher was of the opinion that Old Testament preaching should be confined to the Messianic passages quoted by Jesus and the apostles.[29] Although Luther preached frequently on the Old Testament, more than a few Lutheran preachers have shown a tendency to slight it. As conservative an American Lutheran as M. Reu thinks it necessary in the Old Testament "to distinguish between those parts that lend themselves and those that do not lend themselves to homiletical treatment."[30] And Ernst Christian Achelis, of the Reformed Church of Germany, by no means an extreme leftist, has recommended preaching on the historical portions of the Old Testament and on the Psalms, but held that Old Testament ethics presents "a mixture of Christian and unchristian views."[31]

That there is progress in divine revelation and that the New Testament contains a fuller revelation than does the Old, admits of no doubt. Fosdick's *The Modern Use of the Bible* hails this as a discovery of Modernism, but the Reformed faith has shown awareness of it for centuries. The term *history of revelation* is a common-

[29] *Praktische Theologie*, p. 238.

[30] *Homiletics, a Manual of the Theory and Practice of Preaching*, Chicago, 1922, p. 271.

[31] *Lehrbuch der Praktischen Theologie*, Leipzig, 1911, vol. II, p. 164.

place in Reformed theology. The dialectic theology, on the other hand, rejects emphatically the concept of progressive revelation. In the words of Barth, "Biblical history in the Old and New Testaments is not really history at all, but seen from above is a series of free divine acts and seen from below a series of fruitless attempts to undertake something in itself impossible. From the viewpoint of ordered development in particular and in general it is quite incomprehensible—as every religious teacher who is worth his salt knows only too well."[32] Incidentally, Barth's vehement reference to salt, of course, proves nothing. Holmes Rolston is evidently confused when he says: "The Barthians are in harmony with the orthodox thought in their attack on the thought of progressive revelation."[33] What Rolston should say is that Barthianism rejects the notion of progressive revelation as such, while orthodoxy rejects the liberal conception of progressive revelation. Between the orthodox and liberal views of progress in revelation yawns a gulf so wide that bridging it is out of the question. Under progress the Modernist makes room for contradiction, but from the orthodox conception of progress contradiction is definitely excluded.

For that reason the fact of progress in revelation by no means keeps the orthodox minister from preaching on the Old Testament. However, this fact will affect his preaching on the Old Testament. He will consider it his high privilege as well as solemn duty to view every text taken from the Old Testament in the light of the

[32] *The Word of God and the Word of Man*, Pilgrim Press, 1928, p. 72.

[33] *A Conservative Looks to Barth and Brunner*, Nashville, 1933, p. 86.

fuller revelation of the New. In accordance with the divine plan of history the old dispensation belongs to the irrevocable past. In the new dispensation no preacher may be satisfied to occupy the standpoint of the old. A sermon on an Old Testament text must always be a New Testament sermon.

As long ago as 1909 Josiah Royce, that eminent American philosopher, exposed the folly of the saying that Christianity is not a doctrine but a life.[34] He showed conclusively that even from the liberal viewpoint it must be held that Christianity is a doctrine as well as a life. Today that is granted by so many that the demand for emphasis on doctrine is no longer a hallmark of orthodoxy. It comes with great force from the Barthian camp,[35] and even admittedly liberal voices have joined the chorus. That the clamor issuing from these quarters is more often for false doctrine than for true need create no surprise. But what is not nearly so generally granted is that Christianity, prior to being a doctrine and a life, is a story. That is vociferously denied by both Modernists and dialecticians. And yet, historic Christianity has always claimed to be first a story, then a doctrine, and, last but not least, a life. If that claim is just, then the Christian gospel must have a three-fold aspect. It must present history, doctrine and ethics. And only that minister who does justice to all three of these may be said to be preaching the whole Word of God.

The historical portions of Scripture, more than any other, have had to bear the brunt of the attacks of mod-

[34] In an article "What Is Vital in Christianity" in the October, 1909, issue of *The Harvard Theological Review*.

[35] See, *e.g.*, John A. Mackay, *A Preface to Christian Theology*, New York, 1941.

ern criticism. Among the considerations that account for
this fact, two stand out with special prominence. In
Bible history the supernatural plays an important rôle,
but of miracles the critics will, of course, have nothing.
And such historical events as the creation of the universe, the fall of man, the virgin birth and bodily resurrection of Christ, to name but a few—constituting, as
they do, the foundation of Christianity—have for that
very reason drawn the fire of the heaviest artillery of
unbelief.

Not only Modernism has violently assailed Christianity as a religion of facts; the dialectic theology too has by
no means left Bible history unscathed. Barth's view of
the relation of history to revelation has been summed up
pointedly in these words: "God does not reveal Himself
in the Bible sense in history, not even in Jewish history.
He reveals Himself at special times, in special events,
to special individuals, and in His own special Word. . . .
Revelation, therefore, comes into history, but is not of
it. History is from beneath, Revelation from above.
Revelation precedes history, determines history, is manifest in history, but is distinct from history."[36] Barthianism has brought forth the category of the "supra-
historical." By this is meant, for example, that the fall
of man was not an event that transpired on a certain
day thousands of years ago in a certain garden on the
continent of Asia, when the first man, Adam, as representative of the human race, transgressed a specific
divine commandment, but this Scriptural story is an
account of what occurs in the experience of every individual. Brunner tells us that, when we seek an explanation for the origin of sin, the answer comes "not from a

[36] John McConnachie, *The Significance of Karl Barth*, p. 119.

certain Adam who lived so and so many thousand years
ago, but from myself, just so from yourself and from each
person himself." He says emphatically: "The contrast
'created good . . . fallen' has nothing to do with the
distinction 'earlier . . . later' in the field of empirical
sequence."[37] Rudolf Bultmann, another Barthian, has
dealt more severely with gospel history than some of the
critics who are rated as radical. This was pointed out
convincingly by Dr. N. B. Stonehouse in an address
"Jesus in the Hands of a Barthian," delivered at Westminster Theological Seminary on April 14, 1938, on the
occasion of his inauguration as professor of New Testament to succeed the late Dr. J. Gresham Machen. After
observing that the very stories about Jesus which most
clearly present him as Saviour and Lord are judged by
Bultmann to have originated in Hellenistic Christianity,
and thus at the farthest possible remove from the historic
scene in which Jesus lived and moved, Stonehouse continues:

"Significant as Bultmann's separation of the supposedly
Hellenistic stratum from the gospel tradition is, it is only
when he sets up an antithesis within the Palestinian tradition between Jesus and the Palestinian community that
his skepticism comes to its sharpest expression. In a word
it may be said that while his conception of Hellenistic
Christianity serves as a criterion to eliminate some of the
teachings of Jesus and most of the historical narratives, his
view of the primitive Palestinian church is decisive in the
rejection of the rest of the history and nearly all of the
teaching."[38]

[37] *Der Mensch im Widerspruch*, Berlin, 1937, pp. 78, 413.
[38] *The Westminster Theological Journal*, I, 1 (November,
1938), p. 26.

That it is impossible to reject Christianity as a story and still retain Christianity as a doctrine and a life ought to go without saying. Is not Christian doctrine in large part an interpretation of the Christian story? And did not Christ himself teach that Christian doctrine underlies and determines Christian ethics when he declared that the truth will make men free from sin?[39] If, for instance, the Biblical account of man's fall is either rejected or relegated to the nebulous region of the supra-historical, what remains of the Christian doctrine of original sin? And if it is denied that "by the trespass of the one the many died," how can it be maintained that "much more did the grace of God, and the gift of grace of the one man, Jesus Christ, abound unto the many"?[40] Nor need the slightest surprise be occasioned by Bultmann's typically Barthian statement: "What is God's will, is not stated by an external authority so that the content of the command is its equivalent, but man is trusted and expected to see for himself what is required of him."[41] Both the Modernist and the Barthian do violence to Christianity as a story. In consequence, whatever elements of truth and goodness may lie scattered in their teachings, the claim to Christianity for their doctrine and ethics cannot be sustained.

The conclusion is fully justified that apart from Bible history there can be no gospel. J. Gresham Machen was indisputably right when he insisted with all the power of his keen intellect, his persistent will and his profound emotive nature that in the modern attack on the historical foundations of Christianity nothing less is at stake

[39] John 8:32.
[40] Romans 5:15.
[41] *Jesus*, Berlin, 1926, p. 73.

than Christianity itself and the Christian gospel. Said
Machen:

"If religion be made independent of history there is no
such thing as a gospel. For 'gospel' means 'good news,'
tidings, information about something that has happened. A
gospel independent of history is a contradiction in terms."[42]
Did not the chief of the apostles declare: "If Christ hath
not been raised, then is our preaching vain?"[43]

Scripture teaches, not a number of disconnected
truths, but a system of truth. It hardly could do otherwise, for all truth, being of God, is one. He who preaches
various Scriptural truths as if they were unrelated cannot be said to proclaim the entire Word of God. Only
he who preaches the Scriptural system of truth declares
the whole counsel of God.

The Bible has often been denominated the book of
salvation. By way of differentiation from general revelation, that characterization is correct. General revelation
does not tell man how he may be saved from sin and
death; special revelation tells him all he needs to know
on that supremely important subject. For practical purposes redemption may be said to be the central theme
of Holy Writ. Now the Scriptural teaching of redemption is adequately summed up in the phrase *salvation
by grace*. It follows that the system of truth taught in
the Bible and the Biblical doctrine of salvation by grace
are one.

What is salvation by grace if it be not salvation by
God? The psalmist said succinctly: "Salvation belongeth
unto Jehovah,"[44] and the apostle Paul declared un-

[42] *Christianity and Liberalism*, New York, 1924, p. 121.
[43] I Corinthians 15:14.
[44] Psalm 3:8.

equivocally: "By grace have ye been saved through faith; and that not of yourselves, it is the gift of God."[45] Scripture throughout insists that the determining factor in the sinner's salvation is the will of God, not the will of the sinner. God initiates salvation by regenerating the spiritually dead sinner, and in this experience the sinner is of necessity passive. But also in the succeeding process of salvation, in which the sinner becomes an active agent, he remains utterly dependent on the grace of God. It is indeed his solemn duty to work out his own salvation with fear and trembling, but this duty is grounded in the fact that it is God who works in him both to will and to work.[46] Pointedly put, *salvation by grace* and *the sovereignty of God in salvation* are interchangeable terms. More fully expressed, God the Father before the foundation of the world chose certain sinners to eternal life according to the good pleasure of his will;[47] God the Son wrought salvation for these elect by vicariously enduring in his passion and death the divine curse which was due to them and by meriting for them eternal life through his active obedience to the divine will;[48] God the Holy Spirit applies salvation to those chosen by the Father and purchased by the Son as he implants new life within them and grants them the gift of faith, by which they lay hold on Christ and all his saving benefits.[49] Thus the triune God saves the sinner completely. Although man has a definite responsibility in the matter of his salvation, it is incorrect to

[45] Ephesians 2:8.
[46] Philippians 2:12, 13.
[47] Ephesians 1:4, 5.
[48] Galatians 3:13; Romans 5:18, 19.
[49] John 6:44; I Corinthians 12:3.

speak of man's "part" in his salvation. If salvation is a chain consisting of a million links and but one of these links is dependent on man for its forging, man is lost eternally. As Spurgeon has aptly remarked, "If there be but one stitch in the celestial garment of our righteousness which we ourselves are to put in, we are lost." And because it is God who saves the sinner from beginning to end, the saved sinner owes it to God to offer up to him in loving gratitude all he has and is. Grace so amazing, so divine, demands his soul, his life, his all. Of God, through God and unto God is the whole process of salvation. To him be the glory forever.

If the doctrine of salvation by grace is the system of truth taught in Holy Scripture, it must be admitted that few preachers indeed declare the whole Word of God. Modernism is thoroughly Pelagian, and Pelagianism is pagan. Paganism, Pelagianism and present-day religious liberalism are alike autosoteric in their teaching. And, exceedingly sad to say, most of that which styles itself fundamentalist preaching also does great violence to the Biblical doctrine of salvation by grace. Almost all of American Fundamentalism is Arminian, and Arminianism is a compromise with autosoterism. The great majority of fundamentalist preachers, while stressing the precious truth that the death of Christ was a vicarious sacrifice for the sin of man, deny unconditional election; teach that Christ's death merely made salvation possible for all, but certain for none; ignore the positive aspect of salvation, which is dependent on Christ's active obedience; and insist that faith, instead of being a fruit of the new birth, is the means by which regeneration is effected, thus making faith an act of unregenerate man's free volition rather than a gift of the sovereign Spirit of God. In a word, according to prevalent fundamentalist preaching, God merely gives man a chance to be saved, and it is for the individual to grasp the opportunity and make his salvation actual. But thus salvation is made dependent on the will of man. It is not of God that showeth mercy, but of him that willeth.[50]

Calvinism, on the other hand, has upheld without compromise the sovereignty of God in salvation. Historically it is simply a rediscovery of the Pauline and Augustinian doctrines of grace. The Reformed doctrine of salvation is consistent supernaturalism and, by that very token, Christianity in its purest form. And it is the glory of Reformed preaching that it has steadfastly refused to add even a little water to the pure wine of the Biblical teaching of salvation by grace.

That Scripture teaches a system of truth does not imply that man will necessarily find this system fully comprehensible. Contrariwise, the fact, on the one hand, that Scripture is the self-revelation of the infinite God, and the facts, on the other hand, that man's reason is finite in its nature and has been darkened by sin, make it a foregone conclusion that this system will contain elements which are irreconcilable before the bar of human reason. In other words, that this system would contain paradoxes the solution of which transcends the powers of the human intellect is precisely what might be expected. One of these is the well-known and oft-discussed paradox of divine sovereignty and human responsibility. Another is that of divine reprobation and the sincerity of the divine offer of salvation to all to whom the gospel comes. Still another is the union of the divine and the human in the person of the incarnate

[50] *Cf.* Romans 9:6.

Son of God. The greatest Reformed theologians have stood in awe before these paradoxes and have reverently confessed their inability to solve them.

It must not be thought that the Reformed conception of paradox is identical with the Barthian. Any one at all familiar with the dialectic theology knows that it gives great prominence to the idea of paradox. It is a corollary of the Barthian view of God. God is said to be the Altogether Other, who cannot be known by man. The Reformed theology, however, has always held that, although finite man cannot possibly comprehend God, the Infinite, yet he may have a true knowledge of God, and the believer actually possesses such knowledge. According to Barthianism, man's truest and purest conceptions of God are inevitably self-contradictory, and this is the Barthian teaching of paradox. But to that the Reformed Faith refuses to subscribe.

The difference between the Reformed and Barthian conceptions of paradox aside, it is clear that he who would proclaim the whole counsel of God must, in case he cannot harmonize the elements of a Biblical paradox, take pains to stress both elements. He may not preach one element to the exclusion of the other. Nor may he stress one element at the expense of the other. Again, he fails of performing his duty if he dilutes both. Concretely, the minister who preaches human responsibility so as to rule out divine sovereignty, or *vice versa,* is not proclaiming the whole Word of God. Neither is he who stresses human responsibility to the detriment of divine sovereignty, or *vice versa.* Nor again is he who emasculates both of these Scriptural teachings. Only he proclaims the whole Word who declares that God is absolute in his sovereignty and that for this very reason he holds men accountable for whatever they do or leave undone, so that on the day of reckoning even he who did not his Lord's will because he knew it not will be beaten, albeit with fewer stripes than he who knew it and did it not.[51] The minister of the Word must declare unequivocally that for man's salvation God is entitled to all the glory, and for man's damnation man deserves every whit of the blame.

A distinction is often made between the gospel's *Diesseitigkeit* and its *Jenseitigkeit*. The distinction is valid, but the two are inseparable. The gospel points men both to the way that leads to heaven and to the way in which they should walk here and now, and these two are one. Christ is the way. Only that preacher whose message is at once *jenseitig* and *diesseitig* does justice to the Word of God as a whole.

For some decades now the social gospel has been much in vogue in liberal pulpits. Usually it is exclusively *diesseitig*. The orthodox gospel is taken to task for stimulating a narrow and selfish interest in personal salvation and for anesthetizing the underpaid, ill-housed, underfed and ill-clothed with a vision of the city with pearly gates and golden streets, the Father's house with its many mansions, the tree of life bearing twelve manner of fruits and the flowing white robes, rather than advocating specific ways and means by which they may be provided generously with the comforts of modern civilization and "the abundant life." Typical of the social gospel is Garvie's dictum: "Men are saved by Christ, not for safety hereafter, but for service here."[52] This position is so obviously unscriptural that its ad-

[51] See Luke 12:48.
[52] *Preachers of the Church*, p. 190.

vocates seldom lay claim to Scripturalness for it. The
Bible throughout places tremendous emphasis on personal salvation and teaches that this salvation will not
be complete until the soul, fully sanctified at death, and
the body, resurrected on the last day, are reunited and
go to be forever with the Lord.

On the other hand, much fundamentalist preaching
falls short of doing full justice to the gospel's *Diesseitigkeit*. Modern Dispensationalism in particular is guilty
of this sin of omission. It would, for example, bar the
discussion of social problems from the pulpit. The
kingdom age, we are told, waits upon Christ's return
and so lies in the future. For the present, Satan is prince
of the world. Hence, for the preacher to manifest interest in the betterment of society is preposterous. It is
not for him to attempt to extinguish the conflagration
of society, but rather to rescue from it as many individuals as he may. In a review of Walter Rauschenbusch's
Christianity and the Social Crisis, I. M. Haldeman said
apodictically: "According to the Word of God, the work
of the Church in this age is not to save society but individuals out of it."[53] But this view also stands condemned at the bar of Holy Writ. Jesus did indeed in
three instances describe Satan as "prince of the world,"
but in each of these instances he predicted that his
crucifixion would mark Satan's defeat as prince of the
world.[54] Although the kingdom of Christ will not be
consummated until his return, it is a present reality. He
himself declared: "All power is given unto me in heaven

[53] *Prof. Rauschenbusch's Christianity and the Social Crisis*, New
York, p. 36.
[54] John 12:31; 14:30; 16:11.

and in earth."[55] And we have God's Word for it that, when he raised Christ from the dead and set him at his own right hand in the heavenly places, he "put all things under his feet and gave him to be the head over all things to the church."[56] If Christ is the head over all things, it is the preacher's business to demand recognition of this fact. Small wonder, then, that Scripture deals with social problems. To give but a few examples, Jesus said much about divorce,[57] and Paul defined the Christian's relationship to the state[58] as well as the mutual obligations of employers and employees.[59]

It cannot be gainsaid that only he declares the whole counsel of God who stresses both the gospel's *Jenseitigkeit* and its *Diesseitigkeit*. Plainly put, the preacher must tell men both how they may get to heaven when they die and how they are to live here from day to day. And, while he must stress strongly the matter of individual salvation, he may by no means neglect the gospel's social implications.

One more demand of the *Scriptura tota* principle of preaching must be named. Preaching the inscripturated Word involves preaching the personal and living Word, Jesus Christ. All of Scripture revolves about him. Truly Scriptural preaching, therefore, cannot but be christocentric. And as Christ is God manifest in the flesh, the terms *christocentric preaching* and *theocentric preaching* are interchangeable. However, not all preaching on

---

[55] Matthew 28:18.
[56] Ephesians 1:20-22.
[57] *E.g.*, Matthew 5:31, 32; 19:3-12.
[58] *E.g.*, Romans 13:1-7.
[59] *E.g.*, Colossians 3:22-4:1.

Christ can truthfully be described as proclamation of the Christ in all his fullness. Yet precisely that is demanded by the principle under discussion.

Such older liberals as Renan and Strauss stressed Christ's prophetic activity to the practical exclusion of his priesthood and his kingship. Present-day liberal preachers still exalt Christ as prophet but are wont to place major emphasis on his kingship, while destroying his priesthood with their false theories of the atonement. The recent preaching of E. Stanley Jones affords an outstanding example of the liberal emphasis on Christ's kingship.[60] The dispensationalist preacher, on the other hand, honors Christ as prophet and glories in his substitutionary sacrifice, but, for reasons already stated, virtually denies his present kingship. The theology of crisis too insists that the kingdom of God is exclusively eschatological. In a discussion of the Biblical phrase *the fullness of time* Barth says that Scripture teaches only that the kingdom has come nigh, not that it has come, and he declares it folly to say that at Christ's first advent the kingdom of God came and that it is now present in the church and Christendom.[61]

It is clear that one cannot deny Christ's priesthood without insulting him as prophet or teacher. Was it not his teaching that he came to give his life a ransom for many?[62] It is equally clear that, if Christ's kingship be severed from his priesthood, his kingdom can be only an air castle. Because he poured out his soul unto death

[60] See, *e.g.*, his *Is the Kingdom of God Realism?*, Nashville, 1940.

[61] *Zwischen den Zeiten*, 1932, pp. 458ff.

[62] Matthew 20:28.

God divided him a portion with the great.[63] And it is no less clear that he who denies Christ's present kingship cannot but ignore his claim to all authority in heaven and in earth and so can at best preach only a truncated gospel. The kingdom was founded on Calvary. To remove it from Calvary is to destroy it. Conversely, Christ's death may never be severed from his resurrection, nor the hellish agony which he endured on the cross from his ascension into heaven and session at the right hand of God.

Surely, it is indisputable that only he declares the whole Word of God who proclaims the whole Christ—the divine prophet, the only high priest, the eternal king.

II. The Construction of the Scriptural Sermon

The requirement of Scripturalness for preaching concerns primarily the content of the sermon. But it can also be shown without much effort to bear directly upon the construction of the sermon.

To be sure, the Bible does not present a set of rules for the composition of the sermon. And, although much can be learned on this subject from a careful study of the inspired sermons contained in the Bible, there is no reason to suppose that they were intended as so many precise models for homiletic construction. It follows that the preacher has a measure of liberty in this regard. And yet there may be said to be certain Scriptural requirements also for the construction of the sermon. These requirements are bound up inseparably with the

[63] Isaiah 53:12.

Scriptural requirements for the sermon's content. It is now proposed to look to them from that specific viewpoint. It will be shown that certain methods commonly employed in composing sermons cannot but make havoc of the Scriptural content of preaching for the simple and conclusive reason that they do not expound Scripture. Since exposition of Scripture is of the essence of preaching, the expository method has exclusive validity. Attention will further be called to some types of expository preaching, all of which are more or less conducive to Scripturalness of content. And by way of still further anticipation, it may already be said that it will be pointed out that one type of expository preaching in particular is indicated by the orthodox evaluation of the Bible, the historic Christian doctrine of Holy Scripture.

The Exclusive Validity of Expository Preaching

There is a method of preaching which lays claim to a high degree of Scripturalness but in reality does the greatest violence to Holy Scripture. Ever since Origen advocated the allegorical method of interpretation for the discovery of the supposedly deeper meaning of Scripture,[64] allegorical preaching has been widespread in the Christian church. The Alexandrian school, in distinction from the Antiochian, recommended it. Influenced as he was by the former of these schools, even the great Augustine fell into this evil. In the middle ages allegorical preaching was extremely prevalent, and so eminent a scholar as Thomas Aquinas succumbed to it. Not even Martin Luther escaped from it altogether. Today it is

[64] In his Ὁ Ἡγεμών, said to be the earliest Christian treatise on Hermeneutics.

practiced by countless liberal and fundamentalist preachers alike.

An example of allegorical preaching is afforded by two sermons by Aquinas on the story, as related in Matthew 8:23-27, of Jesus and the disciples in a storm on the sea of Tiberias. Following is an outline of the first sermon. Four things are to be considered in this gospel: (1) The entering of Christ and his disciples into a ship. (2) The great tempest in the sea. (3) The prayer of the disciples. (4) The obedience of the storm to the command of Christ. Morally we are taught four things: (1) To enter into holiness of life. (2) That temptations rage after we have entered. (3) In these temptations to cry unto the Lord. (4) To look for a calm according to his will. The plan of the second sermon, which aims to point out how a ship symbolizes holiness, runs thus:

I. The Material. (1) The wood represents righteousness. (2) The iron, strength. (3) The oakum, by which leaks are stopped, temperance. (4) The pitch, charity.

II. The Form. (1) Smallness at the beginning represents grief for sin. (2) Breadth of the middle, hope of eternal joy. (3) Height of the stern, fear of eternal punishment. (4) Narrowness of the keel, humility.

III. The Uses. (1) To carry men over seas; in holiness we go to heaven. (2) To carry merchandise; in holiness we carry good works. (3) To make war; in holiness we fight against the demons.[65]

Examples of present-day allegorical preaching are numerous. A few may be given. R. C. H. Lenski tells of a preacher of national prominence who chose as his text for a high school commencement the words of John

[65] The outlines are taken from E. C. Dargan, *A History of Preaching*, New York, 1905, vol. I, p. 242.

11:44, "Loose him and let him go." with which Jesus directed the bystanders to relieve resurrected Lazarus of his grave clothes. The point of the address was that, when young people reach a certain age, their parents should no longer attempt to control them but should permit them to shape their own lives.[66] Not many years ago a preacher with a reputation for both orthodoxy and eloquence read as his text "the destruction that wasteth at noonday"—Psalm 91:6—and then announced as his theme *The Perils of Middle Age*.

That allegorical preaching appeals to many audiences cannot be denied, but that is hardly an argument in its favor. Likely it owes its appeal to two factors—the ingenuity of the preacher displayed in it and the spiritual depth to which it lays claim. However, it lacks sanity. To describe it as sacrilegious is no exaggeration. To interpret as allegories portions of Scripture which are not allegories is to make God's Holy Word a plaything. There is no limit to the absurdities which allegorical preaching may present as the truth of God. At its worst it reduces preaching to a vaudeville act. At its best it is still an abomination.

Another method of preaching which is prevalent in our day and must unhesitatingly be rated as unscriptural is that of using the text as a mere peg, so to speak, on which to hang one's own thoughts, with no more organic connection between the text and the sermon than exists between a hook and the coat suspended from it. Ozora S. Davis, of the Chicago Theological Seminary, liberal though he was, used to ridicule this use of Scripture by likening it to the use which a swimmer is wont to make of a diving-board. He jumps from it. And yet it

[66] *The Sermon, Its Homiletical Construction*, Columbus, p. 13.

is precisely the Modernist who most frequently resorts to this manner of preaching. The reason lies at hand. He does not regard the Bible as the very Word of God. Then why should he consider himself bound in his preaching by this or that verse of Scripture? However, the suggestion is in order that, in case he does not intend to preach on a certain Biblical text, he might in the interest of ethics dispense with the reading of that text. On Saturday, January 22, 1944, there appeared in the Philadelphia *Evening Bulletin* a "sermon" by Samuel W. Purvis under the text, "He hath not dealt so with any nation"—Psalm 147:20. The discourse dealt with blessings which we Americans enjoy above the people of other nations. But about that the text says exactly nothing. Its one theme is the favor of special revelation which Jehovah bestowed upon Israel in distinction from all other peoples. How much more honest it would have been in this instance either to omit the text, or to choose another, applicable to the subject in the preacher's mind.

The type of preaching just described is unscriptural because it fails to expound Scripture. And allegorical preaching is unscriptural because it presents exposition so thoroughly unsound as not to deserve to be called exposition. Exposition of Scripture, exposition worthy of its name, is of the very essence of preaching. It follows that it is a serious error to recommend expository preaching as one of several legitimate methods. Nor is it at all satisfactory, after the manner of many conservatives, to extol the expository method as the best. All preaching must be expository. Only expository preaching can be Scriptural.

Two Historical Types of Expository Preaching

In the early church the usual method of preaching was that of the informal homily. After the Scripture lesson had been read, the preacher would give a running commentary on it, and this commentary, interspersed with bits of application, was known as the homily. The great Chrysostom preached thus.

That this method of constructing the sermon tends to Scripturalness of content need hardly be argued. Nor can it be denied that it was especially suited to the needs of the early church. Ignorance of Scripture was rife among the laity and a considerable part of the clergy. Now the analytic homily presented to the clergy an opportunity to acquaint both themselves and their audiences in a comparatively short time with the general content of Holy Writ. It is significant that, when Protestantism faced a similar condition in the Reformation age, it resorted to the same method of preaching. In view of prevalent ignorance of Scripture in our day, there is something to be said for another resuscitation of this method.

At the same time it must be granted that the analytic homily has its drawbacks. Conducive as it is to extensive study of Scripture, it cannot be said to be conducive to intensive Bible study. Ordinarily the length of the text renders detailed exegesis impossible. Little more can be expected of the analytic homily than that it will give a bird's-eye view of the text. Another disadvantage of this method is that the text itself usually offers so much material for consideration that little time, if any, is found for comparing Scripture with Scripture and, consequently, little stress is put on the teaching of

Scripture as a system. A third defect of this type of preaching is that almost invariably it will be found to be lacking in unity. This results from the characteristic emphasis on analysis at the expense of synthesis. A. L. C. Coquerel's description of the effect of the usual analytic homily on the audience is perhaps best taken with a grain of salt, but it contains more than a modicum of truth. Said this eloquent preacher: "When the hearers go home, they carry with them an unorganized, confused heap of remarks, assertions, wishes, exhortations, and so forth; and what is the impression which the whole has made upon the hearer? That he must make the sad admission: I don't know exactly on what the minister has preached."[67] Nor may it be supposed that unity is an extra-Biblical requirement for preaching. Not only do Jesus' sermon on the mount, Peter's Pentecostal sermon and the sermon preached by Paul in the midst of the Areopagus excel in unity; it is also true that insistence on unity in the sermon is but one application of the broad Scriptural principle that the natural must serve as a background for the spiritual. Why does rhetoric demand unity in a discourse if it be not because lack of unity is unpedagogical, unpsychological, unnatural?

As early as the second century a new type of preaching made its appearance in the Christian church. The name *thematic preaching* describes it accurately, and it is also appropriately styled *synthetic preaching*. Instead of giving a running commentary on an extended portion of Scripture, the preacher would announce a theme and proceed to discuss this theme in the light of Scripture. As might be expected, discourses of this type were better

[67] Quoted from Coquerel's *Observations Pratiques sur la Prédication* by T. Hoekstra in his *Gereformeerde Homiletiek*, p. 386.

organized than were the usual homilies. Thus the formal synthetic sermon came to take its place alongside the informal analytic homily. The recognition of the Christian church by the emperor Constantine, early in the fourth century, proved a decided boon to the new method of preaching, inasmuch as a great many who had been influenced by Greek culture now entered the church and demanded literary preaching, and also because the schools of the ablest Greek rhetoricians in the empire, among them the famous school of Libanius, were thrown open to the preachers of the church. In modern times synthetic preaching was strongly advocated by the able Swiss homilete, Alexander R. Vinet.

In course of time the term *synthetic preaching* has come to be used with a variety of connotations, not all of them favorable. But it surely can be used to describe a type of homiletic construction which is consistent with Scriptural content. A few examples will make this clear. A minister reads as his text: "By grace have ye been saved"—Ephesians 2:8. He then announces as his theme: *Salvation by Grace*. After stating that salvation by grace is equivalent to salvation by God, he proceeds to discuss his theme under three heads:

I. *God the Father planned salvation.*
II. *God the Son wrought salvation.*
III. *God the Holy Spirit applies salvation.*

By the time he finishes he should have given a respectable summary of the Scriptural doctrine of salvation by grace. Or let us suppose that a minister wishes to preach on the Biblical doctrine of justification by faith. Perhaps he reads several portions of Scripture bearing on this subject and, without choosing a text, states that on these and similar passages of Holy Writ is based the doctrine which constitutes his theme: *Justification by Faith*. Now he proposes to discuss:

I. *The nature of justification.*
II. *The content of justification.*
III. *The ground of justification.*
IV. *The means of justification.*

Under the first head he will point out at some length that justification is a forensic act of God; under the second, that he who is justified receives both the forgiveness of sins and the title to eternal life; under the third, that the sinner is justified only because of the merits of Christ; under the fourth, that justification is by faith. Again, when the preacher has finished, he should have given a fairly thorough presentation of a Scriptural doctrine.

The synthetic sermon has some definite advantages over the analytic homily. That it makes for unity is self-evident. It is clear also that it offers a better opportunity for the comparison of Scripture with Scripture and so lends itself admirably to the setting forth of the system of truth taught in the Bible. That accounts for the fact that this method has been employed with considerable success in doctrinal preaching. Most of what is known as catechismal preaching is synthetic.

But also this method of constructing the sermon has its weaknesses. Like the analytic method, it provides little room for detailed exegesis and is less conducive to intensive knowledge of Scripture than to superficial acquaintance with its content. Again, the question may well be asked whether the synthetic sermon, as outlined above, on the clause, "By grace have ye been saved," does not violate one of the most basic principles of Scriptural hermeneutics. Instead of viewing the text in the light of the context, the preacher at the very outset lifts the text, as it were, out of the context. Thus is suggested a grave peril to which the preacher of synthetic sermons stands exposed. Because the theme is all-important and the text is relatively unimportant, the danger is great that this type of discourse will be dogmatic rather than exegetical. In other words, the synthetic preacher is beset by a strong temptation to neglect the careful searching of Scripture and, instead, to proclaim as gospel truth the official teaching of the church or the unofficial teachings of notable churchmen. The history of preaching tells us that relatively few synthetic preachers have found it possible to resist this temptation. More than a few have ended up with proclaiming the opinions of philosophers, statesmen, sociologists, physicists and themselves.

Expository Preaching at Its Best

The foregoing discussion makes it clear that both the analytic homily and the synthetic sermon are possible modes of Scriptural preaching. That is to say, there is no compelling reason why the content of sermons constructed along these lines should not be Scriptural. But it has also been demonstrated that neither deserves to be recommended as the ideal method of proclaiming the Word. And it is well to bear in mind that no mode of construction can guarantee Scriptural content. Not even a perfect method would preclude errors of exegesis.

However, there is a method of preaching which,

from the viewpoint of conduciveness to Scriptural content, approaches ideality. It is known by different names. It has been called *textual preaching* because the sermon is based squarely on the text, both the theme and the heads that fall under it being derived from the text. It has been denominated *exegetical preaching* because it requires a thoroughgoing exegesis of the text. And it is described as *analytic-synthetic preaching* because it demands both an analytic study of the concepts of the text in relation to one another and a synthetic study of the text in relation to the Biblical system of truth. A brief description of this method of preaching, together with one or two examples, will show that all of these names are applicable. But *analytic-synthetic preaching*, no doubt, is its most distinctive and, therefore, most accurate designation.

A text of moderate length is chosen, but its brevity is of less concern than its unity. Unity is indispensable. The central thought of the text, which cannot be discovered without a careful study of the text in the light of the context, is made the theme of the sermon. The main divisions of the sermon are likewise arrived at through textual exegesis. These divisions must be subordinate to the theme, coördinate with each other, and collectively, so far as possible, exhaustive of the text. In the development of the divisions, use is made in the first place of material contained in the text itself, but relevant material from any other portion of Scripture is also employed freely.

The following outline of a sermon on John 3:16 will serve as an example. The text reads: "For God so loved the world that he gave his only begotten Son, that

whosoever believeth on him should not perish, but have
eternal life." The theme is: *The Greatness of God's
Love*. It is revealed in:

    I. *The object of his love* (the world).
   II. *The gift of his love* (his only begotten Son).
  III. *The purpose of his love* (the salvation of be-
       lievers).

Both the theme and the divisions are derived from the
text. The divisions are subordinate to the theme and
coördinate with each other. Together they exhaust the
text, at least quantitatively. And in the elaboration of
the divisions, the preacher will consult both the text and
the general teaching of Scripture. Only by consulting
both can he discover the precise meaning, for instance,
of the terms *world, gave* and *believeth*.

Another example is a simple outline of a sermon on
Genesis 1:1—"In the beginning God created the heavens
and the earth." *The Origin of Things* may well serve as
the theme. Under that head, the text falls quite naturally into four parts:

    I. *What things were originated* (the heavens and
      the earth).
   II. *By whom they were originated* (by God).
  III. *When they were originated* (in the beginning).
  IV. *How they were originated* (by creation).

Obviously, this plan is analytic. But each division also
leaves room for considerable synthesis. In fact, it may be
questioned seriously whether any one of the divisions
can be developed adequately without reference to the
Biblical system of truth.

This type of expository preaching has great advantages

over the two types already discussed. It may be said to avoid their weaknesses and to combine their virtues. It makes for unity—more so than the analytic method. It makes for maintenance of the *Scriptura sola* principle—more reliably so than the synthetic method. It makes for emphasis on Scripture as a system of truth and so for maintenance of the *Scriptura tota* principle—more so than the analytic method. And it makes for intensive study of Holy Writ—more so than either the analytic or the synthetic method.

Analytic-synthetic preaching cannot but seem foolishness to him who denies the verbal inspiration of Holy Scripture. Why should he take pains to discover the precise meaning of certain words if these words be not God's. Again, this method of preaching must be foolishness in the estimation of him who regards the Bible as a book to which many fallible men have contributed notions that are often contradictory, and not as a book to which many human authors have contributed, each, to be sure, without doing violence to his personality, but all of them alike so controlled by the Holy Spirit as to write the Word of God. If Scripture denies itself, to interpret Scripture with Scripture can only result in confusion worse confounded.

But for him who is convinced that the Bible is "God-breathed"[68] in all its parts and that for this very reason the parts together constitute a perfectly harmonious whole, there is no better method of preaching than this. Because he is convinced that every part of the Bible

[68] Θεόπνευστος—II Timothy 3:16. For a thorough study of this word see B. B. Warfield, *Revelation and Inspiration*, New York, 1927, pp. 229-280.

is the Word of God, he would analyze. Because he is convinced that the whole Bible is the Word of God, he would synthesize. The combination of correct Scriptural analysis and sound Scriptural synthesis insures Scriptural preaching *par excellence*.

NATURE AND SCRIPTURE

By Cornelius Van Til

WE HAVE been dealing, in this book, with the doctrine of Scripture. But Scripture claims to come to sinners. And sinners are such as have, through the fall of Adam, become "wholly defiled in all the faculties and parts of soul and body." Man made himself "incapable of life" by his disobedience to God's original revelation of himself in paradise. It is in order, then, that a discussion of the doctrine of Scripture should include an investigation of God's revelation in nature. Moreover, Scripture does not claim to speak to man, even as fallen, in any other way than in conjunction with nature. It is therefore of the utmost importance that the two forms of revelation—revelation through nature and revelation in Scripture—be set in careful relationship to one another. Do the two forms of God's revelation to sinners cover two distinct interests or dimensions of human life? Do they speak with different degrees of authority? Just what, we are bound to ask, is the relation between them?

It is well known that Reformed theology has a distinctive doctrine of Scripture. It is our purpose in this chapter to show that for this reason it has an equally distinctive doctrine of natural revelation. To accomplish this purpose we shall limit ourselves largely to the Westminster Standards. Dividing our discussion into two main parts, we shall first set forth positively the doctrine of natural theology that is found in these standards and then contrast this natural theology with another natural theology, the natural theology that has its origin in Greek thought.

I. The Natural Theology of the Confession

The distinctive character of the natural theology of the Westminster Confession may be most clearly brought to view if we show how intimately it is interwoven with the Confession's doctrine of Scripture. And this may perhaps be most easily accomplished if it is noted that, just as the Confession's doctrine of Scripture may be set forth under definite notions of its necessity, its authority, its sufficiency and its perspicuity, so the Confession's doctrine of revelation in nature may be set forth under corresponding notions of necessity, authority, sufficiency and perspicuity.

A few general remarks must therefore first be made with respect to the concepts of necessity, authority, sufficiency and perspicuity as these pertain to the Confession's doctrine of Scripture.

According to the Confession, Scripture speaks to sinners in terms of a covenant. It tells us that man was originally placed on earth under the terms of the covenant of works. It informs us further that man broke this covenant of works and that God was pleased to make a second covenant with men that they might be saved. Thus Scripture may be said to be the written expression of God's covenantal relationship with man.

The four characteristics of Scripture enumerated above may now be regarded in relation to this general covenant concept. The necessity of Scripture lies in the fact that man has broken the covenant of works. He therefore needs the grace of God. There is no speech or knowledge of grace in nature. God has accordingly condescended to reveal it in Scripture.

The revelation of grace can be seen for what it is only if it be seen in its own light. The light of grace outshines in its brilliance the light of nature as the sun outshines the moon. The kind of God that speaks in Scripture can speak only on his own authority. So the authority of Scripture is as basic as its necessity.

To this necessity and authority there must be added the sufficiency or finality of Scripture. When the sun of grace has arisen on the horizon of the sinner, the "light of nature" shines only by reflected light. Even when there are some "circumstances concerning the worship of God, the government of the church, common to human actions and societies, which are to be ordered by the light of nature and Christian prudence," they are to be so ordered "according to the general rules of the word, which are always to be observed." The light of Scripture is that superior light which lightens every other light. It is also the final light. God's covenant of grace is his final covenant with man. Its terms must be once for all and finally recorded "against the corruption of the flesh, and the malice of Satan and of the world."

To the necessity, authority and sufficiency of Scripture must finally be added its perspicuity. The distribution of God's grace depends in the last analysis upon his sovereign will, but it is mediated always through fully responsible image-bearers of God. God's being is wholly clear to himself and his revelation of himself to sinners is therefore also inherently clear. Not only the learned but also the unlearned "in a due use of the ordinary means" may "attain unto a sufficient understanding" of God's covenant of grace as revealed in Scripture.

With this general view of Scripture in mind, we turn to the question of God's revelation of himself in nature. The first point that calls for reflection here is the fact that it is, according to Scripture itself, the same God who reveals himself in nature and in grace. The God who reveals himself in nature may therefore be described as "infinite in being, glory, blessedness, and perfection, all-sufficient, eternal, unchangeable, incomprehensible, every where present, almighty, knowing all things, most wise, most holy, most just, most merciful and gracious, long-suffering, and abundant in goodness and truth."[1] It is, to be sure, from Scripture rather than from nature that this description of God is drawn. Yet it is this same God, to the extent that he is revealed at all, that is revealed in nature.

Contemplation of this fact seems at once to plunge us into great difficulty. Are we not told that nature reveals nothing of the grace of God? Does not the Confession insist that men cannot be saved except through the knowledge of God, "be they ever so diligent to frame their lives according to the light of nature; and the law of that religion they do profess"?[2] Saving grace is not manifest in nature; yet it is the God of saving grace who manifests himself by means of nature. How can these two be harmonized?

The answer to this problem must be found in the fact that God is "eternal, incomprehensible, most free,

[1] *The Larger Catechism*, Q. 7.
[2] *The Confession of Faith*, Chapter X.

most absolute." Any revelation that God gives of himself is therefore absolutely voluntary. Herein precisely lies the union of the various forms of God's revelation with one another. God's revelation in nature, together with God's revelation in Scripture, form God's one grand scheme of covenant revelation of himself to man. The two forms of revelation must therefore be seen as presupposing and supplementing one another. They are aspects of one general philosophy of history.

1. *The Philosophy of History*

The philosophy of history that speaks to us from the various chapters of the Confession may be sketched with a few bold strokes. We are told that man could never have had any fruition of God through the revelation that came to him in nature as operating by itself. There was superadded to God's revelation in nature another revelation, a supernaturally communicated positive revelation. Natural revelation, we are virtually told, was from the outset incorporated into the idea of a covenantal relationship of God with man. Thus every dimension of created existence, even the lowest, was enveloped in a form of exhaustively personal relationship between God and man. The "ateleological" no less than the "teleological," the "mechanical" no less than the "spiritual," was covenantal in character.

Being from the outset covenantal in character, the natural revelation of God to man was meant to serve as the playground for the process of differentiation that was to take place in the course of time. The covenant made with Adam was conditional. There would be *additional* revelation of God in nature after the action of man with respect to the tree of the knowledge of good and evil. This additional revelation would be different from that which had preceded it. And the difference would depend definitely upon a self-conscious covenant act of man with respect to the positively communicated prohibition. We know something of the nature of this new and different revelation of God in nature consequent upon the covenant-breaking act of man. "For the wrath of God is revealed from heaven against all ungodliness and unrighteousness of man" (Rom. 1:18).

Thus God's covenant wrath is revealed in nature after the one all-decisive act of disobedience on the part of the first covenant head. But, together with God's wrath, his grace is also manifest. When the wrath of God made manifest in nature would destroy all men, God makes covenant with Noah that day and night, winter and summer, should continue to the end of time (Gen. 9:11). The rainbow, a natural phenomenon, is but an outstanding illustration of this fact. But all this is in itself incomplete. The covenant with Noah is but a limiting notion in relation to the covenant of saving grace. Through the new and better covenant, man will have true fruition of God. And this fact itself is to be mediated through nature. The prophets, and especially the great Prophet, foretell the future course of nature. The priests of God, and most of all the great High Priest of God, hear the answers to their prayers by means of nature. The kings under God, and most of all the great King of Israel, make nature serve the purposes of redemption. The forces of nature are always at the beck and call of the power of differentiation that works toward redemption and reprobation. It is this idea of a supernatural-natural revelation that comes to such eloquent expression in the Old Testament, and particularly in the Psalms.

Here then is the picture of a well-integrated and unified philosophy of history in which revelation in nature and revelation in Scripture are mutually meaningless without one another and mutually fruitful when taken together.

To bring out the unity and therewith the meaning of this total picture more clearly, we turn now to note the necessity, the authority, the sufficiency and the perspicuity of natural revelation, as these correspond to the necessity, the authority, the sufficiency and the perspicuity of Scripture.

2. *The Necessity of Natural Revelation*

Speaking first of the necessity of natural revelation we must recall that man was made a covenant personality. Scripture became necessary because of the covenant disobedience of Adam in paradise. This covenant disobedience took place in relation to the supernatural positive revelation that God had given with respect to the tree of the knowledge of good and evil. God chose one tree from among many and "arbitrarily" told man not to eat of it. It is in this connection that we must speak of the necessity of natural revelation. If the tree of the knowledge of good and evil had been naturally different from other trees it could not have served its unique purpose. That the commandment might appear as purely "arbitrary" the specially chosen tree had to be naturally like other trees. For the supernatural to appear as supernatural the natural had to appear as really natural. The supernatural could not be recognized for what it was unless the natural were also recognized for what it was. There had to be regularity if there was to be a genuine exception.

A further point needs to be noted. God did not give his prohibition so that man might be obedient merely with respect to the tree of the knowledge of good and evil, and that merely at one particular moment of time. He gave the prohibition so that man might learn to be self-consciously obedient in all that he did with respect to all things and throughout all time. Man was meant to glorify God in the "lower" as much as in the "higher" dimensions of life. Man's act with respect to the tree of the knowledge of good and evil was to be but an example to himself of what he should or should not do with respect to all other trees. But for an example to be really an example it must be exceptional. And for the exceptional to be the exceptional there is required that which is regular. Thus we come again to the notion of the necessity of natural revelation as the presupposition of the process of differentiation that history was meant to be.

So far we have spoken of the necessity of natural revelation as it existed before the fall. Carrying on this idea, it follows that we may also speak of the necessity of natural revelation after the fall. Here too the natural or regular has to appear as the presupposition of the exceptional. But the exceptional has now become redemptive. The natural must therefore appear as in need of redemption. After the fall it is not sufficient that the natural should appear as merely regular. The natural must now appear as under the curse of God. God's covenant wrath rests securely and comprehensively upon man and upon all that man has mismanaged. Before the fall the natural as being the merely regular was the presupposition of the supernatural as being pre-redemptively covenantal; after the fall the natural as under the covenant wrath of God is the presupposition of the supernatural as redemptively covenantal. Grace can be recognized as grace only in contrast with God's curse on nature.

Then too the idea of the supernatural as "example" is again in order here. Grace speaks to man of victory over sin. But the victory this time is to come through the obedience of the second Adam. The regeneration of all things must now be a gift before it can become a task. The natural must therefore by contrast reveal an unalleviated picture of folly and ruin. Nor would the Confession permit us to tone down the rigid character of the absolute contrast between the grace and the curse of God through the idea of "common grace." Common grace is subservient to special or saving grace. As such it helps to bring out the very contrast between this saving grace and the curse of God. When men dream dreams of a paradise regained by means of common grace, they only manifest the "strong delusion" that falls as punishment of God upon those that abuse his natural revelation. Thus the natural as the regular appears as all the more in need of the gift of the grace of God.

Yet the gift is in order to the task. The example is also meant to be a sample. Christ walks indeed a cosmic road. Far as the curse is found, so far his grace is given. The Biblical miracles of healing point to the regeneration of all things. The healed souls of men require and will eventually receive healed bodies and a healed environment. Thus there is unity of concept for those who live by the Scriptural promise of comprehensive, though not universal, redemption. While they actually expect Christ to return visibly on the clouds of heaven, they thank God for every sunny day. They even thank God for his restraining and supporting general grace by means of which the unbeliever helps to display the majesty and power of God. To the believer the natural or regular with all its complexity always appears as the playground for the process of differentiation which leads ever onward to the fullness of the glory of God.

3. *The Authority of Natural Revelation*

So far we have found that the Confession's conception of the necessity of Scripture requires a corresponding conception of the necessity of revelation in nature. It is not surprising, then, that the Confession's notion of the authority of Scripture requires a corresponding notion of the authority of revelation in nature. Here too it is well that we begin by studying the situation as it obtained before the entrance of sin.

In paradise, God communicated directly and positively with man in regard to the tree of life. This revelation was authoritative. Its whole content was that of a command requiring implicit obedience. This supernatural revelation was something exceptional. To be recognized for what it was in its exceptionality, a contrast was required between it and God's regular way of communication with man. Ordinarily man had to use his God-given powers of investigation to discover the workings of the processes of nature. Again, the voice of authority as it came to man in this exceptional manner was to be but illustrative of the fact that, in and through the things of nature, there spoke the self-same voice of God's command. Man was given permission by means of the direct voice of authority to control and subdue the powers of nature. As a hunter bears upon his back in clearly visible manner the number of his hunting license, so Adam bore indelibly upon his mind the divine right of dealing with nature. And the divine right was at the same time the divine obligation. The mark of God's ownership was from the beginning writ large upon all the facts of the universe. Man was to cultivate the garden of the Lord and gladly pay tribute to the Lord of the manor.

Man's scientific procedure was accordingly to be marked by the attitude of obedience to God. He was to realize that he would find death in nature everywhere if he manipulated it otherwise than as being the direct bearer of the behests of God. The rational creature of God must naturally live by authority in all the activities of his personality. All these activities are inherently covenantal activities either of obedience or of disobedience. Man was created as an analogue of God; his thinking, his willing and his doing is therefore properly conceived as at every point analogical to the thinking, willing and doing of God. It is only after refusing to be analogous to God that man can think of setting a contrast between the attitude of reason to one type of revelation and the attitude of faith to another type of revelation.

By the idea of revelation, then, we are to mean not merely what comes to man through the facts surrounding him in his environment, but also that which comes to him by means of his own constitution as a covenant personality. The revelation that comes to man by way of his own rational and moral nature is no less objective to him than that which comes to him through the

voice of trees and animals. Man's own psychological activity is no less revelational than the laws of physics
about him. All created reality is inherently revelational
of the nature and will of God. Even man's ethical reaction to God's revelation is still revelational. And as
revelational of God, it is authoritative. The meaning of
the Confession's doctrine of the authority of Scripture
does not become clear to us till we see it against the
background of the original and basically authoritative
character of God's revelation in nature. Scripture speaks
authoritatively to such as must naturally live by authority. God speaks with authority wherever and whenever
he speaks.

At this point a word may be said about the revelation
of God through conscience and its relation to Scripture.
Conscience is man's consciousness speaking on matters
of directly moral import. Every act of man's consciousness is moral in the most comprehensive sense of that
term. Yet there is a difference between questions of
right and wrong in a restricted sense and general questions of interpretation. Now if man's whole consciousness was originally created perfect, and as such
authoritatively expressive of the will of God, that same
consciousness is still revelational and authoritative after
the entrance of sin to the extent that its voice is still the
voice of God. The sinner's efforts, so far as they are done
self-consciously from his point of view, seek to destroy
or bury the voice of God that comes to him through
nature, which includes his own consciousness. But this
effort cannot be wholly successful at any point in history. The most depraved of men cannot wholly escape
the voice of God. Their greatest wickedness is meaningless except upon the assumption that they have

sinned against the authority of God. Thoughts and deeds of utmost perversity are themselves revelational, revelational, that is, in their very abnormality. The natural man accuses or else excuses himself only because his own utterly depraved consciousness continues to point back to the original natural state of affairs. The prodigal son can never forget the father's voice. It is the albatross forever about his neck.

4. *The Sufficiency of Natural Revelation*

Proceeding now to speak of the sufficiency of natural revelation as corresponding to the sufficiency of Scripture, we recall that revelation in nature was never meant to function by itself. It was from the beginning insufficient without its supernatural concomitant. It was inherently a limiting notion. It was but the presupposition of historical action on the part of man as covenant personality with respect to supernaturally conveyed communication. But for that specific purpose it was wholly sufficient. It was *historically* sufficient.

After the fall of man natural revelation is still historically sufficient. It is sufficient for such as have in Adam brought the curse of God upon nature. It is sufficient to render them without excuse. Those who are in prison and cannot clearly see the light of the sun receive their due inasmuch as they have first abused that light. If nature groans in pain and travail because of man's abuse of it, this very fact—that is, the very curse of God on nature—should be instrumental anew in making men accuse or excuse themselves. Nature as it were yearns to be released from its imprisonment in order once more to be united to her Lord in fruitful union. When nature is abused by man it cries out to her creator for vengeance and through it for redemption.

It was in the mother promise that God gave the answer to nature's cry (Gen. 3:15). In this promise there was a two-fold aspect. There was first the aspect of vengeance. He that should come was to bruise the head of the serpent, the one that led man in setting up nature as independent of the supernatural revelation of God. Thus nature was once more to be given the opportunity of serving as the proper field of exercise for the direct supernatural communication of God to man. But this time this service came at a more advanced point in history. Nature was now the bearer of God's curse as well as of his general mercy. The "good," that is, the believers, are, generally, hedged about by God. Yet they must not expect that always and in every respect this will be the case. They must learn to say with Job, be it after much trial, "Though he slay me, yet will I trust in him" (Job 13:15). The "evil," that is, the unbelievers, will generally be rewarded with the natural consequences of their deeds. But this too is not always and without qualification the case. The wicked sometimes prosper. Nature only shows tendencies. And tendencies point forward to the time when tendencies shall have become the rules without exception. The tendency itself is meaningless without the certainty of the climax. The present regularity of nature is therefore once again to be looked upon as a limiting notion. At every stage in history God's revelation in nature is sufficient for the purpose it was meant to serve, that of being the playground for the process of differentiation between those who would and those who would not serve God.

5. *The Perspicuity of Natural Revelation*

Finally we turn to the perspicuity of nature which corresponds to the perspicuity of Scripture. We have stressed the fact that God's revelation in nature was from the outset of history meant to be taken conjointly with God's supernatural communication. This might seem to indicate that natural revelation is not inherently perspicuous. Then too it has been pointed out that back of both kinds of revelation is the incomprehensible God. And this fact again might, on first glance, seem to militate strongly against the claim that nature clearly reveals God. Yet these very facts themselves are the best guarantee of the genuine perspicuity of natural revelation. The perspicuity of God's revelation in nature depends for its very meaning upon the fact that it is an aspect of the total and totally voluntary revelation of a God who is self-contained. God's incomprehensibility to man is due to the fact that he is exhaustively comprehensible to himself. God is light and in him is no darkness at all. As such he cannot deny himself. This God naturally has an all-comprehensive plan for the created universe. He has planned all the relationships between all the aspects of created being. He has planned the end from the beginning. All created reality therefore actually displays this plan. It is, in consequence, inherently rational.

It is quite true, of course, that created man is unable to penetrate to the very bottom of this inherently clear revelation. But this does not mean that on this account the revelation of God is not clear, even for him. Created man may see clearly what is revealed clearly even if he cannot see exhaustively. Man does not need to know exhaustively in order to know truly and certainly. When on the created level of existence man thinks God's thoughts after him, that is, when man thinks in self-conscious submission to the voluntary revelation of the self-sufficient God, he has therewith the only possible ground of certainty for his knowledge. When man thinks thus he thinks as a covenant creature should wish to think. That is to say, man normally thinks in analogical fashion. He realizes that God's thoughts are self-contained. He knows that his own interpretation of nature must therefore be a re-interpretation of what is already fully interpreted by God.

The concept of analogical thinking is of especial significance here. Soon we shall meet with a notion of analogy that is based upon the very denial of the concept of the incomprehensible God. It is therefore of the utmost import that the Confession's concept of analogical thinking be seen to be the direct implication of its doctrine of God.

One further point must here be noted. We have seen that since the fall of man God's curse rests upon nature. This has brought great complexity into the picture. All this, however, in no wise detracts from the historical and objective perspicuity of nature. Nature can and does reveal nothing but the one comprehensive plan of God. The psalmist does not say that the heavens possibly or probably declare the glory of God. Nor does the apostle assert that the wrath of God is probably revealed from heaven against all ungodliness and unrighteousness of men. Scripture takes the clarity of God's revelation for granted at every stage of human history. Even when man, as it were, takes out his own eyes, this act itself turns revelational in his wicked hands, testifying to him that his sin is a sin against the light that lighteth every man coming into the world. Even to the very bottom of the most complex historical situations, involving sin and all its consequences, God's revelation shines with unmistakable clarity. "If I make my bed in hell, behold thou art there" (Psalm 139:8). Creatures have no private chambers.

Both the perspicuity of Scripture and the perspicuity of natural revelation, then, may be said to have their foundation in the doctrine of the God who "hideth himself," whose thoughts are higher than man's thoughts and whose ways are higher than man's ways. There is no discrepancy between the idea of mystery and that of perspicuity with respect either to revelation in Scripture or to revelation in nature. On the contrary the two ideas are involved in one another. The central unifying concept of the entire Confession is the doctrine of God and his one unified comprehensive plan for the world. The contention consequently is that at no point is there any excuse for man's not seeing all things as happening according to this plan.

In considering man's acceptance of natural revelation, we again take our clue from the Confession and what it says about the acceptance of Scripture. Its teaching on man's acceptance of Scriptural revelation is in accord with its teachings on the necessity, authority, sufficiency and perspicuity of Scripture. The Scriptures as the finished product of God's supernatural and saving revelation to man have their own evidence in themselves. The God who speaks in Scripture cannot refer to anything that is not already authoritatively revelational of himself for the evidence of his own existence. There is no thing that does not exist by his creation.

All things take their meaning from him. Every witness to him is a "prejudiced" witness. For any fact to be a fact at all, it must be a revelational fact.

It is accordingly no easier for sinners to accept God's revelation in nature than to accept God's revelation in Scripture. They are no more ready of themselves to do the one than to do the other. From the point of view of the sinner, theism is as objectionable as is Christianity. Theism that is worthy of the name is Christian theism. Christ said that no man can come to the Father but by him. No one can become a theist unless he becomes a Christian. Any God that is not the Father of our Lord Jesus Christ is not God but an idol.

It is therefore the Holy Spirit bearing witness by and with the Word in our hearts that alone effects the required Copernican revolution and makes us both Christians and theists. Before the fall, man also needed the witness of the Holy Spirit: Even then the third person of the Holy Trinity was operative in and through the naturally revelational consciousness of man so that it might react fittingly and properly to the works of God's creation. But then that operation was so natural that man himself needed not at all or scarcely to be aware of its existence. When man fell, he denied the naturally revelatory character of every fact including that of his own consciousness. He assumed that he was autonomous; he assumed that his consciousness was not revelational of God but only of himself. He assumed himself to be non-created. He assumed that the work of interpretation, as by the force of his natural powers he was engaged in it, was an original instead of a derivative procedure. He would not think God's thoughts after him; he would instead think only his own original thoughts.

Now if anything is obvious from Scripture it is that man is not regarded as properly a judge of God's revelation to him. Man is said or assumed from the first page to the last to be a creature of God. God's consciousness is therefore taken to be naturally original as man's is naturally derivative. Man's natural attitude in all self-conscious activities was therefore meant to be that of obedience. It is to this deeper depth, deeper than the sinner's consciousness can ever reach by itself, that Scripture appeals when it says: "Come let us reason together." It appeals to covenant-breakers and argues with them about the unreasonableness of covenant-breaking. And it is only when the Holy Spirit gives man a new heart that he will accept the evidence of Scripture about itself and about nature for what it really is. The Holy Spirit's regenerating power enables man to place all things in true perspective.

Man the sinner, as Calvin puts it, through the testimony of the Spirit receives a new power of sight by which he can appreciate the new light that has been given in Scripture. The new light and the new power of sight imply one another. The one is fruitless for salvation without the other. It is by grace, then, by the gift of the Holy Spirit alone, that sinners are able to observe the fact that all nature, including even their own negative attitude toward God, is revelational of God, the God of Scripture. The wrath of God is revealed, Paul says, on all those who keep down the truth. Man's sinful nature has become his second nature. This sinful nature of man must now be included in nature as a whole. And through it God is revealed. He is revealed as the just one, as the one who hates iniquity and punishes it. Yet he must also be seen as the one who does *not yet* punish to the full degree of their ill desert the wicked deeds of sinful men.

All this is simply to say that one must be a believing Christian to study nature in the proper frame of mind and with proper procedure. It is only the Christian consciousness that is ready and willing to regard all nature, including man's own interpretative reactions, as revelational of God. But this very fact requires that the Christian consciousness make a sharp distinction between what is revelational in this broad and basic sense and what is revelational in the restricted sense. When man had not sinned, he was naturally anxious constantly to seek contact with the supernatural positive revelation of God. But it is quite a different matter when we think of the redeemed sinner. He is restored to the right relationship. But he is restored in principle only. There is a drag upon him. His "old man" wants him to interpret nature apart from the supernatural revelation in which he operates. The only safeguard he has against this historical drag is to test his interpretations constantly by the principles of the written Word. And if theology succeeds in bringing forth ever more clearly the depth of the riches of the Biblical revelation of God in Scripture, the Christian philosopher or scientist will be glad to make use of this clearer and fuller interpretation in order that his own interpretation of nature may be all the fuller and clearer too, and thus more truly revelational of God. No subordination of philosophy or science to theology is intended here. The theologian is simply a specialist in the field of Biblical interpretation taken in the more restricted sense. The philosopher is directly subject to the Bible and must in the last analysis rest upon his own interpretation of the Word. But he may accept the help of those who are more constantly and more exclusively engaged in Biblical study than he himself can be.

II. THE NATURAL THEOLOGY OF GREEK ORIGIN

With these main features of the idea of a natural revelation that is consistent with the concept of Biblical revelation as set forth in the Confession before us, we must look by way of contrast at another view of natural theology. This other view is characterized by the fact that it allows no place for analogical reasoning in the sense that we have described it. Instead of boldly offering the idea of the self-contained God as the presupposition of the intelligent interpretation of nature, it starts with the idea of the self-contained character of nature and then argues to a god who must at best be finite in character. Instead of starting with the wholly revelational character of the created universe, including the mind of man, this natural theology starts with the non-revelational character of the universe and ends with making it revelational of the mind of would-be autonomous man.

This sort of natural theology has had its origin in Greek speculation, and more particularly in the systems of Plato and Aristotle. With no lack of appreciation for the genius of these great Greek thinkers it must yet be maintained that they, with all men, inherited the sinfulness of Adam and, accordingly, had their reasons for not wishing to hear the voice of God. With all men they assume that nature is self-sufficient and has its principles of interpretation within itself.

The pre-Socratics make a common monistic assumption to the effect that all things are at bottom one. They allow for no basic distinction between divine being and human being. With Heraclitus this assumption works itself out into the idea that all is flux. With Parmenides this same tendency works itself out into the idea that all is changeless. In both cases God is nature and nature is God.

The natural theologies of Plato and Aristotle are best viewed against this background. Neither of these men forsook the monistic assumption of their predecessors.

1. *The Natural Theology of Plato*

As for Plato this may be observed first from the hard and fast distinction that he makes between the world of being that is wholly known and the world of non-being that is wholly unknown. For Plato any being that is really to exist must be eternal and changeless. Similarly any knowledge that really can be called knowledge must be changeless, comprehensive knowledge. It is in terms of these principles that Plato would explain the world of phenomena. This world is intermediate between the world of pure being that is wholly known and the world of pure non-being that is wholly unknown. The being that we see constitutes a sort of tension between pure being and pure non-being. So also the learning process constitutes a sort of tension between pure omniscience and pure ignorance.

Plato's view of the relation of sensation and conceptual thought corresponds to this basic division between the worlds of pure being and pure non-being. The senses are said to deceive us. It is only by means of the intellect as inherently divine that man can know true being. The real philosopher bewails his contact with the world of nonbeing. He knows he has fallen from his heavenly home. He knows that he is real only to the extent that he is divine. He seeks to draw away from all contact with non-being. He seeks for identification with the "wholly Other," which, for the moment, he can speak of only in negative terms. When Socrates speaks of the Good he can only say what it is not.

The Ideal Table is never seen on land or sea. Piety must be defined as beyond anything that gods or men may say about it. True definition needs for its criterion an all-inclusive, supra-divine as well as supra-human, principle of continuity. Ultimate rationality is as much above God as above man.

The result is that for Plato, too, nature is revelational. But it is revelational as much of man as of God. To the extent that either of them is real, and known as real, he is wholly identical with the rational principle that is above both. On the other hand, as real and known in the rational principle, both are face to face with the world of non-being. And this world of non-being is as ultimate as the world of pure being. So God and man are wholly unknown to themselves. Thus both God and man are both wholly known and wholly unknown to themselves. Reality as known to man is a cross between abstract timeless formal logic and equally abstract chance. Yet in it all the ideal pure rationality as pure being dominates the scene.

It requires no argument to prove that on a Platonic basis there can be neither natural nor supernatural revelation such as the Confession holds before us. Natural revelation would be nothing more than man's own rational efforts to impose abstract rational unity upon the world of non-being. Supernatural revelation would be nothing more than that same task to the extent that it has not yet been finished or to the extent that it can never be finished. Those who undertake to defend Platonism as a fit foundation for Christianity are engaged in a futile and worse than futile enterprise.

2. The Natural Theology of Aristotle

As over against Plato, Aristotle contends that we must not look for rationality as a principle wholly beyond the things we see. Universals are to be found within particulars. All our troubles come from looking for the one apart from the other. We must, to be sure, think of pure form at the one end and of pure matter at the other end of our experience. But whatever we actually know consists of pure form and pure matter in correlativity with one another. Whenever we would speak of Socrates, we must not look for some exhaustive description of him by means of reference to an Idea that is "wholly beyond." Socrates is numerically distinct from Callias because of pure potentiality or matter. Rational explanation must be satisfied with classification. The definition of Socrates is fully expressed in terms of the lowest species. Socrates as a numerical individual is but an instance of a class. Socrates may weigh two hundred pounds and Callias may weigh one hundred pounds. When I meet Socrates downtown he may knock me down; when I meet Callias there I may knock him down. But all this is "accidental." None of the perceptual characteristics of Socrates, not even his snub-nosedness, belong to the Socrates that I define. By means of the primacy of my intellect I know Socrates as he is, forever the same, no matter what may "accidentally" happen to him. And what is true of Socrates is true of all other things.

Aristotle's philosophy, then, as over against that of Plato, stresses the correlativity of abstract rationality and pure Chance. Aristotle takes Plato's worlds of pure being and pure non-being and insists that they shall recognize a need of one another. Neither Plato nor Aristotle speaks of limiting concepts in the sense that modern philosophers use this term. Yet both Plato and Aristotle in effect use such limiting concepts and Aristotle more so than Plato. That is to say, the notion of God as transcendent is ever more clearly seen to be inconsistent with the accepted principle of interpretation.

It follows that the God of Aristotle is very difficult to handle. If he exists as a numerical unit, he exists as such because he is utterly potential or non-rational. For all individuation is by means of pure potentiality. Hence, if God

exists, he exists or may exist in indefinite numbers. As
Gilson says, Aristotle never escaped from simple polytheism.[8] On the other hand, Aristotle's God is the very opposite
of pure potentiality or pure materiality. He must have none
of the limitations that spring from pure potentiality. He
must therefore not be a numerical individual. He must be
the highest genius. And as such he must be utterly devoid
of content. He is to be described in wholly negative terms.
He is not this and he is not that. When we speak of him in
positive terms, we know that we speak metaphorically. God
did not really create the world. He does not really control
the world. He does not even really know the world.

What then of God's revelation to man? The answer is
plain. If he exists as a numerical individual, he must be
revealed to himself by means of a principle beyond himself.
He cannot reveal himself without utterly losing his individuality. But if he so reveals himself, if he is identified
with abstract rationality, he needs once more to hide himself in pure existential particularity. If he does not so hide
himself, he is revealed to no one, not even to himself. Such
is the fruit of Aristotle's potential identification of the
human intellect with the divine. Aristotle's natural theology
is but the precursor of modern phenomenalism. And the
polytheism of post-Kantian anti-intellectualism is but the
great-grandchild of the polytheism of Aristotle's intel-
lectualism.

3. The Natural Theology of Thomas Aquinas

It appears then that the natural theology of Aristotle is,
if possible, still more hostile to the natural theology of the
Confession than the natural theology of Plato could be.
Yet the Roman Catholic Church has undertaken the task
of harmonizing Aristotle's philosophic method with the

[8] E. Gilson, *The Spirit of Medieval Philosophy,* tr. by A. H. C.
Downes (New York, 1936).

Christian notion of God. Rome has sought to do so by means of its doctrine of analogy of being (*analogia entis*). Thomas Aquinas thinks it is possible to show that the mysteries of the Christian faith are not out of accord with the proper conclusions of reason. And by reason he means the form-matter scheme of Aristotle as we have spoken of it. These mysteries, he contends, may be above but cannot be said to be against reason.

Reasoning, according to Thomas, must be neither wholly univocal nor wholly equivocal; it must be analogical.[4] If with Aristotle he warns us against the definition-mongers, with Aristotle he also warns us against those who are no better than a plant.

First then, as over against those who reason univocally, Thomas insists that when we speak of God's essence our principal method must be that of "remotion," that is, of negation. "For the divine essence by its immensity surpasses every form to which our intellect reaches; and thus we cannot apprehend it by knowing what it is."[5] Form without the idea of pure potentiality is empty. For all positive knowledge we require the idea of pure contingency. Nature requires that there be luck or chance. Nature includes the wholly non-rational as well as the wholly rational. If it were not for pure contingency we should be driven with Parmenides to define being in such a way as to make it virtually identical with non-being. We should be going 'round in circles of pure analysis.

Then as over against those who would reason equivocally, Thomas argues that, though we need the idea of pure con-

[4] By "univocal" Thomas means reasoning based on the idea of a complete identification of man with God while by "equivocal" reasoning he means reasoning based on the idea of the complete separation of man from God.

[5] Saint Thomas Aquinas, *The Summa Contra Gentiles*, Literally Translated by the English Dominican Fathers From the Latest Leonine Edition (London, 1924), vol. I, p. 33.

tingency, we never meet it in actual experience. Generation, corruption and change must be kept within rational control. Our irrationalism must not go so deep as to endanger our rationalism. "For it is clear that primary matter is not subject to generation and corruption, as Aristotle proves."[6] The matter that we meet is not pure matter; it is "proper matter" that adjusts itself quite readily to reasonable ends. Potentiality and actuality belong to the same genus. The soul is not destroyed by the action of a contrary, "for nothing is contrary thereto, since by the possible intellect it is cognizant and receptive of all contraries."[7] Determinate predication presupposes the idea of a principle of continuity that is as extensive as potentiality itself. If we do not hold to this we have, Aristotle would say, given up rational inquiry itself; we are then no better than a plant.

In the system of Thomas, then, true knowledge demands that we hold pure univocation and pure equivocation in perfect balance with one another. Rationality must never be permitted to go off by itself and contingency must never be permitted to go off by itself. The result is a sort of pre-Kantian phenomenalism. "Now being is not becoming to form alone, nor to matter alone, but to the composite: for matter is merely in potentiality, while form is *whereby* a thing is, since it is act. Hence, it follows that the composite, properly speaking, is."[8]

Thus the very notion of being is virtually reduced to that which is known *to us*. Thomas presents us with a sort of pre-Kantian deduction of the categories. There is to be no awareness of awareness without the idea of pure potentiality.[9] On the other hand, the possibility of reaching reality at all requires a validity that is objective at least *for us*. The harmony is found in the idea of *act*. *"The*

[6] *Op. cit.*, vol. II, p. 229.
[7] *Op. cit.*, vol. II, p. 222.
[8] *Op. cit.*, vol. II, p. 98.
[9] *Op. cit.*, vol. III, pp. 105ff.

intellect in act and the intelligible in act are one, just as *the sense in act and the sensible in act.*"[10] Erich Przywara contends that by the *analogia entis* concept Rome is in the fortunate position of standing with one foot in, and with one foot outside, the tangle of problems that confronts the natural reason of man.[11] Our reply will be that the Thomistic procedure has but prepared the way for the modern forms of pure immanentism. Thomas is not able to escape the dilemma that faced Aristotle. His God too exists and is unknown, or is known but does not exist. Thomas accords existence to God by means of pure potentiality, and knowability by abstract rationality. The result is that God is virtually identified with nature as phenomenal reality to man.

The sharp distinction Thomas makes between the truths of reason and the mysteries of the faith may, at first sight, seem to militate against this conclusion. The two acts of believing and reasoning are said to be diverse. In consequence the objects to which these acts are directed are also said to be diverse. Reason deals with universals that appear in the particulars of sense; faith deals with the wholly unconditioned above sense. Only that which is exhaustively conceptualized is really known and only that which is wholly unknown can be the object of faith. It might seem that the two could never meet. But the Aristotelian form-matter scheme is made for just such emergencies. Harmony is effected by a sort of pre-Kantian limiting concept. In the hereafter, by the "light of glory," we shall see the essence of God. If in this life we are the most miserable of men because faith and reason stand in contradiction to one another, in the hereafter potentiality will be actuality. We posit the idea of an intellect that is comprehensive

[10] *Op. cit.,* vol. II, p. 149.

[11] Erich Przywara, *Polarity,* tr. by A. E. Bouquet (Oxford, 1935).

enough to describe all particulars and a will controlling enough to make all facts fits the requirements of such an intellect. Thus all becoming will have become being; luck and chance themselves will be subject unto us. But then thunder breaks forth in heaven. Lest we should be swallowed up of God, lest the definition-mongers should have their way after all, Thomas once more brings in pure contingency. The light or the vision of God, he says, must still be distinguished from conceptual knowledge. The vision of God must be a sort of global insight, a sort of representative *Wesensschau,* by which we see intuitively the first principles of demonstration. If these first principles were themselves demonstrable, we should after all be going 'round in circles with Plato. Thus though the numerical infinite remains wholly unknowable, the infinite of global vision is wholly known.

It is by means of these principles, all summed up in the one idea of analogy as a cross between pure univocation and pure equivocation, that Thomas makes reasonable to the natural reason such mysteries of the faith as the trinity, the incarnation, the church and the sacraments. The living voice of the church is required inasmuch as all revelation of God to man is subject to historical relativity and psychological subjectivity. The necessity, the authority, the sufficiency and the perspicuity of both the revelation of God in nature and the revelation of God in Scripture are subordinate to this living voice, the voice of Aristotle speaking through the Pope. Herein lies the guarantee of certainty for the faithful. But lest these faithful should be compelled to go around in circles of pure analysis, this certainty is always counterbalanced by pure contingency. The certainties of the church, such as the sacraments, have an ideal operational efficiency on their own account. Yet all differentiation has its source in pure potentiality. The gifts of God are ideally efficient. The grace of God is irresistible. All men, inclusive of Esau, may therefore be saved. Yet all men may fall from grace. Thus univocity and equivocity always maintain their balance.

4. *The Natural Theology of Pre-Kantian Modern Philosophy*

The two types of natural theology, with their utterly diverse concepts of analogy, the one represented by the Confession and the other represented by Thomas Aquinas, now stand before us. In modern times there has been a fearful conflict between these two. Only a few words can now be said about this modern war.

It has been suggested that the natural theology of Thomas Aquinas, conceived after the form-matter scheme of Aristotle, was but the forerunner of modern phenomenalism. The basic differentiation of Romanism is abstract impersonal form or logic and abstract or ultimate potentiality kept in correlativity with one another. The same may be said for modern phenomenalism. It is this modern phenomenalism that must now briefly engage our attention.

Only a brief remark can be allowed for the period preceding Kant. In this period there is, first, the line of rationalism coming to its climax in Leibniz and there is, second, the line of empiricism coming to a head in Hume.

The period as a whole may be said to be one of transition. It is the period when men begin to realize that their immanentistic principle of interpretation should lead them to deny the unconditioned altogether, while yet they are not fully prepared to do so. Their reasoning is to all intents and purposes anti-metaphysical in the post-Kantian sense of the term, while yet they bring God as somehow self-existent into the picture all the time. Men were beginning to feel that it was time for an open declaration of independence from God while yet they dared not quite accept the consequence of such a step. It was not till Kant that modern philosophy became self-consciously anti-metaphysical.

The rationalistic view, exhibited at its highest and best by Leibniz, represents the idea of univocal reasoning in its first modern garb. By means of refined mathematical technique, Leibniz hopes to reach that for which the ancients strove in vain, namely, individuation by complete description. God stands for the idea of pure mathematics by means of which all reality may be described as seen at a glance. All historical facts are essentially reducible to the timeless equations of mathematical formulae. Such is the nature and consequence of his ontological proof for the existence of God. There could be no revelation of God to man on such a basis. How could God tell man anything that he was not able eventually to discover by means of the differential calculus? God becomes wholly revealed to man, but with the result that he is no longer God.

In opposition to the position of Leibniz, the rationalist, stands that of Hume, the skeptic. Concepts, he argued, are but faint replicas of sensations, and the laws of association by which we relate these concepts are psychological rather than logical in character. As Leibniz sought to be wholly univocal, so Hume sought to be wholly equivocal in his reasoning. As in the philosophy of Leibniz God lost his individuality in order to become wholly known, so in the philosophy of Hume God maintained his individuality but remained wholly unknown.

To be sure, neither Leibniz nor Hume was able to carry his position to its logical conclusion. Leibniz paid tribute to brute fact as Hume paid tribute to abstract logic. Leibniz maintained the necessity of finite facts and therefore of evil, lest his universal should be reduced to the blank identity of Parmenides, lest he should have all knowledge of a being that is interchangeable with non-being. Hume, on his part, virtually makes universal negative propositions covering all objective possibility. To make sure that no God such as is found in the Confession, a God who controls all things by the counsel of his will, would speak to him, Hume had virtually to assert that such a God cannot possibly exist and that there cannot at any point in the past or future be any evidence of the existence of such a God. So Leibniz, the rationalist, was an irrationalist and Hume, the irrationalist, was a rationalist. It is impossible to be the one without also being the other.

5. *The Natural Theology of Pre-Kantian Apologists*

It was Kant who told the world this fact in unmistakable terms. Before examining his phenomenology it is well that a word be said here as to what Christian apologists were doing during the period of rationalism and empiricism. The answer is that by and large Protestant apologists followed closely after the pattern set by Thomas Aquinas. With Thomas they walked the *via media* between abstract univocal and abstract equivocal reasoning.

Two outstanding instances may be mentioned in substantiation of this claim. Bishop Butler's *Analogy* is plainly patterned after the *analogia entis* concept already analyzed. And Paley in his *Natural Theology* follows in the footsteps of Butler. Both Butler and Paley depend for their positive argument upon pure univocism and for their negative argument upon pure equivocism. For both, God is known to man to the extent that with man he is subject to a specific unity and God is above man to the extent that he is wholly unknown.

By a "reasonable use of reason," that is, by a carefully balanced mixture of univocism and equivocism, Butler contends, it may be shown that Christianity is both like and unlike the "course and constitution of nature." The atonement of Christ is like that which we daily see, namely, the innocent suffering for the guilty. Yet the atonement is also wholly other than anything that appears in nature.[12]

---

[12] *The Works of Joseph Butler*, ed. by The Right Hon. W. E. Gladstone (Oxford, 1896), vol. I, p. 272.

According to Paley God's providence is fully patent in the world, patent even in spite of poisonous reptiles and fleas. This is a happy world after all. Yet the God whose providence is so plain cannot be known except by way of negation. " 'Eternity' is a negative idea, clothed with a positive name . . . 'Self-existence' is another negative idea, namely, the negation of a preceding cause, as a progenitor, a maker, an author, a creator."[13]

In view of what has been said it is not surprising that the supernatural theology of both Butler and Paley has basic similarities to that of Aquinas. Butler and Paley hold to an abstract Arminian sort of theology which, like the theology of Rome, deals with abstract possibilities and classes rather than with individuals. For Butler and for Paley, as for Thomas Aquinas, the objective atonement is an abstract form that is somehow present in and yet meaningless without the initiative taken by utterly independent individuals. Whatever there is of true Christianity in Rome, or in such positions as those of Butler and Paley, is there in spite of, rather than because of, the Aristotelian form-matter scheme that controls the formation of their natural theologies. A true Biblical or covenant theology could not be based upon such foundations as Butler and Paley laid.

6. *The Natural Theology of Kant*

The field has now been narrowed down considerably. The natural theology of the Confession, derived as it was largely from the theology of Calvin, stands over against the natural theology as it has come from Aristotle through Rome into much of Protestant, even orthodox Protestant, thought. These two types of natural theology are striving for the mastery in our day.

The Aristotelian form of natural theology has, moreover,

---

[13] William Paley, *Natural Theology and Horae Paulinae* (Philadelphia, 1831), p. 289.

been greatly strengthened in our times by the critical philosophy of Kant. Indeed it may be asserted that the typical form of that natural theology which we have found to be inconsistent with the Confession is identical with some form of critical phenomenalism. The main concepts of this phenomenalism must therefore be analyzed.

Kant's great contribution to philosophy consisted in stressing the activity of the experiencing subject. It is this point to which the idea of a Copernican revolution is usually applied. Kant argued that since it is the thinking subject that itself contributes the categories of universality and necessity, we must not think of these as covering any reality that exists or may exist wholly independent of the human mind. By using the law of non-contradiction we may and must indeed determine what is possible, but the possibility that we thus determine is subjective rather than objective. It is a possibility *for us*. To save rationality, Kant argues, we must shorten the battle-line and reduce its claims even in its own domain. Hereafter reason must claim to legislate only in that area that can always be checked by experience and even in this area it must ever be ready to receive the wholly new. The validity of universals is to be taken as frankly due to a motion and a vote; it is conventional and nothing more. Thus the univocation of Leibniz is to be saved by casting it into the sea of equivocation stirred up by Hume.

Again stressing the original activity of the thinking subject, Kant argued that it is impossible ever to find the entirely single thing of Hume. Like a sausage-grinder, the mind of man forms things into molds as it receives them. We never see either pork or beef; we see only sausages that, according to the butcher's word, contain both. Thus we always make facts as much as we find them. The only facts we know are instances of laws.

Kant's argument against the rationalists was like the

argument of Aristotle against the "definition mongers" who wanted to know all things. His argument against Hume was like Aristotle's arguments against Protagoras, the skeptic, who went on speaking even when his principle allowed him to say nothing determinate. Science, Kant argued, does not need and could not exist with such objective universality as Leibniz desired, but it does need and actually has the subjective validity that the autonomous man supplies in the very act of interpretation. Kant argues, as it were, that Aristotle was right in seeking for universals in the particulars rather than above them, but that he did not have the courage of his convictions and did not go far enough. Science requires us to have done once and for all with all antecedent being, with all metaphysics except that which is immanentistic. Hereafter the notions of being, cause and purpose must stand for orderings we ourselves have made; they must never stand for anything that exists beyond the reach of our experience. Any God who wants to make himself known, it is now more clear than ever before, will have to do so by identifying himself exhaustively with his revelation. And any God who is so revealed, it is now more clear than ever before, will then have to be wholly hidden in pure possibility. Neither Plato nor Aristotle were entitled, by the methods of reasoning they employed, to reach the Unconditioned. The Unconditioned cannot be rationally related to man.

There is no doubt but that Kant was right in this claim. Plato and Aristotle no less than Kant assumed the autonomy of man. On such a basis man may reason univocally and reach a God who is virtually an extension of himself or he may reason equivocally and reach a God who has no contact with him at all. Nor will adding two zeros produce more than zero. The addition of pure pantheism to pure deism will not bring forth theism. It was Kant's great service to the Christian church to teach us this. No theistic proof,

either of the *a priori* or of the *a posteriori* sort, based on
Platonic Aristotelian assumptions could do anything but
disprove the God of the Confession.

But if Kant has done so great a service, his service has of
course been wholly negative. Orthodox apologists have all
too often overlooked this fact. Did not Kant make room for
faith? Did he not challenge the pride of the rationalist in
its denial of a God whose thoughts are higher than man's
thoughts? Is not the scientist who today works on the basis
of his principles a very humble sort of person, satisfied with
the single dimension of the phenomenal, leaving the whole
realm of the noumenal to the ministers of religion? And
does not Scripture itself ascribe to reason the power and
right to interpret at least an area of reality, restricted though
it be, in its own right? Surely the God of Scripture does
not mean to dictate to the man who merely describes the
facts as he sees them in the laboratory.

In all this there is profound confusion. Nor is this to
be blamed primarily on Kant. Kant knew well enough what
sort of Christianity is involved in the natural theology of his
Critique of Pure Reason. His own statement of it is unmistakable and frank. To him the only Christianity that
accords with the principles of his thought is a Christianity
that is reduced from its historic uniqueness to a universal
religion of reason. And modernist theologians working with
his principles today make similar reductions of historic
Christianity. We can but admire their consistency. The very
idea of Kant's Copernican revolution was that the autonomous mind itself must assume the responsibility for making
all factual differentiation and logical validation. To such a
mind the God of Christianity cannot speak. Such a mind
will hear no voice but its own. It is itself the light that
lighteth every man that comes into the world. It is itself
the sun; how can it receive light from without? If Plato
and Aristotle virtually identified the mind of man with
that of God, Kant virtually identified the mind of God with

that of man. Such a mind describes all facts as it sees them, but it sees them invariably through colored lenses. The miracles of Scripture are always reduced to instances of laws and laws themselves are reduced to conventional and purely contingent regularities. Prophetic prediction that has come *true* is always reduced to pure coincidence in a world of chance. Conventional law and brute fact are the stock in trade of the Kantian philosopher and scientist. His phenomenal world is built up of these.

7. *The Natural Theology of Post-Kantian Phenomenalism*

Working out the consequences of the Kantian position, Heinrich Rickert has stressed the fact that modern science has virtually abolished the distinction between the description and the explanation of facts. The facts which the scientist thinks he merely describes are such as have already been explained by his philosophical *confrères*.[14] Philosophers have so thoroughly canvassed the field of possibility that the scientist will never meet any facts that will not inevitably turn out to be instances of conventional, wholly man-made laws.

Modern phenomenalism then, it must be stressed, is comprehensive in its sweep. It is a philosophy covering the whole of reality. It may be anti-metaphysical, but this is only to say that it is against such metaphysics of transcendence as the Confession presents. Modern phenomenalism cannot by its principle admit of any of the facts and doctrines of historic Christian theism.

Dialectical theology has, to be sure, made the attempt to combine the main *Critique* of Kant and the *Institutes* of Calvin. But the magnitude of its undertaking is itself the best instance in proof that such a thing cannot logically be done. Barth and Brunner have satisfied the requirements

[14] *Die Grenzen der naturwissenschaftlichen Begriffsbildung* (Tübingen, 5. Aufl., 1929).

of Kant's criticism, but in so doing they have at the same time denied the God of Calvin.

Largely influenced by the phenomenalism or existential- ism of such men as Kierkegaard and Heidegger, Barth and Brunner have been consistently anti-metaphysical in the Kantian sense of the term. That is to say, they have insisted that God is wholly unknown as a numerical individual and that he is wholly identical with his revelation as a specific unity. In other words, the God of the Confession is for Barth and Brunner nothing but an idol. The God of the Confession claims to have revealed himself directly in nature and in Scripture. And all direct revelation, Barth and Brunner continually reassert, is paganism. Barth and Brunner are as certain as was Kant that the Unconditional cannot make himself known as such in the phenomenal world. They could not maintain such a position except upon the assumption of the idea of the autonomous man which legislates, at least negatively, for the whole field of possibility.

Dialectical theology then fits in well with the natural theology of the Aristotle-Thomas Aquinas-Kant tradition. In fact, it may be said to be nothing more than a natural theology cut after this pattern. It is as hostile to the natural as to the special revelation concepts of the Confession. And the same must also be said with respect to such modified forms of dialecticism as are offered by Reinhold Niebuhr, Richard Kroner, Paul Tillich, Nels Ferré and John Mackay.

Certain lines have now been drawn in the modern chaos. The modern chaos is not so chaotic as it may at first sight appear. There are at bottom only two positions. There is the position of the Confession. This position consists of a natural theology that serves as the proper foundation for the full theology of grace that is found in the Reformed Confessions alone. It consists of a natural theology whose fundamental meaning and significance is found in the very fact of its being the field of exercise for the historical differentiation of which the Reformed theology of grace is but the narrative. There is, on the other hand, the position of Plato, Aristotle, Thomas Aquinas and Kant. It consists of a natural theology that must, according to the force of its interpretative principle, reduce the historic process of differentiation, as told in the Confession, to dialectical movements of a reason that is sufficient to itself.

Between these two there is and can be no peace. And the natural theology of the Confession, though unpopular now both within and beyond the church, cannot but be victorious at last. For all its vaunted defense of reason, the natural theology of Aristotle and his modern followers destroys reason. The autonomous man cannot forever flee back and forth between the arid mountains of timeless logic and the shoreless ocean of pure potentiality. He must at last be brought to bay. He cannot forever be permitted to speak of nothing that reveals itself exhaustively into nothing and yet pretend to convey meaning in his speech. The autonomous man has denied the existence of a rationality higher than itself that has legislated for all reality. In so doing it has itself legislated for all reality. Yet it also allows for pure potentiality that is beyond all rational power. It has undertaken to do, or rather claims already to have done, what it also says is inherently impossible of accomplishment. On the other hand, the natural theology of the Confession, with its rejection of autonomous reason, has restored reason to its rightful place and validated its rightful claims. In recognizing the Sovereign God of grace, the God who is infinite, eternal and unchangeable in his being, wisdom, power, goodness, justice and truth, as its chief and ultimate principle of interpretation, the natural theology of the Confession has saved rationality itself. Without the self-contained God of the Confession, there would be no order in nature and no employment for reason.

I. Names

II. Scripture References